The Digital Photography Handbook

DOUG HARMAN

Photography by
David Jones and Doug Harman

Quercus

How to be a
digital photographer

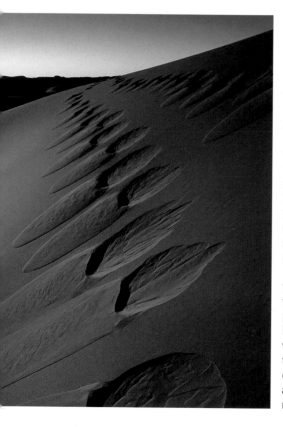

Digital photography offers many advantages – practically, technically, creatively and even economically – over traditional film photography. Over 98% of cameras sold today are digital, but it is the minority of photographers who make the most of the power at their disposal. With a digital camera, you can shoot and store hundreds of photos and high-quality video with sound at practically no cost; instantly review and re-shoot your images or video; achieve great picture quality; improve your images on computer, correcting badly lit pictures and even repairing old photos; adjust colours and apply special effects; or set up a photo website ... the possibilities are exhilarating and nearly limitless.

The Digital Photography Handbook will allow you to make the most of all the advantages your camera has to offer. Assuming no prior knowledge, it will help you quickly become a true digital photographer – whether you want to improve your basic technique to get error-free holiday snaps or to learn professional photo techniques and image manipulation tips and tricks for maximum creativity.

This book will take you step-by-step through the four key areas you'll want to master:

1. **Going digital** – the basics, including choosing a camera and equipment, and getting started

2. **Using your digital camera** – how to take great pictures

3. **The digital darkroom** – improving your images on a computer

4. **Output** – getting the best end result, on-line or in print

But although this handbook offers a complete beginner's course in digital photography, you don't have to work through all of its pages to make progress. Each topic makes sense read individually, and you can use the table of contents and comprehensive index to jump to anything you want to know. Cross-references in italics direct you to any other useful topics related to a particular subject.

Wherever you start, this book offers comprehensive advice and is packed with information. But it also draws your attention to the most important things – grey and black hint boxes give you instant dos and don'ts to improve your results. Blue highlight boxes are marked with an 'i' and focus on the key techniques and knowledge for each topic, speeding up the learning process. Whilst a beginner's guide, *The Digital Photography Handbook* does not avoid any of the seemingly difficult concepts you'll need to know. It demystifies traditionally complex topics such as pixels, depth of field, F-numbers and cloning, explaining them in simple language and demonstrating them in practical situations. Any key technical terms you come across can also be found in the glossary for quick reference. In addition, this book will take you, in illustrated steps, through numerous image editing examples, allowing even the novice computer user, working at their own pace, to produce professional results.

Your digital adventure begins here. Enjoy!

Doug Harman

Contents

The digital darkroom

Improving your images on a PC

Basic digital techniques

Advanced digital techniques

Masterclasses

Output

Getting the best end result

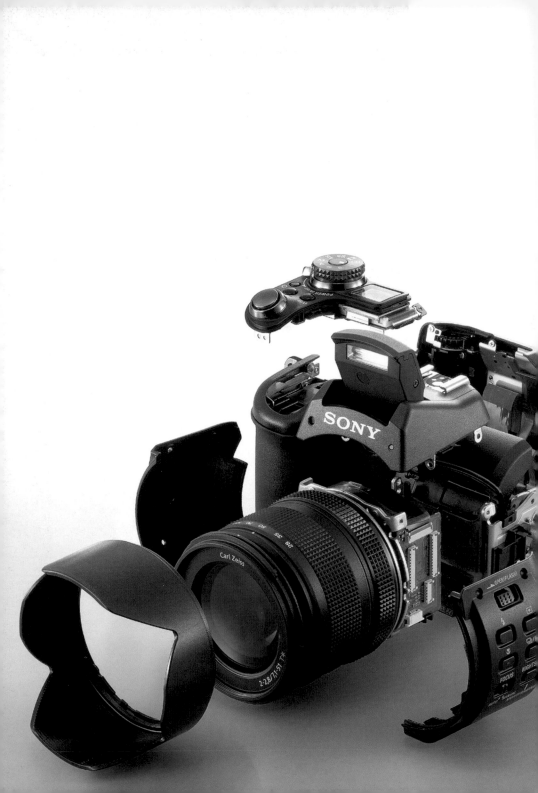

Going **digital**

In this section, you'll find all you need to get started, including:

- **How to choose the right camera** for you

- **The basics** – digital camera features and operation, and camera care

- **Camera essentials** – what you need to know about memory cards, power and lenses

- **Advice** on computers, software, printers and other useful equipment

- **Explanations** of megapixels, focal lengths, zoom ratios, resolution, modes and menus, connection speeds, gigabytes, D-SLRs …

Camera features explained

Digital cameras are designed to be familiar to anyone who's ever used a film camera. But they have many extra helpful features too ...

Most digital cameras have similar basic features. Here we'll introduce you to the typical features of a compact digital camera, and will go on to discuss more specialised functions later in the book. You should check the manual supplied with your camera to see which additional features your camera has.

1 AF assist emitter

This small port has an LED that can emit a beam of bright light to help focusing in low light situations and is also used to help reduce the redeye phenomenon.

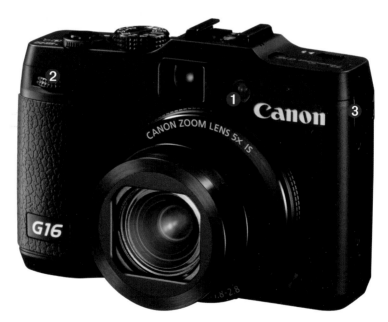

2 Control dial

A dial (or wheel) turned with the thumb to adjust previously selected functions such as shutter speed.

3 Strap lug

Here you attach the camera strap, or the wrist strap on smaller compacts.

1 Lens

Most digital cameras come equipped with a zoom lens that enables more or less of a scene to be included by 'zooming' in and out. These changes in focal length are reflected in the viewfinder and/or on the large display screen on the back of the camera.

2 Built-in flash

Most digital cameras have a built-in automatic flash unit that can be used to provide extra light if it's dark, or to reduce shadows on heavily shaded subjects in bright sunlight.

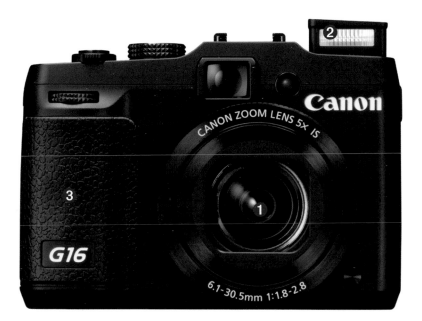

3 Battery and memory card housing

Safely tucked away under a cover on the camera's base (or its side) you'll find a place to insert batteries and a socket for inserting the camera's memory card.

1 Accessory/hotshoe

If present, here you can attach accessories for your camera, usually an external flashgun.

2 Mode dial

A dial that you turn to select different camera shooting modes, such as Aperture Priority (shown here as 'A') or movie mode (the movie camera icon).

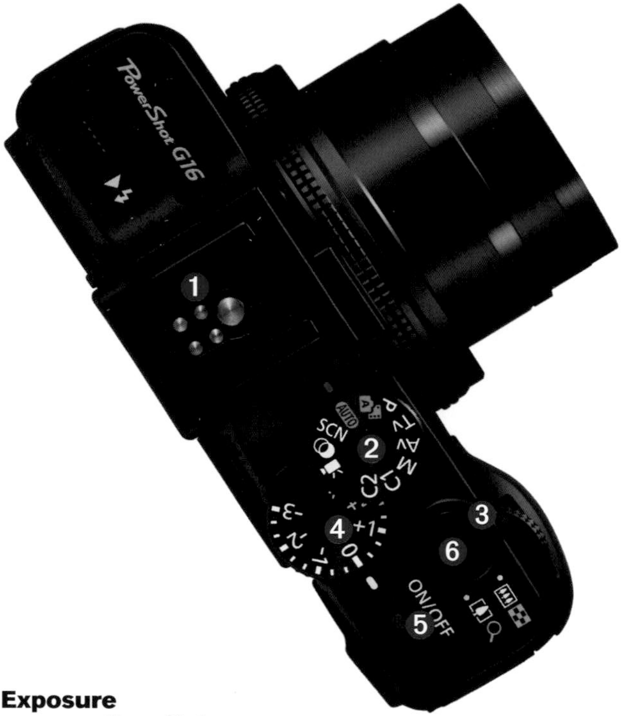

3 Lens zoom control

The lever surrounding the shutter release is moved left or right to make the lens zoom in or out. This makes it easy to adjust the view when framing a shot. Some cameras have a zoom button on the back instead.

4 Exposure compensation dial

The exposure compensation dial allows you to quickly increase (lighten) or decrease (darken) the exposure on the camera without altering any other settings.

5 On/off button

Your digital camera is electrically powered using batteries and will have a power switch: usually an on/off button.

6 Shutter release

The most important button on the camera: it takes the pictures. The shutter release will have two pressures. A half-press (and hold) activates the focus system and all the electronics that measure the amount of light available (the light metering system). A little beep, or an 'OK' indicator on the colour screen and/or an illuminated green light next to the viewfinder, will indicate that focus has been achieved. Fully pressing down the button will fire the shutter and take the photo.

1 Viewfinder (rear view)

This is the part of the camera you use to compose a shot. It also has two small indicators that show the focus and flash status. A green light means the focus is okay, red shows that it is not. If the flash indicator flickers, the flash is charging; when it is steady, it means the flash is ready to fire. However, not all cameras will have optical viewfinders.

2 Video control button

Depending on the camera model, you may be able to shoot video by pressing this button. Some cameras will combine video capture control with the shutter release as well as having a separate video control button, as is the case here.

3 Shortcut button

A button that can be assigned one of a number of features selected from the camera menus to make using the camera more flexible.

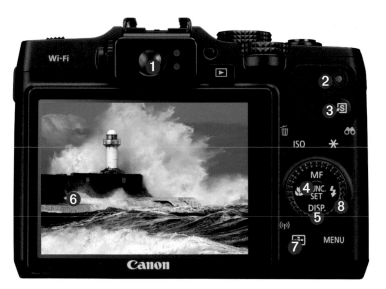

4 Func./Set button

The Func./Set button either sets a feature chosen in a menu or activates the function controls on the display when shooting.

5 Disp. button

This enables you to switch between the various display modes on the screen or to turn the display on and off. If your camera has an electronic viewfinder it will also switch between that and the display.

6 Colour screen (LCD)

The colour screen on a digital camera is great for instantly reviewing your photos to make sure they're okay or for showing them off to others. It can display your camera's settings, menus and picture information. The screen also gives you a live display of your subject, making correct composition easy.

7 Other adjustment buttons and controls

Depending on your camera model, there will be several other buttons on the camera that will be used to control frequently used functions without having to go through on-screen menus. Such functions could include control of the flash, the focus mode, movie mode activation, focus modes (activating macro focusing, for example), image playback (shown here), menus and display modes.

8 Jog buttons or dial

This type of 'jog' button or dial is common to digital cameras and allows you to scroll through your images on the screen. It is used to navigate through the camera's on-screen menus and can be used to activate or adjust various camera features, such as image quality settings. The central Func./Set button is used to confirm selection of other choices within further menus for control of camera set-up options such as date and time.

Types of **digital camera**

What kind of camera do you need? Here's a simple guide.

The basic digital camera

A basic digital camera has everything you need to take great photos but in a package that's very simple to use. It will have few – if any – manual photographic controls to play with and most functions will be automatic. These are often called 'point-and-shoot' cameras.

It will include a built-in flash. It will probably have automatic shooting modes you can select, such as landscape or portrait settings, and it will have either a fixed focal length lens of around 35mm or it might sport a modest zoom lens.

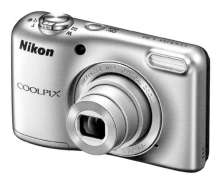

The resolution is likely to range from 10 megapixels (10MP) to as many as 16MP but could be more or less depending on the type you buy (see *How many megapixels?* for more about resolution). It's worth mentioning that a camera with 10 megapixels can print images that range in size from standard 6x4-inch prints right up to A2 size.

The mid-range digital camera

The most obvious differences between basic and mid-range digital cameras, apart from an inevitably higher price tag, are likely to be in the resolution and the lens. A mid-range camera will probably have a higher resolution of around 12MP to 16MP (although some of the latest mid-range cameras may have fewer and larger pixels on a larger sensor instead) and almost certainly have a longer built-in zoom lens such as a 5x zoom ratio or greater. For more on resolution, again see *How many megapixels?*

However, some mid-range models come equipped with 'super' and 'ultra' zoom lenses. Hence digital cameras can have lenses that provide anywhere from a fixed focal length to zoom ratios of up to 16x and even higher (see *Zoom lenses*).

There will be manual controls to put you in charge of the photo taking and enhanced features such as automatic scene assessment, a wider variety of scene modes and high definition (HD) movie modes rather than standard resolution ones. Build quality is likely to also be noticeably better than on basic cameras.

The high-end digital camera

Designed primarily for the advanced snapper, high-end digital cameras (also known as 'Prosumer' or 'Bridge' cameras) are expensive pieces of equipment and feature a multitude of manual controls, backed up by an even more enhanced range of automatic settings.

This camera will have superior internal software that speeds up image capture and processing, making the camera faster and more efficient than mid-range models. The lens may not have a better zoom ratio than cheaper models, but will be crafted from the camera maker's premium optical glass which brings improvements in light-catching ability. Special lens coatings and optical configurations are employed to give improved performance and results.

High-end models will tend to have high-resolution sensors, often between 10MP and 16MP or higher, though some will have a larger sensor and fewer bigger pixels, as with some of the mid-range models. They are likely to have ruggedised or toughened build, for example weatherproofing, and they'll have improved focusing, metering and flash set-ups, the latter enabling the use of external flashguns; for some models professional studio flash equipment can be used. Improved computer connections for faster download and, in some cases, multiple memory card slots will also be in there, depending on the camera you buy.

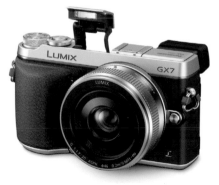

Compact system camera

Compact System Cameras (CSCs) are a new fast-growing group of smaller system cameras (see above). CSCs offer all the advantages of a larger D-SLR system (interchangeable lenses, manual controls, improved image quality) but in a smaller format.

The digital single lens reflex (D-SLR) camera

D-SLRs are the very top of the digital camera tree. They are expensive enthusiast- and professional-level high-resolution digital cameras.

'SLR' is the name given to a camera (digital or film) which lets you view the scene you're photographing through a single 'taking' lens, via a reflex mirror. The reflex mirror directs light through the viewfinder (usually) through a special prism called a pentaprism which is mounted inside the camera. This provides the photographer with an exact view of the subject – through the viewfinder – as 'seen' by the lens. The mirror flips up out of the way when a shot is taken, allowing light to reach the sensor. Some of the new, smaller D-SLRs, called hybrid or mirror-less compact system D-SLRs, have removed the mirror assembly and the optical viewfinder usually associated with it. Instead, they'll have electronic viewfinders or just use the screen for composition – to help keep the system as compact and light as possible.

D-SLRs can use interchangeable lenses, not available on a compact digital camera, and this flexibility provides unparalleled shooting versatility. You'll also get all the high-tech gadgetry found on high-end digital cameras, only it will be more specialised or enhanced to give even better performance, including resolutions from 10MP to 36MP and beyond.

Added to this are a brick-like build quality, anti-dust systems and Live View, which allows you to use the camera's large screen to compose a shot in the same way as you can on a compact digital camera.

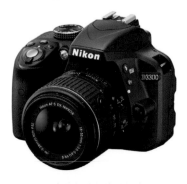

How many **megapixels?**

When looking at the sales blurb for digital cameras, you'll see endless mention of megapixels, and this is indeed a critical feature of your camera. So here we'll explain what they are – and how many you'll need.

A digital camera contains a special device, known as a sensor (sometimes referred to as a CCD or CMOS sensor), to capture light. This replaces the photographic film used in a traditional camera.

Magnify the surface of a camera's sensor and what you'll see is what appears to be a grid of tiny squares. Each of those tiny square dots is a light receptor or photodiode, more commonly termed a 'pixel' or picture element. A camera with a 10-million pixel sensor (10-megapixels) has 10 million of those tiny photodiodes.

The number of pixels is important because the more a camera has, the more detail it can capture – and the higher its resolution is said to be. Additionally, the more pixels there are, the larger you'll be able to print your pictures.

However, if the whole sensor is larger then more light can be collected overall (see below), which can result in clearer images. Sensors are usually measured in inches, across their diagonal (as with flat-screen TVs) and typical compact camera sensor sizes include $2/3$ inch, $1/2$ inch or $1/3$ inch.

Some newer high-end digital cameras have larger sensors going up to full-frame 35mm, film-sized sensors. If you have two sensors with the same resolution (number of pixels), but one sensor is physically larger, its pixels will be larger too. Larger pixels need less additional help from the camera's systems, resulting in brighter, cleaner images of higher quality than images with the same resolution from physically smaller sensors.

The pixels found on a camera phone are extremely tiny, given that the sensors

Pixel pitch and sensor size

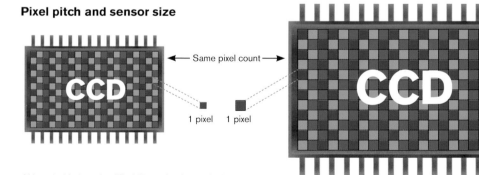

Although this is a simplified illustration it reveals that, although very different in terms of gross size, both sensors have the same number of pixels – their spatial resolution. Each pixel can be thought of as tiny wells collecting photons instead of water. The right-hand sensor's pixels are much bigger in terms of area and so are able to collect light quickly – assuming lenses used on both have the same F/stop ratio – without additional help from the camera's systems. This means that photos with less image noise – a better signal (the light) to noise (interference from camera electronics) ratio – and so better image quality.

High, medium and low resolution

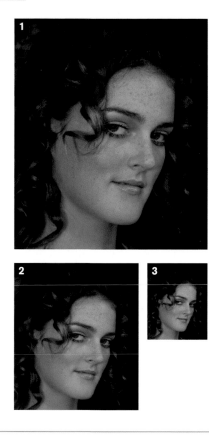

1 High-resolution 16MP image
This image represents a 16MP image with 4608x3456 pixels and has detail and pixels enough for very large prints; colours and detail are finely reproduced and this image could easily be printed at well over A2 (420mm x 594mm) in size.

2 Medium-resolution 10MP image
In this medium-resolution version of the same shot, despite having many fewer pixels (around 4032x3024 pixels), it still has bags of detail; indeed, this resolution was at the very top end of the scale for digital cameras only a year or so ago. It looks almost indistinguishable from the high-resolution 16MP image and can be easily printed at A3 or larger in size.

3 Low-resolution 5MP image
This low-resolution image of the same shot now has only 1400x1400 pixels and is typical of many camera phones or very old basic digital cameras. This would be ideal for email use but could be reduced in size further for use on-line or on screen. However, you will still get a good 6x4-inch print from it.

on which they are housed are (typically) around 2–3mm on the diagonal (although some newer smartphones now have larger sensors). Because they're so very small, their light-gathering power is low and this can seriously affect image quality. Images shot on smartphones may look great on screen, or at smaller print sizes, but you cannot make very large prints from them.

High- and low-resolution image comparison
A single frame of 35mm film contains the equivalent information of around 30MP of data if it were translated across to a digital camera. But it's not always about the numbers, as the human eye can only perceive a finite amount of detail – around 3MP worth of detail when viewing a print at around arm's length. As has been discussed, the more pixels your camera has on its sensor, the more detail it can capture, allowing you to display or print at a larger size. However, you don't always need all that data.

The images in the box above have each been reproduced to (broadly) demonstrate how more pixels can equate to more detail and so lead to differing output (or print) image sizes.

Memory and **memory cards**

Every digital camera uses memory of some sort, sometimes called 'digital film'; it provides storage space for your photos as you take them. Here we'll provide advice on how much and what type you need.

The memory card explained

In simple terms, the memory in a digital camera is a small computer chip called 'flash memory' that retains all the data that makes up the photo. Removable memory cards slot into the camera and can be taken out, allowing you to put in a fresh card. Removing a memory card from a camera does not mean you lose the images; they stay safely ensconced on the memory card for downloading or printing later, for example.

Those digital cameras with built-in memory capacity rarely have more than enough for a few photos – really just enough to get you started. Some digital cameras come complete with a removable memory card (usually of low capacity) included in the box when you buy them. Either way, you'll need to purchase extra cards. The types of cards your camera can use will be indicated in its manual, so check before you buy.

Memory cards at a glance

There are various types of removable memory cards in a range of capacities, measured in megabytes and gigabytes (MB or GB for short), from around 512MB to as high as 128GB, with larger capacities being developed all the time. Some smaller capacity cards previously available (less than 1GB) may be harder to find. One gigabyte is the equivalent of 1024MB so when comparing cards you should note a 1GB card has more memory space than a 512MB card, for example. The bigger the number of bytes indicated on a card, the more space there is, but the more it is likely to cost. Here's a look at the main types.

CompactFlash (CF) Type I and Type II

One of the most popular memory cards, CF has been around for almost as long as digital cameras. They are robust and come in capacities of up to 128GB and are now

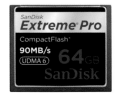

available in higher performance versions with improved write speeds to help deal with the increased data from high-resolution cameras and those that can shoot high-definition video. These are often denoted as having '300x' or '600x' write speeds.

SecureDigital (SD), SecureDigital High Capacity (SDHC) and SecureDigital Extra Capacity (SDXC)

The SD card format has been revamped with a new SDXC variant offering higher capacities, ranging from 32GB to 2TB (terabytes, or 1024GB), and improved performance. SDXC is not backward compatible with SD and SDHC devices, but those older cards will work in SDXC-equipped cameras. The new SDXC cards provide increased storage for today's high-resolution digital cameras and cater to the fact that the newer

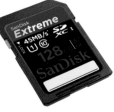

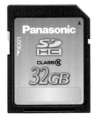

cameras can shoot high-definition video and so require even higher capacities and better performance. Mini and micro versions of the SD card technology are also available; technology borrowed from MP3 players and mobile phones is increasingly finding its way into some of the smaller compacts out there.

Memory Stick (MS)

Memory Stick is Sony's proprietary memory card format used across many of their products, from digital cameras to TVs. Memory 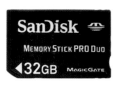 Stick Pro and Duo (including 'Magic Gate' cards) are versions of this MS format, but the type needed depends on the digital camera. Capacities range from 2GB to 32GB depending on the format, with a theoretical limit of 2TB achievable.

xD Picture Cards (xD)

This format was widely used by Fuji and Olympus digital cameras. Whilst small and theoretically able to achieve high capacities, it dropped out of favour in 2010. 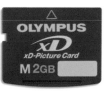 New xD cards are being manufactured but the cameras that use them are not, so availability of new cards will soon become an issue, as the cameras become obsolete.

What capacity cards should I buy?

The number of images you can fit onto a memory card will depend on the card capacity; the level of compression applied to the images in the camera (it varies from manufacturer to manufacturer); any adjustments you make to the image resolution (for different quality shots); and the effective number of pixels the camera has on its sensor.

To give an example, on a 1GB memory card in a 10MP camera you can shoot up to 500 basic quality images. Switch to higher quality settings such as uncompressed RAW (see *Saving your photos*) and that immediately drops to around 45 images.

Whilst having one large memory card for your digital camera might seem attractive and more cost effective than using a number of smaller cards, it's better not to have all your 'photo eggs' in one basket. Imagine the frustration if you had a once-in-a-lifetime holiday, shot all your photos onto one memory card and then lost it! This is a disaster easily averted if you buy two or three medium-sized cards. Instead of buying a single 32GB card, for example, buy two or three smaller (2GB, 4GB or 8GB) cards. It might cost a little more (though not always, as some of the much higher capacity memory cards are still very expensive) but you can be sure you'll have the same total capacity without the risk of losing all your photos if something goes wrong.

- *Some cameras use more than one type of memory card. But not every camera will use every type of card, so check before you buy. You cannot use a CF card in a camera that only uses SD, for example.*

- *Do buy several smaller memory cards to ensure that all your photos are not stored on one card. If something goes wrong, you won't then lose all the images.*

- *Remember: the more pixels your camera has, the faster your memory card will fill up.*

A buyer's guide

Choosing a digital camera can be daunting given the huge number of models on the market and their varied features. Here's a quick guide to help you work out what's really important when you buy.

The first thing to do is to narrow down the many possible buying criteria to a few key ones. Top of the list will probably be budget, and then what you need your digital camera for – holiday or family snaps or more advanced photo tasks.

What to spend?
In terms of cost, the most important factors, in no particular order, are these:

- As with most things in life, you get what you pay for, so don't scrimp on your investment.

- Budget for a decent-sized memory card (see *Memory and memory cards*) or several lower capacity ones.

- Generally, always buy a camera with as many pixels as you can afford (see the following descriptions of different-resolution cameras for more detailed advice on this).

- Buy a digital camera with as large a display screen as your budget allows. Key benefits include easily being able to see the shot as it looks before taking it, instantly reviewing it afterwards and, on newer touch-screen cameras, being able to control the camera via the screen with features such as 'touch snap' in which the camera focuses and snaps a shot at the point where you touch the screen.

What do you need from a digital camera?
Before you buy, you need to decide what you want from a digital camera. Once that's done, it becomes a much easier decision.

The most common things you might use your digital camera images for are:

- Posting on the Internet
- Sending by email
- Viewing on your PC screen or HDTV
- Printing out as photographs
- Using for professional work or to make money

Some digital cameras can provide images that are good for all these uses; some might not give images that are suitable for all of them. Knowing this is the key to buying the right camera.

Essentially, the number of megapixels (10MP or 12MP, for example) that the camera has is the key to the tasks it can perform. It's also worth bearing in mind that the more pixels your camera has, the higher its overall specifications are likely to be and the better its build quality. You'll get bigger pictures and more quality for your money.

8MP to 10MP digital cameras
These digital cameras are more basic, less expensive and have fewer features and (often) plastic build quality compared with some of the higher resolution models. Cameras below 8MP have almost entirely been phased out, but some newer 10MP cameras have arrived that use larger sensors (see *How many*

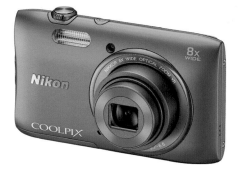

Nikon's COOLPIX S3600 is a great all-round 20MP compact, great for taking anywhere. Its 8x zoom lens adds flexibility and the small size makes it very pocketable.

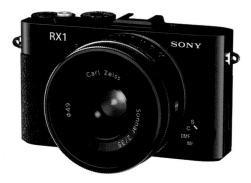

The Sony DSC-RX1 offers a professional level of D-SLR specification and optical quality in a compact body. The 24.3MP sensor allows for great image quality as does the superb Carl Zeiss fixed-focal length lens.

megapixels?), their bigger pixels helping to improve image quality. Most of these digital cameras now have high-definition (HD) video with sound too. These cameras are capable of excellent prints up to and over A3 in size.

10MP to 16MP digital cameras

The most popular and broadest range of cameras fit into this resolution bracket and are widely available. Expect to get enhanced shooting features and high-definition video with stereo sound built in. Very large poster-sized prints can be achieved and the detail these cameras can capture is great for most subjects from detailed landscapes to crisp portraiture. Buy as many pixels as you can afford in this range as often the features and build will be suited to a more professional style of imaging work.

16MP and above digital cameras

Some of the latest professional-level digital cameras have resolutions of 36MP. Many consumer-oriented digital compacts have over 16MP today; the level of detail and image quality they provide is stunning but comes at a price. However, the more pixels you have to play with, the larger the prints can be or the more detailed they can be.

Most of the higher end or professional-level digital cameras, now including most if not all D-SLRs, can shoot HD video with sound, which means you'll need higher performance memory cards to boot.

i More pixels, more detail

In general, it's best to buy a camera with as many pixels as you can afford, as you can always downsize an image if it has more pixels than you need, but you can't upsize an image that doesn't have enough.

For example, if you tried to print a lower resolution image shot at 5MP at the size you could print a 16MP photo, you would quickly see the blocky pixels and lack of detail. You cannot add detail that's not already there in the picture.

Starting to use your camera

Digital cameras are controlled in the same way as a traditional film camera but can also do so much more. Here's a quick guide to the basic operations to help you get started.

Inserting the batteries

Digital cameras are powered by electricity and so first you'll have to insert the batteries. Over 60% of all digital cameras use specially designed battery packs; some use multiple power sources, for example, AA batteries and/or a battery pack. Cameras that use rechargeable battery packs will come with a charger when you buy them. Charging the battery takes a couple of hours, but they should be fully charged before you begin. (See *Batteries and power* for more advice on batteries.) Once the batteries are inserted, you can turn the camera on using the on/off switch.

Inserting memory cards

Your memory card can only be inserted one way into the special slot on the camera. Once the memory card is inserted, you're ready to start shooting.

Memory cards are inserted into a digital camera, in this case a D-SLR camera, which can use both CompactFlash and SD cards.

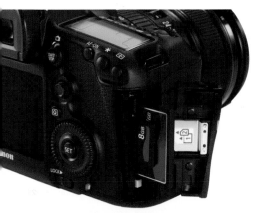

Shooting controls

The controls that actually allow you to take a photo are the shutter button and the 'mode' dial. The former is the most important button on the camera as it allows you to focus and fires the shutter, taking the picture. The latter is used to access different shooting functions, to change between playback and picture taking, and to set scene modes (see below).

The shutter button on your digital camera will have two pressures: the first activates the focusing, the second fires the shutter and, as such, it is the most important button on the camera.

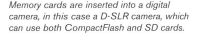

Using scene modes

Scene modes automatically set the camera up for specific shooting situations and are indicated by small icons on the mode dial or in the on-screen menus, or sometimes both, depending on the camera. Expect to find portrait, landscape, sports and night settings, although some digital cameras have many more. When you select the mode that matches your shot (portrait mode for a portrait and so on), the camera does almost all the work for you.

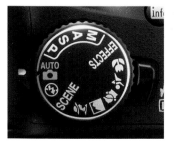

A typical mode dial will include icons such as those shown here, providing fast activation of the camera's various shooting options simply by turning it to the required mode.

Other controls

Other buttons provide control over various functions of your digital camera including the menus (see below), activating the flash, turning the screen on and off, and activating the self-timer.

Using menus

The menus which appear on your camera screen might look daunting at first, but they provide you with a step-by-step series of options for setting the camera up. From changing the date, choosing a resolution or adjusting the brightness of the screen, menus are the heart of your digital camera's settings. Many cameras have touch-screen technology, allowing you to directly interact with menus on the screen without using buttons or dials. However, be aware that this can leave fingerprints on the screen which get in the way when composing or viewing images.

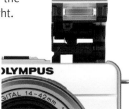

Menus are displayed on the camera's colour screen and provide fast, easy access to its settings.

Built-in flash

The flash lets you add extra, artificial light to a scene when it would otherwise be too dark to take a good photo. It can be set automatically or you can manually select it to flash for a particular shot. Additionally, you can use the flash to lift, or fill in, shadows (see *Creative flash*), and it also helps prevent unwanted silhouettes if the background is very bright.

The built-in flash provides extra light when shooting indoors or when it's dark.

Movies and audio functions

Most digital cameras have a movie mode with sound (many with stereo sound) and audio clip recording capability. Almost all are equipped to shoot HD video but can also shoot at lower resolutions for use on the Internet; some have special YouTube modes for this too. Movie modes allow you to shoot video with sound in short clips or continuously until the memory card is full. Audio clip recording is great for adding short audio annotations to your still photos.

Connecting to a PC or TV

Digital cameras are supplied with the cables needed to connect them to a TV, for viewing images, or a PC for saving images, editing, printing or burning CDs. You can also connect some cameras to compatible printers, tablets and TVs via Bluetooth, although this uses battery power quickly and its reliability and connection distance can vary.

Whichever digital camera you own, you'll be able to plug it into a PC using the leads supplied

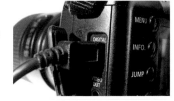

Care, maintenance
and cleaning

If you've invested your hard-earned cash in a digital camera, you'll want to look after it. Here are a few simple pointers to help protect your camera and maintain its performance.

A digital camera is a precision piece of electrical equipment and contains many delicate elements, particularly the optics in the lens, the electrical circuitry and the sensor. Each can be damaged quite easily unless you take care.

Camera bags
The simplest way to protect your digital camera is to keep it in a proper camera bag. A good option is to get a case that's waterproof with decent cushioning and an

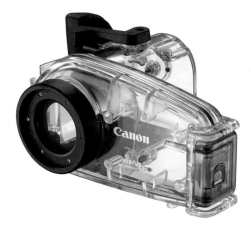

It's a good idea to always carry your camera in a protective case such as this padded, rainproof one from Case Logic.

Protect your digital camera with a waterproof housing such as this one designed for Canon compacts. Not only will your camera be safe from bad weather, sand and knocks, but it means you can take it underwater too.

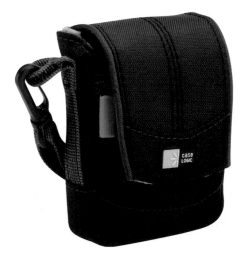

opening that fastens twice: velcro and a zipper, for example. Ensure there's enough room for spare memory cards and a lens cloth.

Protecting against dirt and water
Water and dirt, especially sand, are the digital camera's mortal enemies, unless you own one of the newer ruggedised compacts designed for such conditions. If not and you take your camera to the beach or into the wilds, use a special waterproof 'housing'. This will also keep out sand and dirt. Check with your camera's manufacturer for suitable housings. If you don't have a housing, put the camera back in its bag immediately after use.

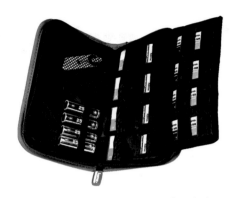

Don't forget to protect your memory cards and other accessories, such as batteries and USB sticks. Cases like this one are great at stopping dirt or dust from ruining delicate electrical connections.

Inserting leads

Many digital cameras come with their own leads made specially for connecting to a PC or TV. Never force a lead into a socket or use the wrong lead. If you damage the socket, the camera will need potentially expensive repairs.

Cleaning

Digital cameras aren't hard to clean – simply wipe them down with a lint-free cloth. Never use solvents or water. If you have a D-SLR and can see dust on the CCD sensor, never, ever clean it yourself. The CCD is very fragile and, despite the fact that you can buy CCD cleaners, if you touch the sensor, it can easily break. Only get a CCD cleaned by a servicing agent certified for your make of camera.

Storage

If you're not going to use a digital camera for a while, store it in its camera bag with a silica gel pack (it will come with one in its packaging when you buy it). These are small packs containing a gel that absorbs moisture very well. Also remove its batteries or you will risk corroding the contacts inside the camera.

Memory card care

Memory cards are NOT affected by airport X-ray machines, but ...

- They are affected by magnetic fields. Keep them away from magnets, (CRT) TV screens and audio speakers.

- Keep cards cool and dry, away from direct sunlight and humidity.

- Keep them away from dust, as this can block the small holes or electrical contacts used to communicate with your digital camera.

- Always keep cards in the protective cases in which you bought them.

- *Don't get sand in your digital camera.*

- *Don't get a digital camera wet. Use a protective housing.*

- *Don't store a digital camera with the batteries still inside.*

Zoom lenses

A zoom lens is a key feature on a digital camera as it adds tremendous flexibility to your photography. Here's what you need to know about them.

Most compact digital cameras have an optical zoom lens: a lens that can vary its field of view in order to magnify ('zoom in') or broaden ('zoom out') a scene. These are ideal for when you cannot get close to your subject or want to include more of it in the shot, making the camera very versatile.

Remember

Buying a digital camera with an optical zoom lens will give you great flexibility in your shot-taking, and the larger the zoom range, the greater the flexibility you will have.

or four times ('4x') and so on. The wider the focal range, the greater the 'x' factor (or 'times' factor) becomes and the greater the apparent magnification.

Here's an example to make all this clear. A digital camera with a zoom lens which has a 35–105mm focal range is said to be a '3x' optical zoom lens, because the highest

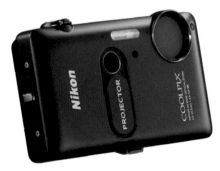

This Nikon is typical of many compact zooms but, unlike many, it also has a built-in projector to display your photos at a large size on a wall or screen.

Focal lengths

Zoom digital cameras have their focal lengths (the range through which the optics in a lens can move) specified by comparison with the focal length of the familiar (35mm) film camera. They are indicated on the camera lens in millimetres.

Whilst this may sound confusingly technical, all you need to know is helpfully simplified in the descriptions of digital cameras by using terms such as 'two times' (abbreviated to '2x')

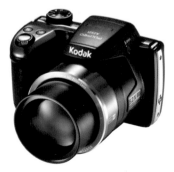

Many digital cameras have long or very long (sometimes called 'ultra') zoom lenses. In the case of this Kodak, it has an amazing 24mm to 1,248mm, or 52x, optical zoom lens.

focal length figure is three times the lowest focal length, i.e. 35 x 3 = 105. A 28–112mm lens would be a '4x', for example, and so on.

The optical zoom range available to digital cameras is growing as lens technology improves and there are now many digital cameras with so-called 'ultra-zoom' ranges with 36x and greater optical zooms, offering a focal range as wide as 24mm in some cases to as long as 1,248mm in the camera shown below left. The most common digital cameras have 3x to 5x zoom lenses and while they can't zoom as much as an 'ultra', they're less expensive and still very versatile.

Optical zoom or digital zoom?

Digital cameras, almost without exception and including those that already have an optical zoom lens, have a feature called digital zoom. This can electronically enlarge a portion of the sensor's image to produce a zooming effect.

Optical zoom works by using the lens to magnify the scene and it utilises the entire sensor area for the image, retaining full image quality and resolution.

Digital zoom enlarges a small central portion of the sensor instead. So it will produce blocky, grainy images and should be avoided if top quality prints are required.

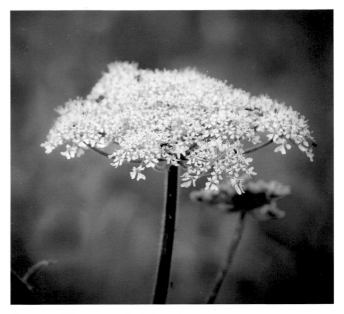

Two widely different images, both shot using a single zoom lens, which show how you can use zoom to improve a shot. By 'zooming out' (below) you can fit everything into a shot: in this case a dramatic beach scene. Zooming out is also particularly good for more confined spaces such as taking pictures indoors. The flower image (above), however, was 'zoomed into' to bring out detail, help the colour composition and add drama.

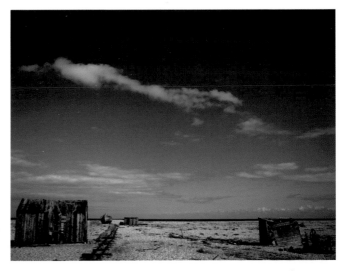

Fixed lenses

Most cameras come with a zoom lens as standard. But you might want to consider the alternative to these – the fixed lens camera. Here we'll explain which is best for you.

We've seen the flexibility a zoom lens has to offer, but there are a couple of benefits offered by a fixed lens digital camera which are not available to most zoom optics, making up for any loss in versatility. These are a higher optical quality and a compact size.

means that the lens is made specifically for that length, making it sharper (for more detail) and brighter (to let in more light) than the zoom lens equivalent. They often have a wider field of view too.

Compact sizes are possible because the design doesn't cater to the mechanisms needed to zoom the optical train back and forth. Battery power lasts longer too for the same reason.

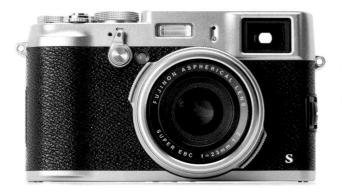

The Fujifilm X100S is typical of a growing number of high-end fixed lens compacts. Robust and largely aimed at enthusiasts, such cameras can be pricey but you get advanced features and a superb lens, in this case a sharp 23mm, f/2 Fujinon lens.

Advantages

Better optical quality results from the lens not being the optical equivalent of a Jack-of-all-trades. A zoom must do a multitude of optical tasks and, in order to achieve them, compromises are made in the lens designs which affect optical quality.

No such compromises are made in a fixed lens. Having one focal length, usually a wide or 'prime' view between 28mm and 35mm,

Disadvantages

Fixed lens digital cameras can seem expensive, largely due to the cost of their optics and the fact that these cameras are often premium models. Another consideration is that there are fewer fixed lens digital cameras on the market. Also, as already discussed, a fixed lens camera doesn't have the convenient flexibility of a zoom. Because of this, most people are willing to live with the compromises involved in a zoom camera.

The cheaper option

There are many very cheap non-zoom digital cameras on the market. They tend to use digital zoom to make up for the lack of an optical zoom. We've discussed the problems with digital zoom already, and with very cheap fixed lens digital cameras you actually get worse optics, poor image processing and potentially poorer results. These are best avoided.

Changing lenses

You're not always restricted to the lens your camera came with. If you're after more shooting flexibility on a compact, you can use an adapter lens. D-SLRs can use any lens made for them, but there are pitfalls. Here's what you need to know to make the right lens choice.

A digital camera with the ability to use any lens offers the photographer two things: unparalleled versatility and access to superb quality optics.

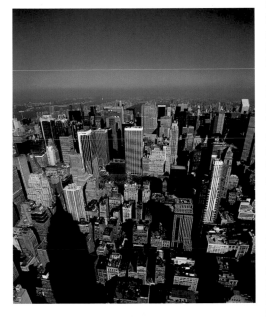
This photo was taken using a wide-angle lens, without which you couldn't fit everything into the shot.

Despite the fact that compact digital cameras come with a predetermined focal length range – or just a single focal length for a fixed lens camera – you can still buy specialist lenses and adapters that enable you to stretch your compact's abilities, including wide or telephoto lens adapters. Unlike on D-SLRs, adapter lenses don't replace the original lens – they fit over it.

The interchangeable lenses on D-SLRs are really their raison d'être, allowing you easily to remove a lens and replace it with another of a different focal length. Let's look at how best to adapt or change the lens on each of these types of camera.

Lens adapters for compact digital cameras

The only way to expand the abilities of a compact's lens when it is an integral part of the camera is to attach something over the front of that lens. Happily, many compact digital cameras come with a screw thread round the front of the lens barrel that provides the means to do just that.

Other types of adapter lenses clip over the front of the camera's entire lens barrel, there are some that strap on, while yet others have special magnetic strips that are used to mount them on the front of cameras. However, the screw-in variety is best as there's less chance of them getting out of alignment and they're less fiddly to use. The other types are, however, cheaper if you're on a tight budget.

Such specialist lens adapters might not offer the same optical quality as a lens made for a D-SLR, but they do provide a way to extend your shooting flexibility quickly and (relatively) cheaply.

Adapter optics are available that provide extra-wide-angle shooting abilities or extend the telephoto end of the lens (the longer focal lengths), providing an increase in optical performance without the drawbacks associated with a digital zoom.

Having said that, optical quality can drop with an attachment, so always buy the lens adapters designed for your camera and, if you can afford it, the ones made by the same camera manufacturer, since they'll be matched to the lens already built into your compact.

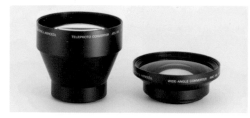

Telephoto and wide-angle converters such as these screw onto the front of your digital camera's lens, providing increased focal range for specific tasks such as zooming closer to your subject or squeezing all of a wide subject into the shot.

Avoiding adapter problems

Because lens adapters are basically a set of new, separate optics that 'bolt' onto the front of an existing lens, there are a few things worth considering before buying.

The lens adapter should be made from high-quality glass of at least as good a quality as that within the camera's lens. If not, expect image degradation.

This could include 'vignetting', where the corners of shots taken with the adapter will go dark, or an overall softness that's apparent on all shots. It could even make your photos suffer from barrel or 'pin cushion' distortion. The former makes the image bulge in a circular fashion around the middle and the latter pinches the image in at its corners.

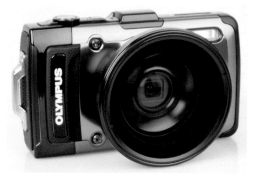

A very wide-angle lens – in this case a fisheye lens adapter fitted to the Olympus Tough TG-1 digital compact.

ℹ Lens filters

Another type of adapter you can attach over an existing lens is a filter. They're not really regarded as a lens but do provide optical 'special' effects. They include UV filters and polarisers which boost colours, and filters that will change the colour of a scene. They're fun to use but you'll first need to check if you need a special mount to use them on your camera.

✔

- *Do buy the lens adapter made specifically for your camera's lens (a 'matched' adapter). This way you'll be able to ensure all the optics are optimised, thus reducing possible distortion.*

- *Do buy screw-mounted adapters. They're very secure and offer a light-tight, seamless join with the camera.*

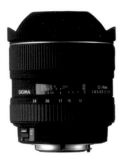

This is Sigma's 12–24mm wide-zoom lens, ideal for squeezing in everyone in a large group at a wedding, for example.

- **Don't forget that the amount of light reaching the sensor will drop if you are using a lens adapter.**

- **Don't buy cheap adapters. Image quality will be impaired, distortion will be apparent and you could get horrible pixel fringing too.**

Specialist lenses for D-SLRs

D-SLRs use interchangeable lenses and each make of D-SLR will accept only those lenses specifically made for it; Canon use one type of lens and mount, Nikon another, for example. Some independent lens manufacturers such as Sigma or Tamron make lenses that can be used across different D-SLR makes and models, each fitted with the correct mount for the camera to which it will be married.

These lenses are designed to provide a solution to specific shooting tasks from the relatively mundane, such as portraiture where a lens is built to provide the optimal focal length (usually around 135mm) and a flattering blurred background, to extreme close-up (macro) shooting or the ability to take very-wide-angle shots. In each case, the lens is optimised for its job, to a greater or lesser degree.

The digital rangefinder mirror-less compact system camera (CSC)

The digital rangefinder is a compact digital camera able to use interchangeable lenses. Fuji's X-Pro1 is one of the latest rangefinder models worth looking at. Meanwhile, the mirror-less compact system cameras, such as the Olympus PEN cameras and the 'G' series from Panasonic, grow apace, with a large range now available from other brands such as Samsung and now Canon has a CSC of its own too.

Nikon also has its Nikon 1. These cameras are small, 10MP, compact mirror-less D-SLRs

that have the latest in Nikon CMOS sensor technology, which allows for very fast AF, high quality stills and superb HD video. At the time of writing, there were eight models available, offering a broad range of specification and kit to fit most budgets.

Mirror-less compact system cameras are more expensive than 'normal' compacts with the equivalent – or better – resolution, but they offer the performance and image quality of larger D-SLRs without the bulk.

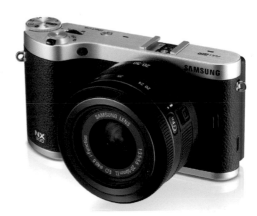

Samsung's NX300 is one of the models within the growing mirror-less compact system camera market, featuring high-speed shooting and focusing, a 20MP sensor and a large touch-sensitive display. Such cameras offer the advantages of larger D-SLR interchangeable lens systems but without the bulk.

Which **computer?**

If you want to create slide shows of your images or edit and print your own photos at home, a computer is essential. So what should you look for when selecting a PC to use for digital photography?

A personal computer (PC) ideal for digital photography can be thought of as a digital darkroom. Anyone keen on getting hands-on with their pictures, particularly when it comes to playing around with printing, creating enlargements or making slide shows with music and special effects, will need a PC. Tablets offer a very portable way to shoot and deal with images using photo apps, but a PC is essential for more complex editing.

What type of PC?

There are two main types of computer on the market – laptops and desktops – but the range of tablets now available, from makers such as Apple, Samsung and HP, mean there are other options albeit with some limitations. Whether you buy a laptop, desktop or tablet is down to the tasks you want to do and whether or not you'll want to do them 'on location' and need portability, or work from a fixed location such as your home. Whatever your need, remember that laptops tend to have slower processors, or will be more expensive than a desktop with equivalent processing power, their hard disk space will have less storage and the screens will (often) be smaller, but all will have built-in wireless connectivity (see *Getting connected*). While tablets offer superb portability, their creativity is limited to the apps you can run. 'Light' versions of some PC software programs are available, but you won't be able to do advanced edits, plus the processing power and storage are limited too.

Mac or Windows?

Whether you buy a desktop or laptop, it will use a specific operating system (OS). This is simply a computer program used to make a computer run.

The most common is the Windows operating system. At the time of writing, around 91% of people who own a PC use a Windows PC. They're made by a variety of manufacturers, of which Dell, Hewlett-Packard and Acer are good examples; and today, most PC makers have PC systems optimised (with a faster graphics processor, say) for specific tasks such as digital imaging or movie playback, as well as PCs for more general tasks; so check before you buy.

The second main type of operating system is the Mac OS used in Apple Macintosh (Mac) computers. Originally designed to be simple enough for children to grasp quickly, Macs do essentially the same job as Windows PCs. Both these types of computer come in laptop and desktop form.

A Mac tends to be more expensive 'off the shelf' but comes loaded with proprietary software – and the right hardware – for image manipulation and all multimedia tasks from making and editing movies to sorting digital photos, storing music and creating slide-shows. It will let you share your work on-line or via the Cloud, but if you want to make a DVD or Blu-ray disc it's worth noting that most new Apple computers don't have a built-in disc writer/reader, so you would need to buy an accessory disc burner.

Windows PCs can look cheaper to buy at first but the cheaper models will probably not have powerful enough graphics abilities to handle the large image files created by today's high-resolution digital cameras. This means you could end up spending just as much on your Windows PC upgrading it, or installing extra software in order to make it perform fast enough to cope, so check before you buy that it is capable of dealing with what you intend to throw at it.

Tablets are different again: they have special OSs such as iOS (Apple iPad) or Android (non-Apple tablets), which use apps. You can check emails, browse the Internet, play games and perform light, fun image editing techniques in readiness for heavier edits on your laptop or desktop.

Compatibility

Traditionally, Mac and Windows software has not been transferable: you could not run a Mac program on a Windows PC and vice versa; but things have changed. Parallels Desktop is a good example of a program that allows you to install and run Windows on a Mac, whilst the free WineBottler application allows you to run Windows applications within the Mac OS, but many applications for PCs, Mac or Windows are 'universal'; they work or have versions for both OSs.

Which features to look for

Whatever type of computer you buy, you need to ensure that it has a large hard disk, as this is where all the programs and files are stored. Images rapidly fill up storage space, so buy a PC with the biggest hard disk you can afford, but ideally a minimum

of around 500GB or 1TB, or more.

Ensure you buy a PC with the 'fastest' processor you can afford, ideally a multi-core processor, for example, Intel's Quad Core processor. The more processors the PC has, the faster it will be able to work.

Most computers today are sold with a high-definition LCD screen, which is thin and saves desk space. Ensure you get a PC with a built-in (or accessory) CD/DVD/Blu-ray drive. Tablets will definitely lack such a drive, but you can usually connect one to them. Without such features you won't be able to write your own slide shows onto a disc, although you will still be able to share them on-line via websites such as Facebook or YouTube once connected to the Internet or another PC.

Maximise the RAM

A simple thing you can do to make your digital imaging experience faster on a PC is maximise the amount of RAM.

Random Access Memory (RAM) is different from storage memory (the hard disk) as your PC uses it to carry out the tasks you give it. All of your commands and the resulting data are processed here. So the more your PC is doing at once, say, processing changes to one image while you try to print another, the more quickly the RAM gets used up, and the slower your PC becomes – no matter how 'fast' your PC processor, or how large its hard disk.

Ensure you have as much RAM installed as you can afford – 4GB or more is a good start. Check what the PC comes with and, if it'll take more RAM, my advice is to add it; it is more cost effective to have extra RAM fitted when you buy rather than later.

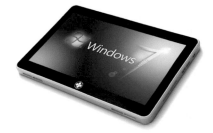

Computer **accessories**

You've got your PC and camera. Now let's see if there are any accessories that will help improve your productivity and make your digital imaging work easier and simpler.

Your PC will come with a standard mouse and keyboard enabling you to input instructions and activate some of your system's many features. But there are other devices available that can help make the imaging process even simpler.

Graphics pads

Using your mouse to carry out image editing tasks is okay, but a graphics pad (shown below) makes things even easier and more precise. You use a digital pen to 'draw' your changes onto the screen. Working this way is more intuitive and ideal for fine adjustments and intricate image editing work. A mouse is also supplied as an alternative to the pen, for less precise, general use.

Memory card reader

A memory card reader is a small device that accepts camera memory cards and usually plugs into a PC's USB port. It's a faster and easier way to download images from your camera to the PC, without connecting it directly, therefore saving camera battery power. Memory card readers range from those which accept one card to those which accept multiple card formats.

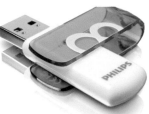

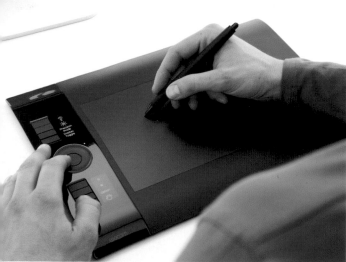

Pen or USB drives

Pen drives are another useful accessory. They are great for quickly swapping data between all your USB-equipped devices, they're relatively cheap to buy, can have large capacities (up to 32GB) and save time and money not having to burn CDs or DVDs.

External hard drives

Also known as external hard disks, these are an ideal way to extend the storage capacity of your PC. With capacities from 20GB for more portable discs to over four terabytes (one terabyte (1TB) is equal to one thousand gigabytes), such drives mean you don't need to clutter your PC's precious hard drive with loads of images and other digital data such as MP3 music files or your digital camera movies. Buy the largest capacity drive you can afford; you'll be amazed how quickly they fill up. Another benefit of having a large-capacity external hard drive is that it makes it simple to back up your data. (See *Backing up*.)

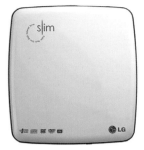

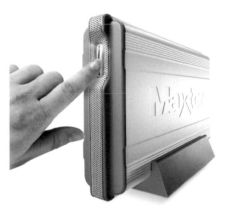

on-line, such as create DVD slide shows, an external burner is invaluable. They're inexpensive too. If you can get a Blu-ray compatible drive, it will be able to write CDs, DVDs and Blu-ray discs, although it will cost a little more to buy.

They're also great for backing up or archiving your data to optical discs (see *Backing up*), particularly the higher capacity Blu-ray discs that fit up to 50GB of data.

Portable burners are available and add even greater flexibility because they can be used on the go with any PC, laptop or compatible tablet. They are powered by USB 2.0 (or higher) ports, by battery or the mains; some by all three.

External CD, DVD or Blu-ray burner

As storage options on the Cloud grow, many newer PCs lack optical drives or disk writers (as do many earlier PCs): Apple has dropped them from its iMac range, for example. This means that if you intend to do more than just share your images

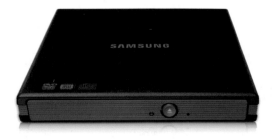

Getting **connected**

It's all very well having a digital camera, PC and other kit, but now you need to get them to communicate with each other. Here's a guide on how best to get everything connected.

USB connections

The most common form of connection for a digital camera to a modern PC is a USB connection. The latest version of this technology, USB 3.1, provides data flow speeds 20 times faster than USB 2.0. Most digital cameras have a USB port and lead as standard, so you can download images to your PC easily. USB also enables 'hot swapping', which simply means you can plug or unplug the cables without needing to restart your computer or the device.

Your camera will also probably come with a video lead which will allow you to connect your camera direct to your TV to show pictures on screen.

There are other forms of interface (connection between digital devices and a PC), and systems will have one, two or all of them, usually depending on price.

FireWire and HDMI

FireWire (or IEEE 1394) is a fast data cable connection common to many digital cameras, almost all PC systems and many printers, camcorders and scanners. FireWire comes in two 'speeds', FireWire 400 and 800. Many cameras are equipped with HDMI ports that

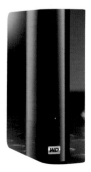

This external hard drive is one of the latest devices to use the super fast USB 3.1 connectivity system, although it will work with older computers with older USB connections.

connect cameras directly to HDMI compatible devices such as TVs or projectors for direct HD playback.

Ethernet and power-line network connectivity

Ethernet is computer network technology typically used to allow a small local network of connected PCs to connect to the Internet with a wired Ethernet connection and an Internet router.

Power-line networking uses special adapters connected to your home's AC electrical wire and your router via Ethernet cable so it simultaneously transmits electrical power and computer data. Any AC socket in the home can be added to a power-line network with additional adapters, to build a fast, robust home network.

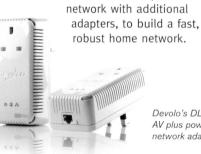

Devolo's DLAN AV plus power-line network adapter.

Wireless connections

Wires abound with all these interfaces, so consider wireless networking or WiFi connectivity. WiFi devices transmit data in a waveform and can connect together multiple devices, such as a printer, PC, tablet or camera, without any cables. You can send images to your PC wirelessly as you shoot

Connection speeds

It's no surprise that the faster the rate at which data is transferred, the faster you can work, and each of the main connection options has different connection speeds. We don't have to worry about the exact rate they work at, but it's useful to know which is fastest.

- **Bluetooth:** *Bluetooth is very slow when compared with cable and other WiFi connections.*

- **WiFi:** *WiFi is getting faster all the time but relatively slow compared with a direct USB 2.0, 3.1 or FireWire connection. Also, WiFi speed is affected by the number of obstacles in the way (number of walls and the size of the room, for example). The latest type (802.11n) is faster than previous versions such as 802.11a, 802.11b and 802.11g, and offers greater range.*

- **USB 2.0/3.1:** *USB 2.0 is faster than FireWire 400 but USB 3.1 is even faster, ideal for larger data transfers, and outperforms FireWire 800.*

- **FireWire 400 and 800/IEEE 1394:** *FireWire is common and fast, although not as fast as USB*

3.1 (see left). But it's still widely used because it is reliable.

- **Ethernet connection:** *There are two main types of Ethernet: Fast Ethernet (IEEE 802.3u) has data transfer (throughput) rates of up to 100Mbits/second, and Gigabit Ethernet (IEEE 802.3ab) up to 1000Mbits/second. The actual throughput rates vary greatly depending on the size and type of your network, the connected devices, number of adapters and your home's wiring if using power-line technology.*

- **Thunderbolt Technology:** *The latest and the fastest connection type being adopted by PC makers, Thunderbolt beats all others in terms of transfer speed and ease of use.*

---

too, using cards such as Eye-Fi's SD/SDHC memory cards with built-in WiFi connectivity. Some also allow automatic geotagging or transfer to the Internet.

You can also connect to WiFi from your smartphone, either at home or via public 'hot spots', such as a café. This enables you to share images on-line without impacting your data usage allowances.

Bluetooth is another example of wireless networking, and can also be found on many modern mobile camera phones. It is a common wireless interface for up to eight devices over a range of about 30 feet (10m). If you have a Bluetooth-enabled printer you could print images directly from a Bluetooth camera without needing a physical wire, for example. Bluetooth is not as flexible as WiFi or Eye-Fi memory cards but still saves on wires and associated clutter.

Cloud computing and connection

Cloud computing or 'the Cloud' is a system giving individual computers (connected via the Internet) the ability to run a program or application at the same time without installing anything on the PC. You can share and save data and buy services, such as off-site back-up storage. Advantages are the ability to access your images and data across multiple devices anywhere in the world (when connected to the Internet) but it can be slow to synchronise large amounts of data and can be expensive.

Thunderbolt Technology

The newest connection type is called Thunderbolt Technology, a very high-speed PC connection running at 10Gbps (10 gigabits per second), which supports both data and HD display data on a single cable.

Which **software?**

Your digital camera will come with a CD-ROM of assorted software, or links to a web page where you can download the software for your camera from the Internet, so which extras do you need?

The software with your camera

The 'proprietary' software that comes with a digital camera is very important as it provides the necessary programs to get your PC and camera talking properly (though depending on the model you buy it may not need – or even have – this software). It will come on a CD-ROM and will be very easy to install by following the instructions in the camera's manual or shown on screen once you insert the disc into your computer's CD drive.

The exact features of the software supplied will depend on your camera model, but it usually includes tools to save images onto your PC, which then make it easy to sort and search through them. It may also allow basic image editing, although there are additional software packages you can buy or download (many for free) that provide more advanced digital imaging tools.

What image editing software can do

Why edit your images? Simply, it's an easy way to improve them, either by subtle correction or by applying more creative effects. For example, you can:

- Resize images for printing or use on a web page
- Improve colour
- Correct exposure problems
- Remove redeye from a portrait
- Crop an image to improve composition
- Make a blurred photo sharp
- Add special effects
- Remove unwanted elements of a scene.

The ways in which image manipulation software can be used to achieve these effects is the subject of Section 3 of this book.

What software to buy or download

The following are some of the best software packages you can load onto your computer to enhance your image editing.

Adobe Photoshop CS

Still seen as the de facto professional-level image editing program, it is expensive but

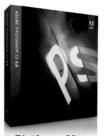

● **Platform: Mac and Windows**

comes loaded with all the latest imaging tools to manipulate your photos on your PC. It's also now included in Adobe's Creative Cloud, which is an alternative to a 'boxed' product that gives access to Adobe's entire suite of media software for a monthly subscription.

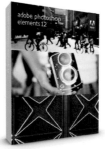

● **Platform: Mac and Windows**

Adobe Photoshop Elements

This is just like a cut-down version of Photoshop CS with only the digital photography 'elements' left in, hence the name. It is inexpensive but very powerful, and as it is tailored for digital photography it's one of the best to use.

Adobe Lightroom

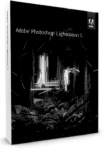

Ideal for both professional and amateur snappers, Lightroom is a fast way to manage, create and display your photos. It has a set of advanced yet simple tools and 'filters' for fast and powerful image editing, as well as advanced organisation tools.

● **Platform: Mac and Windows**

ArcSoft PhotoStudio

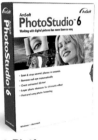

This package contains powerful editing tools married to an enhanced browser interface with a Photoshop-like feel. Auto editing functions such as redeye removal are included. This is very affordable and worth trying.

● **Platform: Windows only**

Corel PaintShop Pro Ultimate

Corel's latest and newest photo editor is PaintShop Pro Ultimate, an affordable alternative to Photoshop CS. It has all the power of PaintShop Pro but with new kit

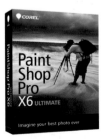

that includes 64-bit processing power, 'Perfectly Clear' image correction technology, improved portrait enhancement tools and a collection of other creative extras including RAW editing, HDR processing and much more.

● **Platform: Windows only**

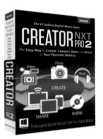

● **Platform: Platform independent – accessed through your web browser**

Pixlr

This is one of a growing number of (free in this case) on-line photo editing services. It is similar to Photoshop but is downloaded and used through a web browser. Mobile variants for compatible smartphones or tablets can also be downloaded, and these have a more limited suite of tools and effects filters.

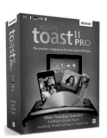

● **Platform: Windows only**

Roxio Creator NXT Pro2

Roxio's excellent media editing suite is the comprehensive Creator NXT Pro2. It has everything you'll need to edit, create and use special effects – for photos and videos – as well as copy, burn, convert and share all your media creations.

Roxio Toast Titanium (and Titanium Pro)

Extremely powerful CD and DVD burner with sophisticated tools for video, slide show and also music creation. Toast comes complete with automatic back-up software, it allows streaming across TiVo for TV on-the-go and lets you sync up folders across multiple computers, folders or external drives. Toast now also allows you to convert your media for playback on the iPad or iPhone and share it directly via YouTube, Facebook and Twitter.

● **Platform: Mac only**

Photo **apps**

Apps for Android, Windows and iOS devices are a great way to edit and transform images shot with or stored on your tablet or smartphone.

Working with photos on our smartphones and tablets has become so much easier as the quality of the apps available has improved.

Whilst not as powerful as full image editing packages such as PaintShop Pro or Photoshop, which are designed for use on a laptop or desktop with plenty of RAM and hard disk space, these apps are fun and very easy to use. Think of them as a way to start playing with your images, in preparation for the real work on your main computer, or just as a way of sharing images straight from the device.

The quality of the images on your smartphone cannot compete with your compact or D-SLR – have a look at the lens on your smartphone and compare it with even a small compact camera and you'll see what I mean – however, the convenience of having a digital camera to hand at all times cannot be argued with.

Specialist apps provide a way to improve phone shots, adding filters or allowing you to mimic the sort of effects possible in a dedicated digital camera. These include adding bokeh (the blurred, out-of-focus effect achieved by shooting with a wide aperture on your lens), lens flare, light trails and other filters to add aged or scratchy looks to shots.

Many of these apps are free and, as a way of creating more beautiful images from your smartphone, without needing to know a lot about the technical aspects of photography, they are very convenient. If you want to learn the traditional camera techniques, however, you can still use apps for inspiration. When travelling without my camera, I often use the visual effects of some of these apps, such as Big Lens (see below), to test out how a subject might look if I were to photograph it properly.

But ultimately apps are best for adding effects to your smartphone snaps ready for sharing.

 Photoshop Touch
A mini version of the full program, this offers some of the core features found in the desktop version of Photoshop. You can create layered images, edit them using Photoshop-like tools, add clever image effects and then share them on YouTube or social media sites such as Facebook and Twitter.
● **Platform: iOS, Android**

Photoshop Express
Differing from PS Touch, this allows you to apply fast edits to images shot with or stored on your device or on-line. Finger gestures on your device's screen do the work, including fixing images with odd colour casts, cropping and rotating. You can also shoot straight from within the app too.
● **Platform: iOS, Android, on-line**

Snapseed
This creative app is designed to help you enhance and share photos on your tablet or smartphone by choosing from a number of filters and effects. Editing is as simple as picking a filter and then using finger gestures to adjust the filter's effect.
● **Platform: iOS, Android, Mac OS**

Instagram

As its name suggests, fast photo-sharing is Instagram's raison d'être. Here you snap a photo on your device, choose a filter or effect to transform its look and feel, and then share it via Facebook, Twitter or Flickr. An easy-to-use, popular and innovative app.

- **Platform: iOS, Android**

Photo Effects Studio

This app lets you quickly and easily change your photos with the aid of hundreds of built-in filter effects, such as glows, fog, rain, lightning and starry night skies. You can also add neat frames or mimic styles like mosaic or cubism.

- **Platform: iOS**

Big Lens

This mimics the effects of shooting photos using a big aperture lens, providing the effect of a narrow depth-of-field blurring the background. Tools include a Smart Focus system, Aperture Control and filter effects for further creativity to add punch to images shot with or stored on your iPad or iPhone.

- **Platform: iOS**

Photosynth

An interactive panorama creation app, this makes vertical and horizontal panoramic images within your iOS device, even shooting a complete 'sphere' effect. You can link the panoramas to the Internet, sharing them on Facebook and other social media sites, or sites like Bing Maps.

- **Platform: iOS**

Aviary Photo Editor

You can capture and edit images quickly with this fast app. Its versatile tools include enhancing and cropping images and adding filters, stickers and frames to the images captured via the app or to those in your gallery/albums.

- **Platform: iOS, Android and Windows Phone7**

Pixlr Express+

Autodesk's Pixlr Express combines its new flash-based web image editor with its original photo app, Pixlr-o-matic, which was similar to Instagram, using filters and effects. Pixlr Express adds in a variety of versatile tools to the mix and you can save photos to the Cloud, so it is great for image editing on the move.

- **Platform: iOS and Android**

Camera+

Combining snapping with excellent editing tools and features, this app will dramatically transform the quality of your images. A standout feature is its Clarity function, where a simple tap corrects colours, adjusts contrast and brightness, and enhances details. Other features include digital flash, brushing and layered effects, borders and captions, as well as standard photo editing tools. The iPad version has even more advanced features, while both iPad and iPhone versions offer syncing with the iCloud.

- **Platform: iOS**

Repix

An intuitive app, this lets you 'remix' photos by using one of many brush effects. With the tip of your finger, paint various effects, colours and artistic flourishes onto your images. A suite of filters and frames finish off your designs. The app allows for direct sharing to Facebook, Instagram, Twitter, Flickr and Tumblr, as well as via email.

- **Platform: iOS and Android**

Slow Shutter Cam

This app lets you capture images that have the effects of slow shutter speed, such as light trails, ghostly images, soft waterfall effects and adding blur to convey movement. Three modes of Automatic, Manual or Light Trail can be selected.

- **Platform: iOS**

Which **printer?**

It's really easy to turn your digital images into photographic prints. But you'll need a printer for this and there are hundreds to choose from. Here's a buyer's guide to what you need.

Most digital cameras can print directly through a compatible printer or via a computer, and printing the images yourself provides great flexibility in terms of the size of the print you can make. We deal with the practicalities of printing images in the topic *Printing*, but first here are some tips on making sure you have the right printer.

Inkjet printers

Inkjet printers are the most common type of printer, designed for general home and office use. They come in many varieties, some more suitable for printing photos than others. Some have WiFi built in too, so you can print directly from compatible cameras or smartphones.

Standard inkjets use a combination of four coloured inks – cyan, magenta, yellow and black – that combine to form the colours we see on a print. But inkjets designed for high quality photo printing use these four colour inks plus special photo inks. All such extra inks are designed to improve the colour rendition on the prints and create finer gradations between light and dark areas.

Inkjet printers come in various sizes: 6x4-inch 'normal' print size, which are dedicated to print just that size photo, A4, A3 and even A2. Some can print on rolls of paper and/or CDs and DVDs, so you can customise discs as you go. A4 (and larger format) printers accept 'normal' letter-sized media, and can therefore be used to print

Printers don't always need to be connected to a computer to print. You can connect cameras (and other devices with cameras such as smartphones or tablets) directly to a printer, insert memory cards into slots built into the printer, or connect wirelessly (depending on your printer). Some of the latest portable printers (shown here) let you print almost anywhere; battery operated or powered by a car charger or the mains, they are self-contained units that allow you to connect your camera and print as you shoot.

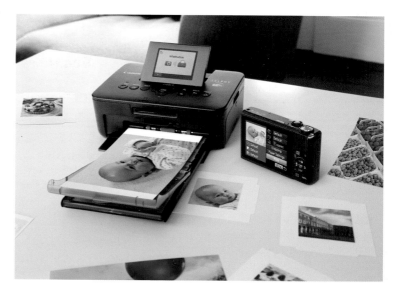

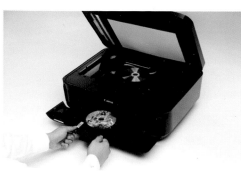

Many printers combine a scanner, copier and printer; some even boast a built-in fax too. The so-called 'all-in-one' combined printer, copier and scanner saves on desk space and will still print high-quality photos and documents and do scanning/copying/faxing as well, depending on the model you buy.

- Look for a printer which is a 'true' photo printer (it'll say on the box); they often use extra photo inks.

- Inkjet printers with separate ink tanks can be more economical to use.

- Dye sub printers cannot be used for anything other than photos.

- Always buy a 'photo-quality' inkjet printer if photos are the main task your inkjet will be used for.

both general work documents and photos. A3 printers offer larger print sizes and (sometimes) better colour and print resolution, providing superb print quality, but are expensive. A2 printers tend to be the preserve of the professional and are designed primarily for studio work; they're expensive but will produce stunning quality.

Dye sublimation printers

Also known as 'dye sub' printers, these are designed specifically for printing photos, and offer excellent quality. They come in a range of sizes from 'normal' print sizes (6x4 inches) up to A4. They use a special film coated in cyan, magenta and yellow dyes, plus a special fixing layer dye. These are transferred to a special paper which is designed to receive the dyes (or 'sublimated'), using heat.

The downside is that dye sub printers cannot be used for general print jobs such as letters, but if you just want 6x4-inch photo prints, a dye sub might be the printer for you.

Printing without a PC

Most photo printers now have direct printing capability. This allows you to connect the camera to the printer via the supplied connecting lead or via Bluetooth or a wireless network to produce prints without needing a computer. So if you don't have a PC, you should check you are buying a printer with such capabilities. Many printers will also have built-in memory card slots into which you can insert your camera's memory card and print from it directly that way. This type of printer can also act as a card reader, allowing you to download images from your memory cards to a connected PC.

i Scanners

Scanners can bring your old film photos into the digital domain and come in two main types. Flatbed scanners have an A4 glass plate on which prints and documents are placed to be scanned onto your PC. You can also get dedicated film scanners, which allow you to scan negatives or slides and create higher quality digital scans than scanning a print on its own, but these cost more. If you think you are likely to want to scan negatives or slides, the best value option is to get a flatbed scanner with a transparency unit (or TPU) built in.

Preventing **camera shake**

It's very easy for camera shake to blur your photos. But there is a range of solutions and support accessories to prevent this.

What causes camera shake?

Camera shake is caused when the shutter speed your digital camera uses is so slow that it is not fast enough to freeze the human body's natural and slight shaking motion – or any other movement for that matter. Such slow shutter speeds come about as a result of using a long focal length which reduces the amount of light reaching the camera's sensor, or just if it is too dark, for example.

Even when you can control the shutter speed on your digital camera, you still need to keep the camera steady in low light and using flash is not always an option. So when taking a portrait shot or photographing city lights at night, or even a sunset when the sun is very low, a support for the camera will ensure you always achieve a sharp image for your troubles.

Here are some of the best support options.

Preventing shake by adjusting shutter speed

To prevent camera shake in your photos always use a shutter speed that's the reciprocal of the focal length in use. Therefore, if you use a 100mm focal length, you should use a shutter speed of at least 1/100th second. If you use a 150mm focal length then the shutter speed will need to be at least 1/150th second and so on.

If you cannot control the shutter speeds on your digital camera, as is the case with very basic digital cameras, then to stop camera shake you will have to support the camera, so a camera support in the form of a tripod or monopod is essential.

Tripods

A tripod (left) is a three-legged support with telescopic legs that the camera screws onto via the screw lug on the tripod's mount and the threaded tripod bush on the base of the digital camera. Tripods are ideal when using very long focal lengths or in low light.

Tripods come in many sizes, from very portable mini tabletop models to massive and bulky professional ones built to keep your camera steady in almost any environment, even in strong winds. Tripods are ideal for shooting landscapes where sharp detail is crucial, long exposures at night or if you want to include yourself in a shot.

A carbon fibre tripod is a good option for saving on weight when carrying, yet maintaining the strength and rigidity needed for crisp shots in any conditions.

Monopods

A monopod – as the name suggests – is similar to a tripod but with only one telescopic leg designed to help support the camera. The camera mounts on top in the same way as on a tripod, via its tripod bush. It helps to keep the camera steady while still providing a large degree of manoeuvrability. Monopods are not as steady as tripods; you have to hold them and they require a little practice to use properly. But they are a lighter and more portable solution.

Monopods are not ideal for long exposures at night but are great if you need to shoot a fast-moving subject with a longer focal length, such as a running child at a school sports day event, for example.

Other supports

It's worth noting that basic digital cameras or those designed to be small enough to fit in a pocket may not have a means of connecting to a tripod. For these cameras you'll have to use an alternative means of support or use BluTack to 'stick' the camera to the tripod head. This is primitive, but it works because such small cameras are very light. Make sure that you take great care that the camera is adequately fixed to avoid it falling.

One good alternative means of support available to buy from many camera shops uses a 'bean bag' construction which you can use to help cradle your camera on fence posts, walls or even the ground. They're waterproof, come in various shapes and sizes and the filling provides a stable cushion into which you can snugly fit the camera. They're extremely versatile, as almost anything in the environment can become your camera's support. But again take care to ensure that the camera is securely supported.

Tripod heads

The 'head' is the part of the tripod where the camera screws into place. Some use a special quick-release mechanism where the camera screws onto a mount that stays with the camera, enabling it to be quickly taken off without unscrewing it. More important, however, are the movements allowed by the head. Some tilt, some turn and some swivel all the way round; some do all three. The more movement you have, the more the tripod will cost, but the greater the flexibility once the camera is nestled neatly in place.

Using a remote release

To avoid exacerbating camera shake when you activate the shutter, you can use the camera's self-timer, or a remote or cable release. Older digital cameras accept a mechanical release that screws into the shutter button to allow you to take a picture.

Some use a special electrical release that works in a similar fashion but costs more. Other digital cameras come complete with a tiny infra-red activated remote control (or have accessory remotes you can buy) that allows you to trigger the camera from another vantage point, including from within the shot.

Optical and digital image stabilisation

Optical image stabilisation (OIS) is a system built into most digital cameras or their lenses, which compensates for and helps reduce the effects of camera shake. It does this by moving around either special 'active' optics or the camera's sensor to compensate for any movement, although there's a limit to the amount of shake it can mitigate against. Lenses with OIS built in will be more expensive, as will cameras with OIS built into their bodies, but for the latter the lenses will be automatically stabilised (and cheaper too).

Digital image stabilisation (DIS) is a similar feature on some cameras but it increases your camera's sensitivity to achieve higher shutter speeds. It is not as effective as OIS, and it can introduce unwanted image noise. However, when combined with OIS you can reduce the effects of both camera shake and subject blur (when the motion of the subject makes it blurred in the shot).

Extra **flash**

Almost every digital camera has a built-in flash unit designed to give a burst of artificial light, though they're small and don't always provide as much illumination as you need. But there are several solutions for too little light.

Most digital cameras' flash units are ideal for subjects close to the camera or as a way of filling in shadows in brighter conditions, but not much beyond this. However, depending on the type of digital camera you own, you can increase the amount of light at your disposal by using an accessory or 'off-camera' flashgun. These are much larger and provide a much brighter, more controllable burst of light than a camera's built-in flash. Several types are available.

Hotshoe flash

Many digital cameras have a hotshoe on their top plate: a secure fitting with electrical contacts. This provides a way to connect an accessory flashgun to your camera. Such flashguns have their own battery power (usually from four AA batteries) and once connected, an on-board computer 'talks' to your camera to get the flash exposure right each time it fires. This computer operates in the same way as it would for the built-in flash, which is automatically turned off when an accessory flash is mounted on the camera. Some more expensive models offer comprehensive manual control.

Many flashguns also have what's called a 'bounce head': these are the best types to use as the flash's head can tilt, turn and swivel in order to redirect (or 'bounce') the light at an angle. This allows control over where the light comes from, for example, bounced off nearby walls or a ceiling. This is useful as it helps to increase creative opportunities (adding neat shadows over a

Buy a dedicated flash

While some, usually less technically complex flashguns can be used on any camera they're attached to, they must be controlled manually. However, if you buy a flashgun made by the manufacturer of your camera or one made specifically for your make of digital camera, then they can provide 'dedicated' control.

Dedication is an advantage because the flashgun and camera work together seamlessly; the camera's metering and focus systems combine to help get better flash exposures. And such flashguns can also provide extra functionality such as stroboscopic flash (it freezes fast moving subjects) and finer control over the amount of light being used.

subject, for example, by bouncing light from one side off a wall) or simply to reduce the harshness of the light hitting the subject if fired 'head on'. The more control and bounce movement a flashgun has, however, the more expensive it will be.

Slave flash

These units are another type of accessory flashgun, which can be triggered by detecting the light emitted by other flash units (or in some cases by using a special radio signal). As such, they are said to be 'slaved' to the

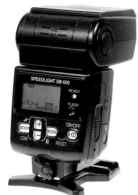

A typical flashgun showing the pivoting 'bounce' head on top of a body that houses the controls and batteries. This flashgun is shown on a small stand for slave flash use. Note the data LCD on the back and many controls that provide all the functions needed to use the flashgun either as a slave or attached to the camera's hotshoe.

main flash doing the triggering. In fact, in some instances, such as some of the more advanced hotshoe flashguns, you can trigger multiple slave flashguns simultaneously.

You can also purchase 'dumb' standalone units too. Dumb freestanding units are inexpensive and can be placed almost anywhere. In either case, slaves are ideal for getting even more light onto a scene such as a very large room or a large group photo where one flashgun cannot cope on its own.

Studio flash

Some high-end digital compacts and most D-SLRs have what's called a 'flash synchro' terminal. This is where a studio flash system can be plugged into, and triggered by, the camera.

Studio flash systems, offering the ultimate control over lighting a subject, comprise large lights, often with reflectors or 'soft boxes' attached (they look like big umbrellas or fabric-covered boxes respectively), and require mains power. Though they tend to be studio-based, some systems are portable and can be used at home.

Left: A ring flash such as this is designed for close-up flash work and can also be used effectively for creative-looking portraits.

The amount of light a flash produces, or its 'power', is rated using Guide Numbers (GN) and is measured at a specific ISO (light sensitivity) and at a specific focal length.

The higher the GN, the more powerful the flashgun. A GN of 11 is typical for most built-in flashes and will provide enough light to illuminate up to around 11 feet (3.3m) from the camera, at a typical ISO (usually ISO 100) and a focal length of 50mm. A flashgun with a GN of 50, on the other hand, will properly illuminate everything up to a distance 50 feet (15m) from the flash.

Manual flash settings

Note that if you alter the focal length, sensitivity or lens's aperture, the GN changes too. Using the GN, it's easy to calculate how close your subject should be at a given aperture or the aperture needed to shoot your subject at a given distance.

To find a GN, you multiply the distance to your subject by the aperture (the F/stop). For example, 20 feet x F/5.6 gives a GN of 112. To find the F/stop needed, divide the GN by the subject's distance. In this example, 112 divided by 20 gives an F/stop of 5.6. To find the maximum flash range, divide the GN by the F/stop, so here that's 112 divided by 5.6, which gives a distance of 20 feet.

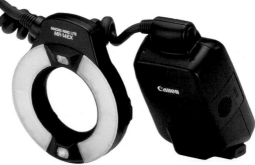

Extra **storage**

Your PC may have a large hard drive seemingly offering plenty of space. But sooner or later you're going to need extra storage, so here's what you should look for.

Today's PCs come with large capacity hard drives, usually over 500GB but increasingly 1TB or greater. However, digital image files can quickly use up this space, as can the applications you use to work on those images. This could slow your PC down too.

External hard drives

These, also known as external hard disks, are the solution to this. They are relatively inexpensive, simple to use and can provide you with an abundance of extra storage space – they're now available in capacities of well over 500GB.

Onto these you can store your photos and any other large media files such as digital music files or videos you've captured on your digital camera. As a rough guide, a 100GB external hard disk can provide enough space for around 50,000 images, depending on their file size.

As with buying a PC, it's important to get as large a capacity disk as you can afford. Although seemingly more expensive at the outset, this actually works out much cheaper than buying several, smaller capacity disks, a situation you may find yourself in as your image library grows.

Once plugged into your computer, the hard disk will appear on your PC's desktop as a small hard disk icon and you'll simply be able to drag and drop onto it in the same way you can with other folders on your PC. They usually don't require any special software to install them and work automatically once plugged in. How to actually store your data is dealt with in more detail in the topic *Backing-up*.

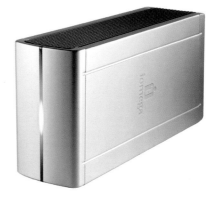

External hard drives, such as this 2TB Iomega USB model, provide simple and fast additional storage for your images by copying data across via your PC.

Speed and connections

Regardless of what capacity disk you buy there are things to look for to help get the most out of your data and working environment. To start with, buy an external hard disk with at least a 7200rpm disk speed. Check the spec on the box before you buy or ask your retailer for advice.

Also buy a disk with either USB 3.0, FireWire (IEEE 1394) 800 or Thunderbolt connectivity, preferably with multiple ports, no matter what the connection type.

This way you can be sure you have fast data transfer rates thanks to the connections, a high speed disk for quick data addressing (that's reading or writing your data) between your PC and the external disk, and you'll be able to 'daisy chain' multiple devices.

An example of the latter is having two external hard disks connected to one another and then to your PC, giving you more total

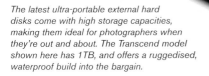

The latest ultra-portable external hard disks come with high storage capacities, making them ideal for photographers when they're out and about. The Transcend model shown here has 1TB, and offers a ruggedised, waterproof build into the bargain.

storage. One external disk plugs into the other, and then that last disk is the one actually connected to your PC. Both disks will still appear as separate hard disk icons on your desktop.

Portable storage

You don't have to confine extra hard disk storage to the desk at home or the office. Today there are a range of portable hard disks that provide you with extra storage capacity on the move, ideal for saving images from memory cards to free up space. Whilst you could use your Android or Windows tablet or iOS device to hold some images (assuming you can connect them wirelessly or with a cable), the memory would rapidly fill up and you might not be able to see images shot in RAW format.

Many portable hard disks provide 'dumb' space: they're just a repository for the images and that's it. The market for portable hard drives with screens has almost entirely gone now, replaced in part by tablet PCs and large screen smartphones and the need for greater capacity portable storage as a simple repository.

The latest portable hard disks come with software built into them to play slide shows of the images. These can also be played on TV. Some can even play DVD-format movies with sound, thanks to built-in speakers.

Portable hard disk capacities tend to be lower than their bigger, non-portable counterparts, but there are a wide range available, with capacities from 20GB to 1TB and beyond.

You can also buy ultra portable external hard disks that will fit in the palm of your hand or snugly into a camera bag; the latest are also ruggedised so they're ideal for outdoor use (see above).

'Cloud' storage

In simple terms, the Cloud is the name given to data storage on the Internet. It's storage space that you buy or rent, for a monthly fee, from a 'host' company, which you connect to and store data with. You'll need an Internet connection to use it (for example, to copy images to or from it), but with an increasing number of free Internet 'hot spots' around today, if you have a WiFi-enabled camera, it can be convenient for extra storage space when out and about. (See also *Backing-up*.)

It's worth bearing in mind, however, that using such storage on the go can be slow. Also, while many external hard disks come with free Cloud storage, some of the paid-for Cloud space can be expensive and if you stop paying your monthly fee, you lose your data.

Other benefits of the Cloud are services such as Dropbox and Google Drive, offering free on-line storage space (typically between 2GB and 5GB – you get more with paid accounts) accessed via a PC or app. Both are designed for sharing and synchronising data across all your devices and between people.

Light meters

Still not getting the lighting right on your pictures? If you're suffering from pictures that are over- or under-exposed or too dark, using a light meter could be the solution.

A hand-held light meter may not seem to be an essential item given that all digital cameras have a built-in light measuring system of some kind. However, built-in meters may not be accurate enough, particularly for the demands of the enthusiast or professional photographer.

Using a light meter

A hand-held light meter can be a useful accessory that allows you to make far more accurate light measurements in order to get better exposures. A light meter can measure the light reflected from a subject, in the same way your camera's metering system works. This is called a reflective light reading.

However, a light meter can also be used to take a measurement of the light arriving at the subject, which is called an incident light reading. You do this by holding the light meter in front of the subject or part of the subject where you want to measure the light. This provides a more accurate light measurement than a reflective reading and so allows you to get a better exposure than would be possible using your camera's metering alone.

You'll need a camera on which you can control the apertures and shutter speeds manually in order to input the exposure readings you measure with the light meter. Light meters are often used in photography studios where fine control over the lighting can be particularly critical for good results.

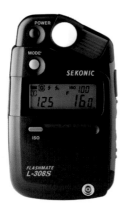

The Sekonic Flashmate L-308S is a (relatively) inexpensive and compact light meter with a moveable globe (for incident and reflective readings) and a flash sync port for use with studio flash.

i Buying guide

Hand-held light meters can be expensive but offer very accurate light measurement that will help improve your results. If you buy a light meter, look for one with these features:

- **Flash and ambient light measurement.**
- **A sliding globe,** *which is a white plastic hemisphere that hides and reveals the meter's light sensor: cover the sensor when taking incident readings, uncover it when taking reflected readings.*
- **Compact in size,** *to save camera bag space.*
- **A flash sync port:** *if your light meter has this you can use it in a studio with studio flash too.*

Batteries and power

There's nothing worse than getting ready to take a photo to find the 'battery low' warning flashing. Here's how to be fully powered up at all times.

Batteries, the lifeblood of your digital camera, are not all made equal. Here are some tips on getting the most from them and your digital camera.

---

i Battery types explained

- **Carbon zinc:** *Disposable batteries not suited to digital cameras.*
- **Alkaline:** *General all-purpose battery, cheap but not ideal for digital cameras.*
- **Lithium:** *Disposable and a third lighter than alkaline batteries. High power, long life and environmentally friendly. Suitable for digital cameras.*
- **Lithium-ion battery:** *Many digital cameras come with this special battery pack and charger, designed specifically for them.*
- **Nickel zinc:** *Disposable battery similar to lithium in its good power delivery and low environmental impact.*
- **NiCad cells:** *Rechargeable batteries, not good for the environment but can be recharged for over 1000 charge/discharge cycles. Can suffer from the 'memory effect' which is a capacity loss if they are over- or partly charged, or not fully discharged before recharging. This means they cannot then hold a full charge or that they 'remember' their last, poor charge state.*
- **NiMH cells:** *Rechargeable batteries that don't have memory effect problems, last a long time but are more expensive. Can be recharged over 1000 times.*

✔ Remember

Always take a spare set of batteries with you when you're mobile with your digital camera. Either charge up a spare set of rechargeable batteries or take new disposable ones along.

- Battery power is measured in mAh or milliamp hours. Only buy high-mAh batteries; 1000mAh is better than 500mAh as they have a higher power density and will last longer. Look for 2500mAh or higher.

- If your digital camera uses four AA cells, you can save thousands of pounds over the lifetime of the batteries if you buy good quality rechargeable ones and look after them properly.

- Always charge your batteries properly, for the correct length of time. You can determine the length of charge by multiplying the mAh figure by 1.4 and then divide that figure by the charger's current, indicated by its mA figure, which is usually displayed on the charger. For example, for a 2000mAh power battery, being charged by a 250mA charger, you would make the following simple calculation: 2000 x 1.4 ÷ 250 = 11.2. So a charge time of 11.2 hours is needed. Failing to do this can reduce the life of batteries.

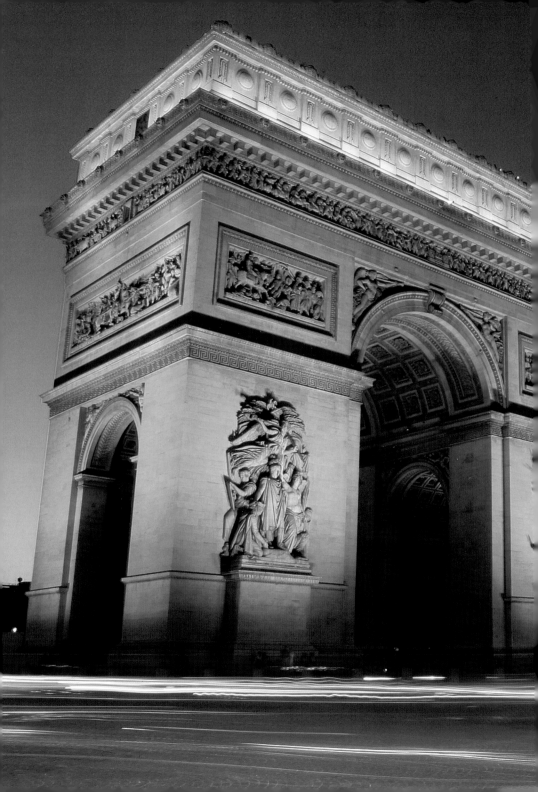

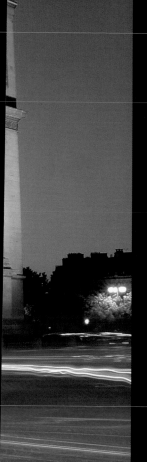

- **Overcoming the common problems** of low light, blurred images, poor framing, under- and over-exposure, washed-out colours and redeye

- **Inspirational photo ideas** to improve your creativity

- **Practical advice** on getting the best results, whatever the subject: portraits, weddings, close-ups, children, travel, flora and fauna, abstracts, and black and white

- **Explanations** of depth of field, exposure, white balance, F-numbers, ISO, shutter speed, aperture width, rule of thirds …

Composition

What makes one image more pleasing than another? By following a few simple steps about where to place elements within your pictures, you'll be surprised at how much you can improve your photography.

Composition is the name given to the combination of all the elements within the photo and their position in the scene. Compositional rules can be thought of as guides to help get better photos. Here are some key techniques to keep up your sleeve.

Framing

Always fill the frame with your subject. If you are photographing a person, then make sure you can see them clearly and that they do not appear too small within the frame. The benefit of this is that you make the most use of all the pixels you have at your disposal: this is particularly important for digital cameras with lower resolution sensors.

Another framing tip is to use frames within frames. When taking a shot, don't be afraid to use elements of your surroundings to frame a more distant part of the scene; shooting through a window including the window frame is a good example, as is including overhanging branches or foliage.

Portrait or landscape?

Like any digital camera, yours can be used horizontally in its normal or 'landscape' position or it can be used upright in the vertical or 'portrait' format. While these names suggest the types of image you'd usually use each format to photograph, experiment to see which works best for a given shot – often what works one way might be made even better simply by turning the camera.

Rule of thirds (or golden section)

Using this 'rule', you can add tension and a dynamic 'feel' to your photos by careful placement of the main elements. First imagine that your digital camera's colour screen is split into a grid of nine equal squares; two lines running vertically and two horizontally across it. Depending on your digital camera, it may have the ability to display such composition lines on your camera's screen for you.

If you place the subject upon any of these lines or, in the case of positioning specific elements within a photo, where the lines intersect (these points are also sometimes called 'golden means'), the image can have more impact. Try placing the horizon across the top (or bottom) horizontal line rather than across the centre of the shot, for example. Or place a person at one of the intersections when you want to put them in context with the background in a landscape-style photo.

Bull's-eye composition

This is when the main subject of the shot is smack in the centre of the frame and should be avoided unless you have a specific reason for doing it. This type of image is less pleasing to the eye and lacks dynamism. However, good uses for such composition might include emphasis of circular subjects in macro work, for dramatic effect.

This shot of potters in Nepal uses the rule of thirds beautifully: both potters' wheels sit on the golden section points. The graphic pattern created by the thrown pots adds interest, and energy comes from the use of a slow shutter speed that has allowed the spinning wheels to blur nicely.

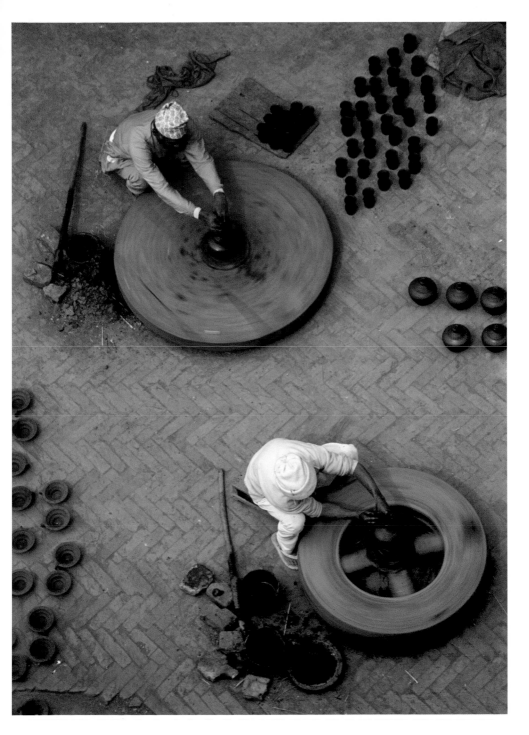

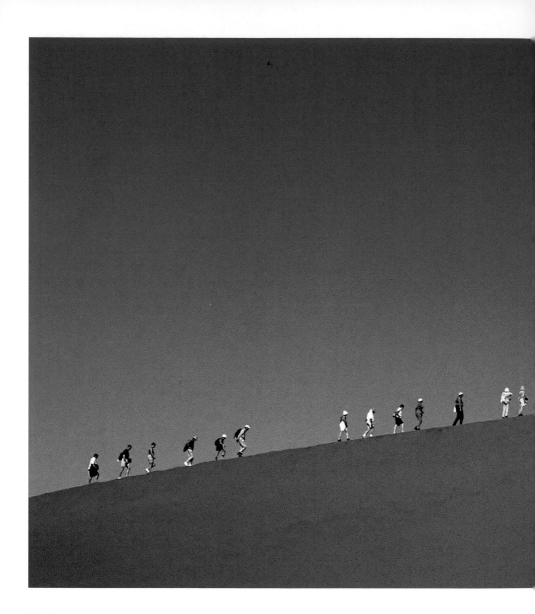

Balance

You can create images with either equal or unequal balance. In the former you have elements within the photo balancing each side of the image, say two buildings of the same size. In the latter, you would have one prominent subject with another element in the scene placed on the other side of the frame that's either closer or farther away (whichever is best for the composition). Place a big tree on one side, then a small rock or bush or person on the other for example. Although a subjective technique, it is one that can prove very successful when the elements are positioned carefully.

Experiment

The last 'rule' and probably the most important is simply to experiment. Like so many rules, these simple techniques can be broken or bent and by mixing them up you'll quickly learn how to get the best from your digital camera and have bags of fun in the process.

This image from the Namib Desert has a very dynamic structure thanks to the flowing curve of the sand dune and the sky. Colour is also very important here, and the teeth-like effect of people walking on the dune's ridge adds both a sense of scale and energy to the composition.

Focus

Getting your images sharply focused is just a matter of pointing the camera at the subject and pressing the button, isn't it?

Focusing is critical to good photos and today's cameras usually have an auto focus system that quickly gets things sharp. However, not using this properly can ruin an otherwise perfect shot.

Most digital cameras have a central auto focus target indicated by a small square on the colour screen or in the viewfinder. Many use multiple focus points, which ensure off-centre subjects stay sharp. But how many times have you taken a picture of family members side by side with a gap between them and the camera has focused on the wall behind? Read on to find out how to prevent such problems …

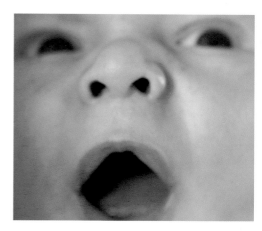

If you don't let the camera focus by half-pressing the shutter button and allowing it to focus properly, you'll get blurry pictures, such as this shot of a baby.

Don't rush the shutter button

All digital cameras that use auto focus have a dual pressure shutter button. A first half-press-and-hold activates the focusing and other in-camera systems. There's a brief pause and then you'll get some form of focus confirmation: a green LED in the optical viewfinder and/or a green icon displayed in the screen or a beep. Only finish pressing the shutter release once you have these confirmations. Trying to take a shot in one big press won't give time for the camera to set itself properly and you'll risk a blurred photo every time.

Portraits

In portraiture, your intention is to take a picture of a person. This usually means a head and shoulders shot or tightly cropped face, so always focus on the subject's eyes. If your camera allows control over which auto focus (AF) points you can use, select the central AF point, or the Face Priority AF system where applicable, and use it to focus (half-press the shutter button), and then recompose the shot, still holding the shutter button halfway down to preserve the focus selection. Complete the press to take the shot once you have the composition right.

Landscapes

To get a good landscape you need to ensure sharp focus from the foreground to the far distance. Begin by auto focusing on a prominent object in the distance. Haziness can hamper AF; if your digital camera uses a wide AF system, ensure it does not set the focus to something nearby or at the edge of the frame. Then keep the camera rock-steady, using a tripod or monopod if necessary.

Use the camera's landscape scene mode – if it has one – as this optimises the camera's settings for landscape work, or select a small aperture if using manual settings.

Macro shots

Digital cameras offer some of their best results in close-up or 'macro' work. Some digital cameras can focus to within one centimetre of the subject, ensuring frame-filling shots of even tiny details. However, you need to ensure the correct part of the subject is sharp. Use a single AF point and recompose once it's in focus. Also use a tripod, which helps keep things stable if you have slow shutter speeds. Remember, for close-up work you can use the camera's macro mode, or select a small aperture if using manual settings.

Small groups

To prevent the problem of the auto focus locking onto the wall behind a group shot, either move the subjects to reduce any gaps between them, or focus on one person's face and then recompose. This way, you'll ensure that the group, and not the wallpaper, is sharp. Again, try the Face Priority AF system.

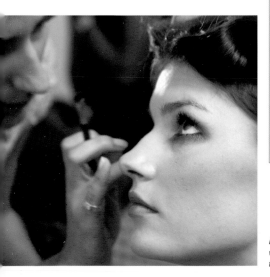

> ### ℹ️ Avoiding auto focus problems
>
> *Some subjects always cause AF systems problems, so here are ways to avoid them.*
>
> - **Parallel lines and regular patterns** *These can be difficult for the AF to 'key' on. Try tilting the camera (from landscape to portrait, for example), refocusing and then recompose for the shot.*
>
> - **The dark** *Unless your digital camera has an 'AF emitter' (it shines a beam of light out to help focusing), darkness or dark subjects provide nothing for the camera to focus upon. The answer is to get more light on the scene: turn on a light or two.*
>
> - **Low contrast** *Fog, haze, a predominantly white or black subject that doesn't provide the AF anything to focus upon – all these can present problems. You cannot change the weather; so try looking for an alternative but prominent element of the scene to focus upon. Also use the camera's landscape mode, which ensures a small aperture is used.*
>
> - **The manual focus solution** *Alternatively, to help prevent any of the above problems, try using your camera's manual focus mode – if it has one. By taking control of the focusing yourself (check your camera's manual for operating instructions), particularly if you have the time to work on the photo, this will provide fine control and you can check the results on the LCD too.*

By concentrating the focus on the model's eye, the viewer's interest is directed to her, the main subject of this reportage-style portrait.

Depth of field

The 'depth of field' is simply how large the focused area in a photo actually is. Let's see how it can be used to help create emphasis in your photos.

Everyone has seen photographs in which everything in the picture is crystal clear, from a foreground flower to the distant mountains. You've also seen pictures where only the main subject is sharply rendered, and everything else is blurry.

These are two examples of the effect which depth of field (DOF) can have. The former is a shot with a deep DOF (more of the scene is crisp) and the latter has a shallow DOF.

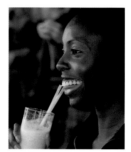

This portrait of a model at work had a very distracting background. A shallow depth of field has emphasised her face and blurred away the busy background.

What is depth of field?

In more accurate technical terms, DOF can be defined as being 'the range of object distances within which objects are imaged with acceptable sharpness'. Thankfully, particularly if using a compact digital camera, you don't need to know the complexities behind the DOF calculations, just how to maximise it to your advantage.

So for simplicity, here are the key practical points about DOF:

- A wide aperture gives a shallow DOF
- A small aperture will give deep DOF
- A telephoto lens (or long zoom, at the 'zoomed' setting) appears to give shallow DOF
- A wide-angle lens appears to give a deep DOF

In points three and four above 'appears to' is used because while the perception in the shot is usually as described, it is not always – technically speaking – accurate. It depends on the subject magnification and scene perspective (or viewpoint), making direct comparison of focal length and DOF difficult.

However, although this may sound complex, you can now start to play with the DOF effect in your images.

When to use shallow DOF

The most common use for a shallow depth of field is in portraiture, where you want to emphasise the subject. By using either a long focal length on your lens and/or a wide aperture, say, F2.8 (see box opposite for explanation of F-numbers), you can get the effect of a sharp subject and blurry background. Use this technique on any shot where you want to separate it from its background. A shortcut is to use the portrait mode on your camera, if it has one.

When to use deep DOF

This is slightly more flexible, but a good example of when to use deep DOF is for landscape photos. Typically, you'll use the wide-angle end of a zoom lens and a small aperture of, say, F8, which will help to ensure that the sharply rendered area in the shot stretches from near the camera to the far distance. A shortcut here is to use your camera's landscape mode, if it has one.

Close-up and DOF

It's worth pointing out that in close-up shooting, particularly if your camera has a good close-up or macro mode, the DOF will be very shallow indeed; a mere millimetre or two at most. Use a smaller aperture, F8 for example, to help deepen DOF if you want more of the small subject to be sharp.

Throwing the background out of focus

By selecting a suitable aperture, it is possible to throw the background out of focus by changing the depth of field. In the example below, the same scene was taken three times using different size apertures for each shot.

Firstly, a small, F16 aperture was used, which gives a sharp image from the gargoyle to the distant Montmartre in Paris. For the second shot, an aperture of F5.6 is used, and now an element of blur has removed much of the sharp detail visible in the first shot. Finally, an aperture of F2.8 was selected and the background detail is almost completely blurred away.

The effect is to divert the viewers' attention increasingly to the foreground. This is in essence why control of DOF can be so powerful.

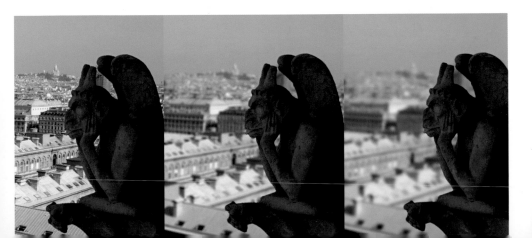

Exposure

Exposure, the amount of light that reaches your camera's sensor, is the key to great photos. Here's how to control it.

Exposure is controlled by three elements: the camera's shutter speed, the lens aperture and the sensitivity. It is calculated by the camera's metering system for any lighting using a specific combination of these three elements. Alternatively, you can manipulate the exposure either to deliberately darken or lighten a scene: this is termed under- or over-exposure.

Shutter speed

The camera's shutter is a small, usually metal curtain that travels across the face of the sensor and helps control the quantity of light hitting the sensor. A fast shutter speed lets through less light, a slow shutter speed more. The faster the shutter speed, the greater the 'freezing' effect it has on motion and vice versa.

Aperture and F-stops

The camera's aperture is a small adjustable circular opening in a diaphragm within the lens through which light must pass to reach the shutter and then the sensor. The aperture's size can be varied (called the iris control) and each position is called an F-stop. The smaller the F-stop number, the larger the aperture. The larger the aperture, the more light is admitted. Aperture settings also have an impact on the depth of field (see *Depth of field* for a fuller description of F-stops).

Sensitivity and ISO equivalence

The digital camera's sensitivity to light can be increased, which is helpful in low light. Digital camera sensitivity is based on a scale similar to that used for 35mm film sensitivity, called ISO: it is typically 100, 200, 400 and upwards. The higher the ISO number, the more sensitive to light the camera becomes (see *Low light* for more explanation of ISO numbers).

Increasing the camera's sensitivity (or its 'ISO equivalence') allows you to use higher shutter speeds or smaller apertures than would otherwise be possible at a given light intensity.

---

i Camera types and levels of control

Being fully automatic point-and-shoot models, basic digital cameras will only offer very limited – if any – manual control.

Some mid-range models offer an aperture priority mode: you set the aperture and the camera sets the shutter speed according to your choice for a correct exposure.

Higher-end models provide control of both (aperture and shutter priority) where you make a selection of one, and the camera automatically sets the other to get a correct exposure. Some, however, do offer full manual control, where both can be independently set by you.

Exposure compensation

This is the ability to adjust the exposure by one or more F-stops (depending on your camera's sophistication), overriding the camera's automatic exposure control system and therefore lightening or darkening the shot. This allows fine-tuning of the exposure without adjusting any other settings. This technique is ideal if extremes of light are 'tricking' the metering into under- or over-exposing.

Auto exposure bracketing

This is an automatic setting on more advanced digital cameras that carries out exposure compensation for you automatically, each time you take a photo. And it does it to a predefined level and on a predefined number of images, usually three.

Exposure bracketing means the camera takes one shot at the metered exposure, then (usually) a single under-exposed and

---

i Exposure effects

The shutter speed and aperture are interrelated when it comes to setting exposure. By combining the two settings – if your camera offers manual control over them – you can adjust the exposure for specific effects. A fast shutter speed and large aperture can freeze motion. A slow shutter and small aperture can help blur motion.

---

another over-exposed shot as well. It takes these three shots (or more depending on the camera) each time you fire the shutter and you can pick the best shot to keep. The amount of under- or over-exposure can be preset by the photographer by up to one or two F-stops and again depends on the camera.

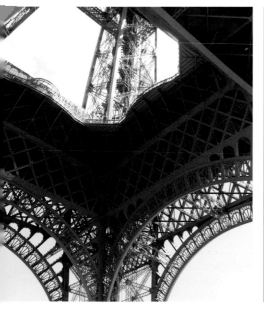

In this over-exposed shot, note how colour has been lost and highlights have been bleached out, making for an insipid-looking picture.

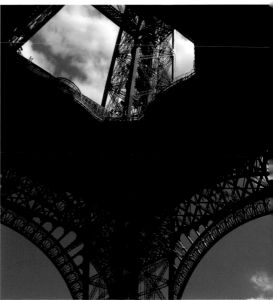

An under-exposed shot such as this one reveals plenty of colour but all the detail has been lost in shadow areas.

White balance

Unlike the human eye, digital cameras can't automatically adjust to compensate for variations in the colour of light, potentially causing unnaturally coloured pictures. But here we'll show you how to adjust your settings for this – and how to use the effect creatively.

When shot with a digital camera, a candle produces a nice warm glow, normal household tungsten bulbs create a yellow colour and fluorescent strip lighting produces a cold-looking cast. Artificial light can produce such unnatural-looking colours because digital cameras are primarily designed to 'see' sunlight – that is, light containing all the colours in the spectrum. They need to have their 'white balance' adjusted to take account of occasions when not all of the colours of the spectrum are present.

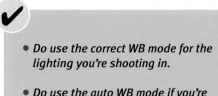

- *Do use the correct WB mode for the lighting you're shooting in.*

- *Do use the auto WB mode if you're not sure about the light or if it's a mixture of various lighting.*

Controlling white balance

Most digital cameras are able to set the white balance for a given lighting in two ways. First, there is an automatic white balance (WB)

The shot below reveals the difference that using the incorrect white balance will have on your photos. From left to right we have:
1 Shade; 2 Tungsten; 3 Fluorescent; 4 Flash (the correct setting for the studio location).

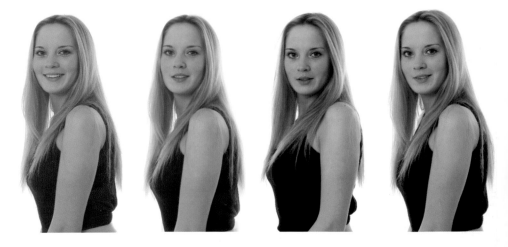

setting that adjusts the colours for you. Such WB settings can be found in the camera's set-up menus.

You will also find a range of possibly four or five other manually selected settings in the WB set-up menu. These will include 'cloudy' (or 'shade'), 'tungsten' and 'fluorescent'. Some might have a 'mercury' setting and all will have a 'daylight' mode. Each setting alters the way the camera's sensor 'sees' and records the light according to the conditions.

Experiment with these settings outdoors and you will be able to see how each mode affects the image in the colour screen. Selecting tungsten, for example, makes daylight images go blue, as this is used to compensate for the warm colour cast attributable to household bulb lighting.

These settings more accurately capture and process the light than the catch-all automatic WB mode, which entails extra processing of the image too. In other words, if you know the lighting you're shooting in, then select one of these WB modes so that you can fine-tune your shots. This will help get better quality shots and save time processing on a PC later

- *Don't worry if you get it wrong, change the WB setting and shoot again.*

- *Don't change the WB setting if you want to capture the mood the ambient lighting has created in the shot.*

when you may feel any colour casts are too intrusive to the photo and need removing.

Creative use of white balance

There's one caveat to all this. Sometimes you might want to take a picture and keep the colour cast, for example when you want to capture the atmosphere the lighting creates, as shown below in this picture of a candle-lit church. In this case, the auto WB setting proved best, but experiment to see if you can get results that are even more creative.

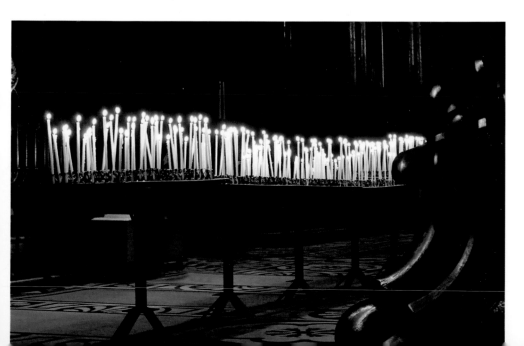

Creative **flash**

Your camera's built-in flash unit has more creative potential than you might imagine. It's not just for use 'in the dark'.

Most cameras automatically apply the flash when it gets dark or whenever more light is needed. Whilst useful in many scenarios, this can limit creative potential. By using flash in bright daylight you can add sparkle to a shot, reduce harsh shadows and boost colour too, so don't always think 'flash equals dark'.

Auto flash

Most digital cameras' default flash setting fires the flash automatically whenever the camera's meter senses that the ambient light has dropped beyond a level at which a reasonable hand-held exposure can be achieved.

The flash fires every time in such conditions, but the small size of the flash and the resulting flash exposure can leave the shot looking flat and dull, and you'll get unattractive dark backgrounds to each photo (see *Flash fall off* overleaf).

Auto flash is quite limiting, particularly if you want a photo that records both the atmosphere of a party and the people (see *Slow sync flash* opposite). So let's consider some alternative ways to use the flash.

Fill-in flash

As its name suggests, this is when the flash is used to fill in parts of the scene with extra light. It's 'forced' to fire each time: ideal for shots of a heavily backlit person or in

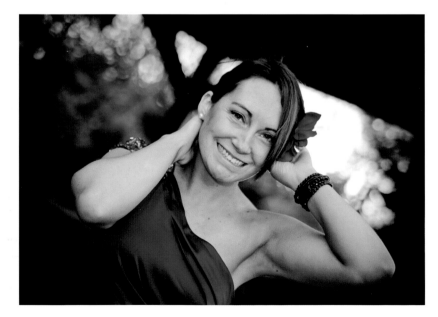

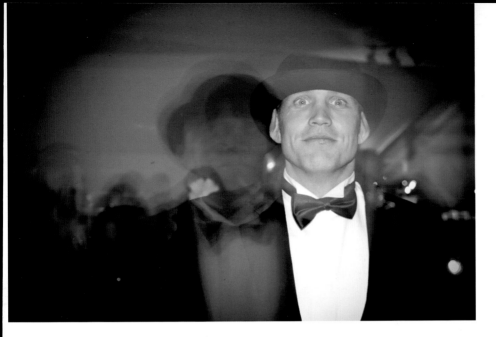

situations where the camera's meter might be fooled by bright surroundings, such as snow or on sunlit beaches.

This technique helps balance the exposure between the flash and the ambient light. Altering the exposure is not always an option: exposing for the shadows in our portrait example on the left would have unacceptably over-exposed everything else, while a non-flash exposure would have left a dark shadow area on the subject's face. A puff of flash has worked a treat. Use this technique to add 'catch lights' in the subject's eyes too; it helps bring portraits to life.

To use fill-in flash, turn on your camera's fill-in flash mode if it has one; if not, switch the flash to its forced flash 'on' mode (it will fire every shot) and the camera's metering system will do the rest. Some cameras will have an auto backlight feature to help out, automatically firing the flash when the background exposure level is much brighter than other parts in a scene.

Slow sync flash

This sounds complicated, but in essence it is just a means to synchronise the flash and shutter at a slow speed to help capture ambient lighting in a flash photo. The flash freezes any movement in the main subject, while the slow shutter picks up the gloomier background. This is ideal when the flavour of an image comes from the ambient lighting, such as a party, but the people in the foreground are the main subject of your photo, as shown in the shot above.

Most digital cameras will have a slow sync flash mode; if not, select a slow shutter speed and fire the flash (use the flash 'on' mode) and it will achieve similar results. Slow shutter speeds mean the camera will need supporting to reduce camera shake, although this can be used to creative effect if you want to add a dramatic dynamic to a shot.

Flash off

Not strictly speaking a flash technique, it's here because there are times when flash is the last thing you want in a photo. These include taking photos through a window, or when taking photos of a flat subject or one with a reflective surface, where the flash would leave a 'hot spot' in the photo where the flash is 'bounced' back into the lens.

We have all seen photos of people taken with flash in which they appear to have bright red eyes. This is caused when flash light reflects directly back into the camera's lens off the eye's retina. It's red coloured because of the blood vessels in the eye. Redeye is most common in low light (the eye's pupil enlarges to let in more light), and when using cameras where the lens and flash are close together – always the case on very small digital cameras! Depending on the camera, whilst in redeye reduction mode the flash either emits a bright beam of light or a series of fast strobe flashes will fire. Both help reduce the pupil size of your subject, lowering the chance of light being reflected back into the lens.

Flash fall off

This is caused by the flash illumination dropping off quickly beyond a certain distance. This happens because the intensity of illumination is inversely proportional to the square of the distance between light and subject. Put more simply, if the distance between light and subject is doubled, the light reaching the subject will be only a quarter of the original intensity.

The result is that light for a correct exposure quickly drops away, leaving backgrounds looking very dark, as shown here in our example picture. The man's perfectly exposed, but there's no detail in the background at all, even though this image was shot in a reasonably well-lit but very large room at a wedding.

To avoid this, use the slow sync flash technique or use an accessory flashgun (if your digital camera has a hotshoe) to provide more light.

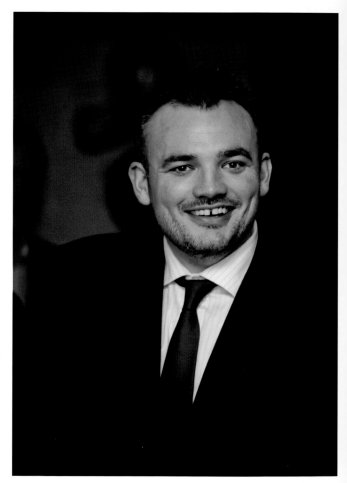

Low light

Shooting in low light or darkness presents real challenges but can be one of the most rewarding photo techniques to get right. Let's look at the best ways to achieve stunning low-light shots.

Typical low-light photo scenarios include shooting cityscapes at night or shooting in a dark interior such as at a party, whilst still capturing the atmosphere created by the available light. Here's how best to shoot different dark scenes whilst avoiding the typical camera shake and image noise problems associated with low light.

Shooting at night

Night photography, say a night landscape scene with the moon in the shot, presents a couple of key problems: keeping the camera stable is one and another is image noise (see below). A tripod or other such support will keep your camera steady. If you don't have a tripod then find a suitable wall, table or similar support on which to place the camera.

Ensure you set the largest aperture on your camera's lens (if you can control this feature on your camera) and turn off the camera's flash. Then set your camera's 10-second self-timer. This way, even if you jog the camera when you press the shutter button, the vibration this causes is gone when the shutter fires 10 seconds later. Select the camera's

---

ℹ Low light and 'noise'

Many lower priced cameras (or those with a lower specification in terms of their sensor technology or image engine and software) have a potential Achilles heel in that they suffer more image noise; higher end compacts or bridge compacts and D-SLRs suffer less in low-light shots. It looks similar to the effect of heavy film grain and is usually characterised by blue or red pixels peppering images shot in low light, particularly those with large areas of even colour. And the darker that colour the more obvious and intrusive it can be.

Noise is created when the signal-to-noise ratio (the difference between the light captured, the 'signal', and the interference or 'noise' created by the camera's electronics, analogous to the hiss you hear if a radio is not tuned properly) is such that there's more noise than signal. Therefore a

high signal-to-noise is good (think lots of light) and the reverse is not.

Increasing the camera's sensitivity (its ISO setting) makes the camera more sensitive to low light but can add image noise. Modern digital cameras have improved image noise characteristics – many top-end digital cameras can shoot in almost total darkness, thanks to settings of up to ISO 25,500, without distracting noise problems. If low-light shooting is key, look for cameras with this capability. To reduce image noise if it does occur, keep the ISO setting as low as possible, and support the camera where needed. Switch on any noise reduction settings too, usually found within main menus. This allows the worst effects of noise to be processed away but may extend processing times between shots and can reduce image details in some circumstances.

landscape scene mode, which ensures correct focus; on many cameras it will automatically deactivate the flash for you too. Also try selecting the camera's night scene mode if it has one.

Low light and flash
The night scene mode can also be used in low light. A slow shutter speed with a burst of flash records any ambient light and the flash illuminates the foreground. You still need to support the camera as a very slow shutter is used and the trick with the self-timer is a good idea too. Remember to use the camera's redeye reduction setting if the fore-ground interest is a person.

Night portraits
Another common setting on many digital cameras is the night portrait mode. If it has one, select this mode when shooting people in low light. This will select a slow shutter speed combined with the flash – similar to that used in the night scene mode – but crucially, the flash exposure will be less powerful, helping to ensure the subject's skin doesn't bleach out (a problem if the flash light is too harsh).

Party pictures
A perennial problem taking pictures indoors and particularly at parties is the relatively low available light. The flash will always want to fire and there's a risk of blurry pictures from camera shake if you turn it off because of the slow shutter speed.

Another problem here is that the small flash will not be able to cope with the areas you're trying to illuminate; even relatively small rooms can be too much for a built-in flash. The resulting photo will have a very dark background: this is called 'flash fall off'. The problem is surmountable by switching the flash to its slow sync mode (see *Creative flash* for more on this). You risk motion blur, but this can, however, appear to be an intentional effect, as in the night-time shot below.

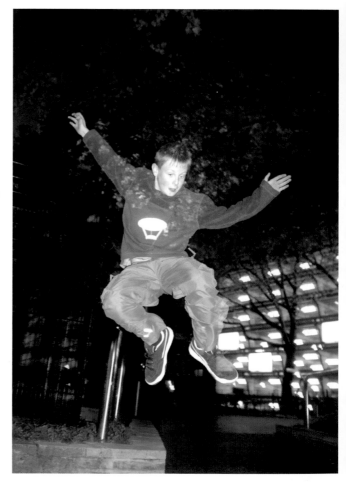

This shot was taken using the camera's night scene mode. The burst of flash has frozen the boy, but the background is blurred by camera shake.

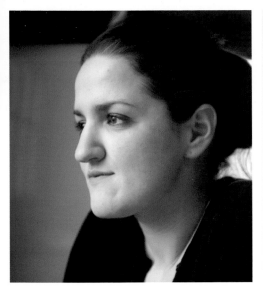

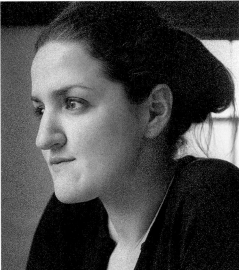

This shot taken at ISO 200 has no noise problems, the image looks 'clean'.

An otherwise identical shot but this time taken using ISO 6400. As you can see here, image noise becomes obvious and seriously undermines the quality of the image, filling it with blue and red speckles.

i Camera sensitivity (ISO)

A camera's sensitivity to light is measured in ISO: the higher the number the greater the sensitivity to light. Today's cameras have very high ISOs available. Here's an at-a-glance guide to ISO settings and what they're good for.

- **ISO 100 (or lower):** *The best all-round setting for top quality photos in bright conditions or where low noise is a key requirement, such as in portraiture.*

- **ISO 200:** *Ideal for slightly less bright lighting where low noise is still a requirement but not key.*

- **ISO 400:** *Provides faster shutter speeds in overcast conditions or low light. Noise might just be visible when printing larger sized photos.*

- **ISO 800:** *Ideal where faster shutter speeds are needed to freeze fleeting action. Noise might be evident even at normal print sizes, so use the camera's noise reduction feature for shots at this ISO.*

- **ISO 1600 (or higher):** *This setting provides very fast shutter speeds in very low light on more advanced digital cameras; some professional D-SLRs might not show image noise even at settings as high as ISO 25,500. If noise is evident, ensure you activate noise reduction to help reduce its effects.*

Close-ups

Close-ups are one of the most practical and creative areas of photography and a real strength of digital cameras. Here's how to make the most of your camera's macro abilities.

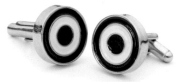

lose-up or macro (its technical term) photography opens new perspectives on our natural world and most digital cameras are very good at it. Even basic models have macro modes built in, enabling this great technique to be used without needing specialist equipment.

Digital cameras are good at macro because they have a combination of small sensor sizes and short focal length lenses. Together these provide closer focusing distances than would otherwise be available with conventional 35mm film cameras.

Some can even focus as closely as half an inch (1 cm) – that means the subject can be almost touching the lens. Even if your digital camera doesn't have a macro mode, as long as you can focus the camera sharply on subjects

within 20cm of the front of the lens (or closer) you can shoot good close-up shots.

How to take close-ups

Just like a 'normal' photo, when shooting close-ups the subject appears in the camera's LCD, which you use to compose and focus your subject properly. If your camera has it, select its macro setting as this helps get focus spot on, and gets metering and depth of field (DOF) to the optimal level for the shot too.

A drawback is that macro results in very shallow DOF, so you will find that just a very

---

ℹ️ Ideas for close-ups

The practical and creative uses for macro shots are almost endless, so here are some simple ideas for you to try.

- *Photographs of your jewellery or stamps in a stamp collection can be shot in close-up for insurance purposes, as well as being attractive images in their own right.*

- *Garden flowers make stunning subjects and are easy to find.*

- *Insects such as bees and butterflies, which you'll find on those garden flowers, can also look great in close-up.*

- *Textures and patterns often look dramatic in close-up too. If it looks bad 'big', think small and close in for a macro shot – it may just be worth it.*

- *Use a tripod. This helps to keep the camera steady at high magnifications and means you can better control depth of field, which can be important when shooting in macro mode.*

More magnification

One way to get greater magnification if you cannot focus really close is to shoot from further away, zooming in to get a closer crop. You can then use software on the PC to crop closer still later. But this means you lose pixels (you've cropped them away) so you won't be able to enlarge the prints as much. Zooming in will also reduce the DOF. If you zoom in, you may need to support the camera using a tripod or other support to stop camera shake due to the longer focal length in use, or bump up the ISO to get faster shutter speeds.

small area is sharp and the rest of the subject will be out of focus (see the shot below) so you may need to shoot several pictures until you're happy with the focus point. Adjusting the aperture to use a smaller F-stop (F8, for example) will help deepen the DOF but will

A shot taken using the camera's macro setting focusing on the water droplets on blades of grass. Note the shallow depth of field.

result in slower shutter speeds, so you may need to use a tripod to steady the camera in order to prevent camera shake.

Subjects such as butterflies or jewellery make for good shots, but insects tend not to sit still for long, so timing is everything. Practise on static subjects such as in our example opposite – of a pair of cufflinks – where you can control the focus and lighting and your subject is not likely to fly away!

Avoiding flash problems

Because the close focus distance on most digital cameras is very close indeed, using the camera's built-in flash will either not illuminate the subject at all or the lens will get in the way and cast a shadow over it. Natural light offers an even lighting over the whole subject, but artificial light from a table lamp is also ideal as you can set the camera's white balance to take away any colour casts (see *White balance*). If you want to use flash, then you may need to use an off-camera flashgun, if your camera will work with one. These can be positioned away from the camera, angled to give the best effect for creative shadows or angled for all-over lighting – whichever you want to use.

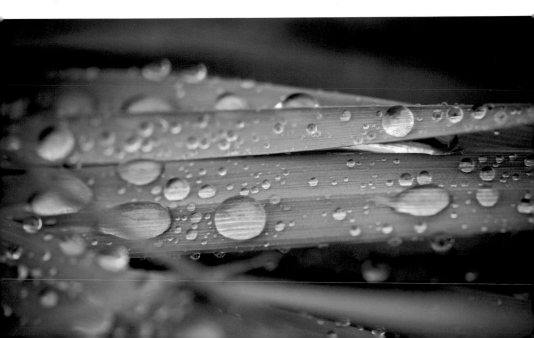

Black and **white**

Black and white photography provides another creative weapon for your digital photo armoury and it's easy with today's digital cameras. Here's how.

Almost all digital cameras have a series of black and white or monochrome ('mono') modes within their menus that provide a host of easy ways to get more creative with your photography. Monochrome simply means the camera uses only one range of tones to make an image, so everything in a picture is shown in shades of just one colour.

Different monochrome modes
The black and white mode is the most popular mono mode, used to add a certain arty flair to otherwise mundane photos.

Sepia is another popular mode that mimics the look of an old faded photograph. It uses a range of brown tones to create an image with an 'antique feel'.

The document mode is another useful mono mode. This is primarily used to shoot documents, as you might have guessed, where you want to make sure the wording is clear and crisp by creating a very high contrast mono image.

Thinking in black and white
Shooting colour is one thing, but a successful black and white shot requires just a little more thought. Although you can still shoot anything in black and white if you wish, what looks good in colour will not always lend itself to this approach. But it is ideal for capturing texture, form and shapes, as these can look better with the more graphic representation that black and white offers.

Good subjects range from stark winter tree lines, rocky mountains, landscape vistas or close-up images of textures such as stone, wood or the walls of buildings. Look out for these and the small details that may stand out to make that 'graphic' look in the shot.

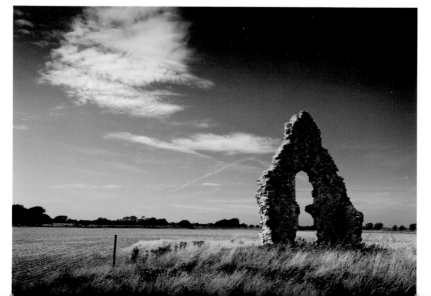

Gradations in tone and texture are great for black and white photography, which lends itself to those types of subject, as this image reveals.

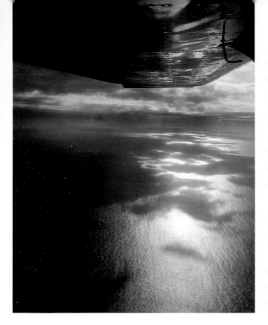

Think laterally, as in this shot taken from a light aircraft. The sky, wing, sea and clouds combine for a great graphic effect in black and white.

camera to its black and white mode, either from its relevant menus or the control assigned to this task (check your camera's manual), you'll see the image in the LCD turn from colour to a greyscale image; that is, an image that has all the colours represented by a range (or 'scale') of greys, from black all the way to white. This is helpful as it lets you see how the image will look when you shoot it in black and white.

Be warned that some colours will look identical once converted into black and white. Yellow and blue end up looking the same shades of grey, for example.

It's worth noting that even very basic image editing software can perform the same sepia or black and white trick on any colour image on a PC, and we'll look at just this technique in the topic *Creating black and white*.

Try to imagine it in black and white. Pick the best angle to exaggerate the lines or rugged bits and it should provide the right look in the shot.

If shooting people, remember to look for those graphic elements such as a craggy, characterful face, or the mood created by shadows, which all help to give the image the right feel. It takes a little practice but once you've taken a few successful black and white shots, switching from colour to black and white will become almost second nature and you'll know just by looking what will look good and what won't. When shooting sepia shots, it's best to try and frame the subject so that modern paraphernalia, such as lamp posts, telegraph poles, cars and pylons are excluded. This helps keep a timeless look and makes the old-fashioned sepia look work more successfully.

Practical advice

Use the camera's LCD in the mono mode of your choice. When you switch your digital

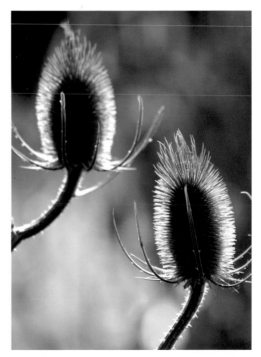

Even common or 'in-the-garden' subjects can lend themselves to black and white, so you don't need exotic locations.

Portraits and people

Taking pictures of people sounds simple enough, but there are key ways to make sure these precious photographs do their subjects justice. First we'll have a look at the basics, and then move on to some great ideas and tips to make your people shots really stand out.

The basics

The most common problem with people pictures is 'amputation'. How many times have you seen photos with a person's head mysteriously cut off or their feet missing?

This is very easily avoided with a digital camera as you can see everything in the LCD screen exactly as it will appear in the photo. Always use the LCD to help you compose correctly: you will be able to see if you have got it wrong, and can delete the shot and try again.

Another basic trick, if you're not doing a close-in portrait, is to put the person in context. This is ideal if you're shooting a candid image of someone working, for example. Rather than cropping in tightly, shoot the subject in their environment to 'tell a story' with the photo.

Don't be afraid to photograph people small in a scene, allowing more of the background in. This gives space around the subject in the shot, and is ideal if you want to convey a sense of scale.

Formal portraits

A formal portrait is any portrait where the shot has been deliberately set up, as opposed to a candid shot (for an example, see overleaf). However, formal portraits don't have to look posed – you can still get your subject to pretend and set up the shot to look like you've caught someone behaving naturally. For any type of pose to be successful, you need to try to relax your subject and get them to be themselves. Try to get a rapport going.

The classic formal head and shoulders crop, where you compose so the subject is cropped across the shoulders just below the collar line, is effective and looks clean. But you don't have to stick to this. Full body portraits can be equally as effective, particularly if you want to convey a character trait, perhaps through flamboyant clothing, for example.

✔

- *Look for character and emphasise such features as a craggy, lined face or flamboyant clothing.*

- *Remember to focus on the eyes.*

- *Use a long focal length: around 100mm can be ideal.*

- *If your camera has Face Priority AF, use it. It will help to focus properly on a person's face.*

Right: *Portraits that are formally posed can be very effective. Use of light and shadow here has given the shot 'mood', as has the sitter's characterful face.*

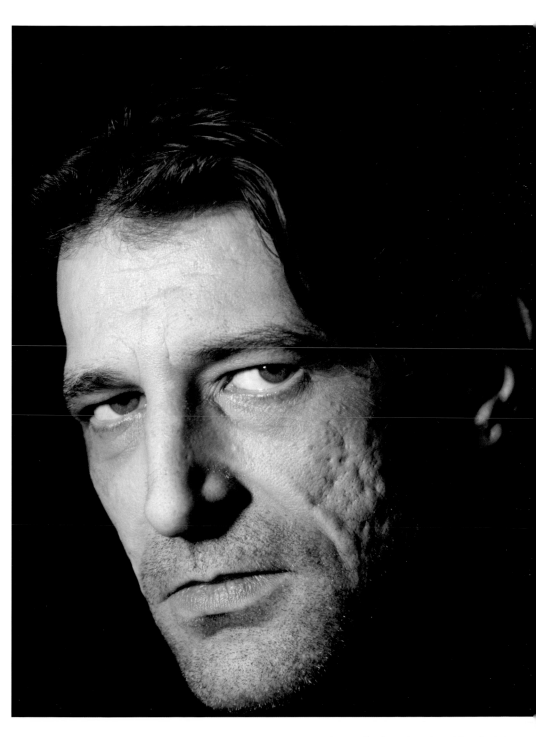

Lighting

If shooting outside in daylight, getting enough light is not an issue, but if shooting indoors the quality of lighting will play a big part in the success of your people shots. Clearly, your camera's built-in flash or additional lighting can help here (see the topics *Extra flash* and *Creative flash*). However, a simple way to get a great lighting effect is to use natural light streaming in through a window. It'll be diffuse and provide nice soft shadows. However, if the light is too bright and shadows too harsh, use a white sheet of paper or card to reflect light onto the face's shaded side as a 'fill-in'.

If you are using flash and the exposure is harsh, lower the flash power (if you have the flash exposure compensation function on your camera) or switch to fill-in flash. Or just turn the flash off and use the available light, remembering to adjust the camera's white balance accordingly to stop unsightly colour casts caused by indoor artificial lighting.

Right: *Candid portraits are best if you can capture the person unawares. Here, the woman appears preoccupied and unaware of the camera, making for a lovely, natural-looking photo.*

Candid portraits

Candid or 'informal' shots of people are probably the most common type of picture you'll take, and include anything that's not posed. To capture a good candid, you'll normally be shooting on the hoof, without a tripod or stopping to 'set up'. Roam around to look for unusual angles or just to capture spontaneous or emotional moments.

A classic environment where candids work is at a wedding. The subjects are usually relaxed, unaware they're being photographed, and you're left to snap away to your heart's content. This spontaneous style of people picture is increasingly being used by professional wedding photographers for just these reasons.

To take a successful people picture, you must think about what, who and how to shoot. Use a focal length suitable for the effect you want: telephoto for longer focal length shots to remove distracting backgrounds; wide lenses for group shots and where you want to include the background of the scene. And don't limit yourself to upright format shots; landscape format images can work too.

If you intend to photograph a stranger, you should be courteous and ask their permission before you snap away. Whilst it's not always possible to do this, it can make the situation more relaxed, so you'll have more time to shoot and get a better snap. If the person poses making the shot look awkward, ask them to ignore you while you shoot for a more natural picture.

- *Don't be afraid to 'grab' a shot. If a scene presents itself in a fleeting moment, go for it. You can always just delete it if it doesn't work. You never know!*

- *Always fill the frame; don't waste a pixel anywhere.*

- *Don't forget to 'think in black and white'. Your digital camera's black and white mode can make the difference on a grey day or if the person in the shot would look great photographed this way, at a historical event for example.*

- *And last but not least, don't be afraid to experiment.*

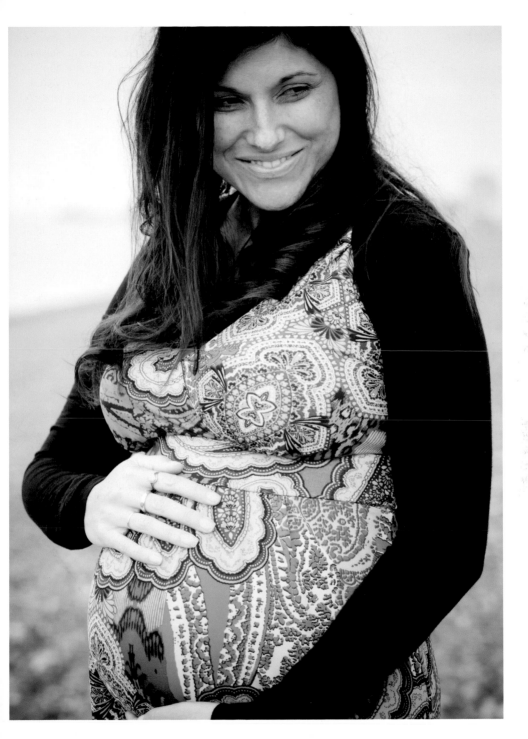

Still life

Still life photos capture everyday objects in a way that can make even the seemingly mundane look beautiful – if handled well. Check out these tips for making the 'still' come to 'life' with your digital camera.

S till life is defined as photographing inanimate objects, and can include almost anything, from flowers in a vase, coloured beads, sliced fruit and vegetables to ornaments and objets d'art.

When shooting still life, you need to consider both the subject and the surroundings. You'll need to think about how you arrange your subject, where you'll place it and then how it will be lit.

Composition

Pay close attention to the subject's arrangement. Don't place objects in a line, for example, as regimented composition rarely works well. Stagger your subjects – but not at equal distances from each other – and if you have to have them in a row then overlap them.

Right: These flowers make a stunning still life image. Note how natural light from a window, controlled by curtains to create shadow, has been allowed to fall across the flowers, which stand in a vase on a simple, plain wooden floor. Also note the depth of field is quite shallow, helping to keep attention on the flowers.

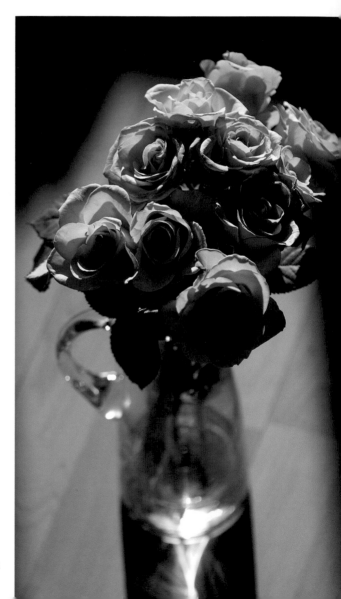

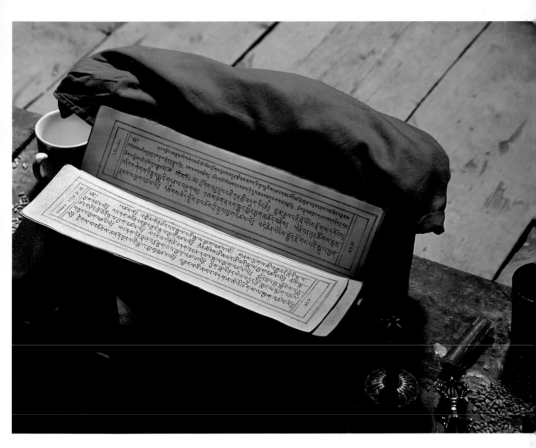

Above: *This is a classic still life image, shot in available light, of a Tibetan monk's scripts and robe shot in situ at a monastery. Again, the background is out of focus due to a shallow depth of field, keeping viewers' attention on the main subject.*

Then try to shoot from an unusual angle such as directly overhead or from very low down. Remember to think about the background. Neutral backgrounds work well, and can be provided simply by a draped cloth. But you may want to include some of the surroundings. Try it and check what looks best in the camera's LCD.

Lighting

Still life subjects tend to be on the small side, so lighting is important. Using your camera's built-in flash may be adequate for this, but if it lacks a flash exposure compensation function, the light it emits may be too harsh and could also create a heavy shadow.

Additional off-camera flash can be helpful here, and you can also exercise more control over this. The light from a flashgun can have its angle adjusted (by bouncing the light with a bounce head flashgun, for example) or be softened with a diffuser. Diffusers are accessories usually supplied with a flashgun that fit over the gun's lamp to soften ('diffuse') the light. If you don't have one, a simple piece of tissue or tracing paper placed over the flashgun's lamp will be just as effective.

If you don't have a flashgun, it's not a problem, because natural light from a window is also ideal for still life. A good idea is to leave a slit in the curtains, allowing a stream of light to flood across the subject. This works really well for glass, coloured or otherwise, and any reflective subjects, where the spectral highlights (the bright, reflective parts of an object) are enhanced and add sparkle.

Alternatively, you can use any suitable table lamp (or even include them in the shot if they're attractive or ornamental) and reset the camera's white balance accordingly. Try the trick of using white card to act as a simple reflector, or aluminium cooking foil to help get dazzling reflections and shadows falling where you want.

As you'll need to use longer focal lengths in more subdued lighting, your camera may need the aid of a tripod or some other support to avoid camera shake. Longer focal lengths also affect the depth of field, so use your camera's aperture control (if it has one) to adjust this as needed.

✔
- *Use natural light from a window or artificial light, adjusting the camera's white balance to compensate for any unwanted colour cast.*

- *Use white card or paper as reflectors to help control the light and shadow on a subject.*

❗
- **Don't use regimented lines of subjects: stagger them or allow them to overlap for a pleasing composition.**

Below left: *This autumn leaf was placed on white paper and lit by a household lamp correcting for white balance not bringing out the rich colour.*
Below right: *This still life of old pots uses natural soft light coming in through a frosted glass window.*
Opposite: *An unorthodox still life of a ceiling light shows it pays to always look around you as you never know what might make a great still life.*

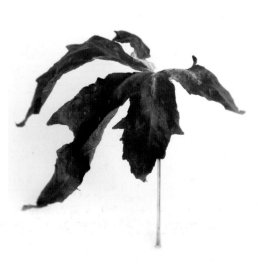

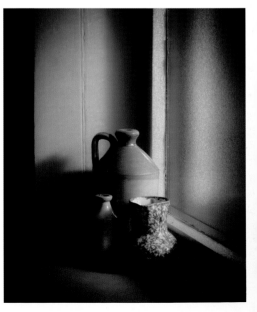

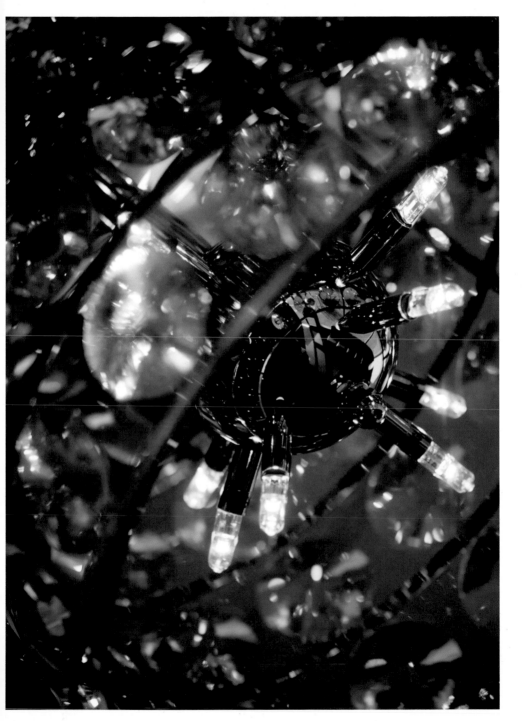

Reportage

Reportage – using your digital camera to tell a story in a series of pictures – is one of photography's greatest uses. Here are some inspirational ideas for projects, and tips on getting the best results.

Project ideas

Almost anything can be given the reportage treatment, but family events such as an important birthday or birth of a new baby are of course very popular choices. If you've ever taken a series of photographs of guests enjoying themselves at a wedding, then you've already tried reportage.

They needn't be one-off events, however. You can just as easily keep a photo record showing how your children grow up, from newborn baby onwards, which would become a fantastic memento. Or maybe you want to record the progress you make as you redecorate your house or work on some other long-term practical or creative endeavour. Projects such as these are the essence of reportage.

Enthusiast photographers might want to tackle more ambitious projects such as changes in their community or home town as it's redeveloped. To make this easier to cover, you could follow the developments in just one part of your locale or the changes to a famous building, for example.

Another good subject to follow is a local historic event. You could even find that your 'documentary' work, particularly if it's comprehensive, can become a valuable social document that local museums or historic societies would be interested in.

In the example shown here, the photographer was asked to capture and explain the hand signals used to transmit betting information to and from trackside

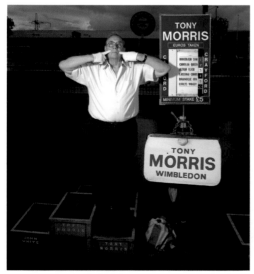

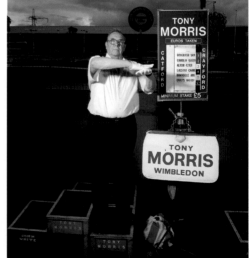

Practical tips

- *Store the photos carefully by date but remember ...*

- *Because your photos are digital, the date and time of each photo is embedded in each shot and can be read on a PC – perfect if you can't remember when a picture was taken.*

- *Take many pictures and try to cover all the 'angles'. It doesn't matter if you 'waste' shots – you can always delete the ones you don't need later.*

- *You may want to re-shoot the same place time and again, over many years in some cases, and from the same viewpoint, so use a tripod and be patient.*

- *Shoot at regular intervals, once a day or week, depending on the subject you're following of course.*

- *Keep a diary of events if photographing something that will be a long-term project. Using your PC it would even be possible to combine your words and pictures and print out your own 'publication' about the project.*

- *With long-term projects, you really don't want to take any risks with all the work you've put in. So don't keep all your images on memory cards alone. Make sure you back them up to your PC or other external memory device (see Backing-up).*

bookmakers in greyhound and horse racing. His aim was to show the different signals the bookmaker uses as the betting progresses. The four shots shown here are just part of an extensive selection that formed a dictionary of bookmakers' gestures used in a national newspaper. You'll need to give your subject a similar 'sequential' treatment.

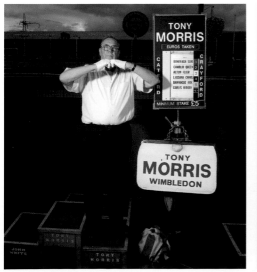

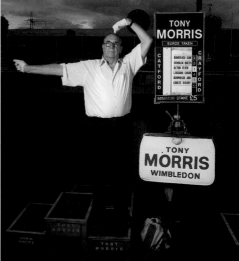

Travel

Travel to foreign climes often presents photo opportunities that will never come your way again. Make sure you make the most of these once-in-a-lifetime images by following these inspirational ideas and our practical travel checklist.

From the plane

If you're flying, there's usually an opportunity to get some stunning images from the aircraft. You won't be able to carry loads of photographic kit into the cabin, of course, but even a simple digital camera with zoom lens can produce good shots. Use the telephoto end of the lens to exclude the porthole in the shot, or go with the wide-angle end of the lens, as in our picture, to include it as an extra framing device. Look for shapes and patterns in the clouds – or on the ground – and turn the flash off, and you'll have a good chance of shooting a breathtaking image before you've even arrived at your destination.

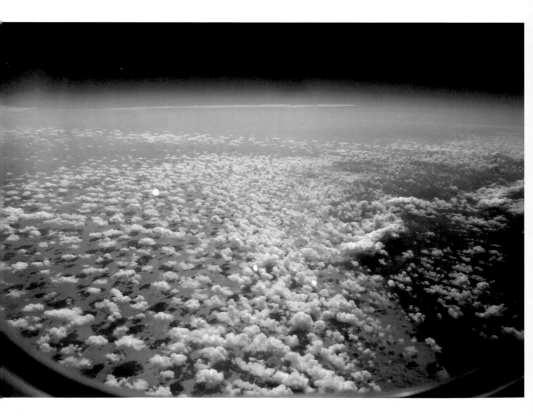

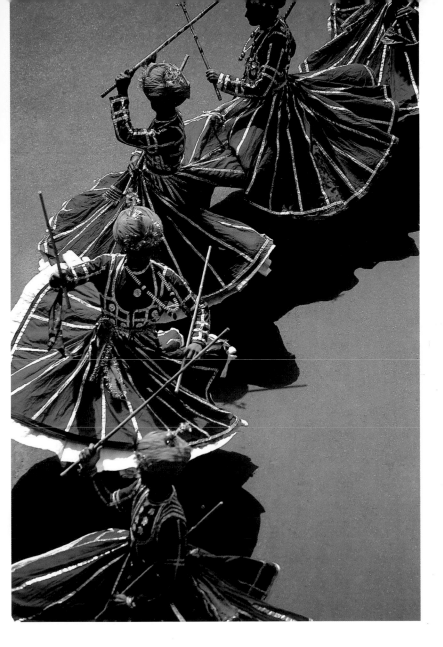

Local flavour

When away from home, it's always nice to capture local flavour. Unusual buildings and architecture make eye-catching images that can tell the viewer where you were in a single shot. But also look out for other elements of the locality. If you travel to an exotic location, don't just shoot the mountains or the local scenery, get shots of the locals too, particularly if there's a festival or local event. This shot, taken at the Jaipur Festival, has captured dancers in traditional clothing.

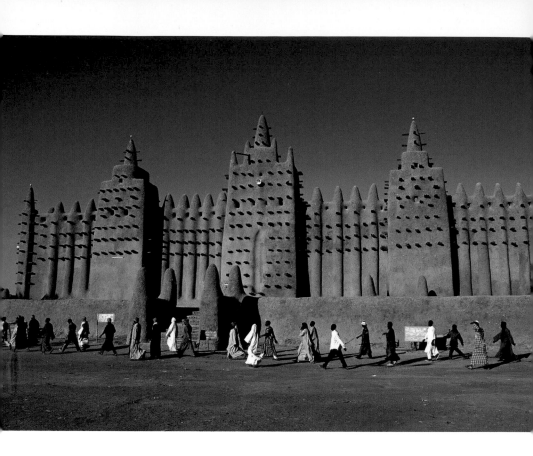

The early bird

Try to get up early on holiday, particularly
if you travel to a country with a very hot
climate. Early morning light is often the best
for any photo. And if it's very hot, the heat
of the day creates haze and dust, which can
lower contrast, reducing your photo's impact.
Another advantage of being an early riser is
simply that with the sun lower in the sky,
you get better shadows, ideal for enhancing
landscapes. The same is true for landscapes
shot later in the day at sunset, though light
tends to be warmer at dusk than dawn.

Sunset shots

A beach holiday abroad can often provide
stunning sunset shots (right), but then so
can a trip to the mountains. Either way, one
sunset can look much like any other unless
you try to include something extra in the
scene. To get spectacular beach sunsets
include other foreground interest, perhaps
someone standing at the water's edge (using
the rule of thirds to place them, the horizon
and the water lapping the shore). Alternatively,
use palm trees arching into the shot to create
a 'frame' for the sun. Even beach huts can
add interest and give the sunset a 'place'.

Away from the beach, the options are
usually more obvious – mountains in the
distance, for example – or once again, a
person placed carefully to 'balance' the
composition. Experimentation is the key, but
remember that low light could mean you
need to use a support for the camera to stop
camera shake.

Travel photography checklist

- Unlike film cameras, digital cameras and their memory cards are NOT affected by airport X-ray machines, but always carry your camera as hand luggage (rather than checked into the hold) so you can shoot from the plane's portholes.

- Carry spare memory cards or a portable storage device to free up space on your memory card. There's nothing worse than running out of memory as a great shot presents itself.

- Take a support of some kind: even a small, table-top tripod is better than nothing if you need to keep the camera steady for a crucial shot.

- Spare batteries are an absolute must, particularly if you're travelling to a country where getting hold of replacements is going to be difficult. If you use rechargeable batteries then remember to take your charger and a travel power adapter.

- Protect your camera from excessive heat and dust. Never leave it in the window of a car in the sun and always keep the camera in a case. You could even buy a waterproof housing which will help protect the camera not just from water but also from dust and sand.

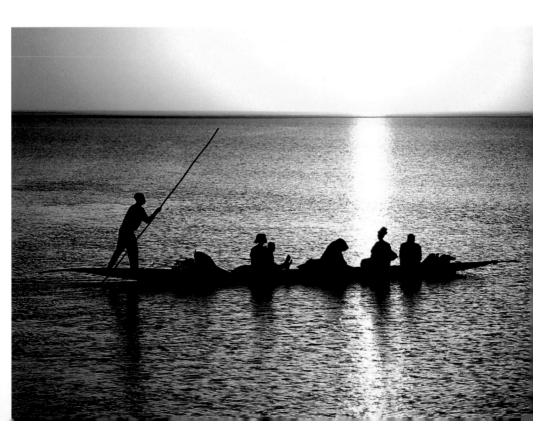

Architecture

Architectural photography is rewarding but also very challenging. It can even be hard to do justice to famous buildings that offer potentially stunning results. Here's how the professionals do it.

Architectural photography can include anything from churches, castles and monuments to bridges and sculpture, so there's plenty to choose from. Whatever your subject, there's a natural temptation to try to cram the whole building into one shot and that urge should be held in check. It *can* work on some buildings but it's often not successful.

Less is more

If you don't have a wide enough lens to take in a whole building from where you stand, you may have to step so far back in order to force everything into the shot that there's no visible detail left. In addition, you can end up with clutter in the foreground that may ruin the shot.

The telephoto end of your digital camera's zoom lens is the solution here. You can use it to crop in close for a more detailed image. You'll quickly find that, with architecture, less is often so much more. Look for the little architectural details that will make an interesting image. Alternatively, shoot only part of the building in context, revealing some of the background.

In this way the building will still be recognisable, particularly if it's a famous structure, but you get a unique view of it that can add interest to an otherwise bland or well-known façade.

Exaggerate perspective

This technique can work really well with tall buildings shot from a low angle, particularly if you have an interesting or clear blue sky. In the tall building image shown opposite, the buildings have been shot to exaggerate the converging verticals, and the clouds in the blue sky above balance the composition.

Go black and white

Don't forget to try out your digital camera's black and white mode. This can work really well on older buildings or where a modern building lends itself to the graphic look that black and white so often creates.

Change your viewpoint

If it's at all possible, change your viewpoint. Some buildings provide access to towers, balconies, basements or viewing platforms – utilise these whenever you can. It will add interest and once up (or down) there, other interesting shots will become apparent.

✔

- *Use the wide-angle end of the lens (that's around 35mm or wider) or get a wide-angle adapter to accommodate broader views. Alternatively, use your camera's panorama feature to stitch many shots together or do this later on your PC.*

- *The telephoto end of your zoom will enable you to crop in closely on a detail if you can't, or don't want to, fit in the entire structure.*

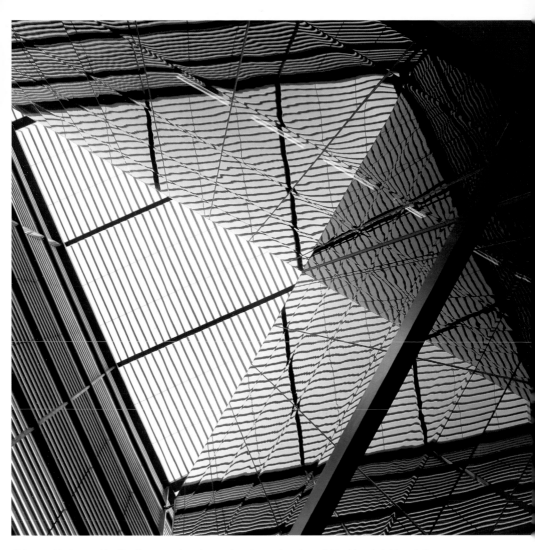

Using a wide lens and looking for unusual angles, such as from a low viewpoint looking straight up, help to exaggerate perspective and create bags of drama, as shown in this image of a colourful building.

Shoot vertically up the wall too, but if you try the reverse of this – from a high vantage point looking down – make sure you always have the camera attached to you via its carry strap. Look for natural frames such as an archway or go for reflections in lakes or ponds: all can make excellent alternative views of buildings.

Bridges can be so huge that you have no choice but to stand well back to fit everything in. Again, look for details and perspectives that offer a new and unique shot. For example, go to the river bank or try to shoot down the length of the bridge to get a receding perspective on the structure.

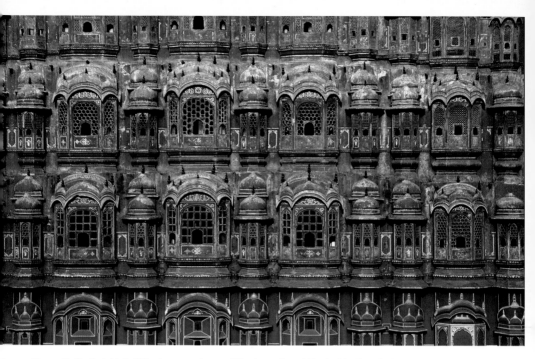

Above: *To fit all of this building into one shot would look very 'busy'. But in this shot, closing in using the zoom lens has helped to give a sense of scale, show detail and make for a superbly graphic image.*

Night shots

Another professional's tip is simply to shoot at night. Even stark or uninteresting buildings can take on a completely new personality at night. A tripod or other support will be needed to hold the camera steady. Also, it's best to survey the building during daylight so you'll already have an idea of the best angles and views.

Shooting statues

Statues can make excellent subjects but involve extra considerations. First, because statues tend to be relatively small, there's a danger of under-exposure as there's usually a large expanse of bright sky behind them which fools the meter. Switch the metering to centre-weighted or spot to ensure the metering is from the statue and not the sky behind.

Walk right around statues to look for the best shot or to see if there's a better background. Try to balance the shot with other compositional elements such as trees or parts of the background to 'set the scene'.

> **!**
>
> - *Watch out for under-exposure, particularly if there's a bright background. Use centre-weighted or spot metering.*
>
> - *Avoid clichéd shots – move around to find a unique view, particularly of famous monuments or buildings.*

Landscapes

Landscapes are ideal images to grace any wall. Here are a few ideas on how to make them as striking as possible.

The single most important thing in landscape photography is to get up early to catch the morning light. Why? Because morning skies are clearer. A lack of haze in the atmosphere produces a better quality of light, and you get raking shadows from the lower angle of the sun which is a good effect. That established, here are some more expert tips to improve your landscapes even further.

Leading the way

One of the best ways to make a success of a landscape shot is to have elements placed within the composition that lead the viewer's eye into the shot. Anything in the foreground such as a plant or rock, then a tree in the middle distance and then, perhaps, a distant hill – these all help.

A swooping hillside with the ridge running across the frame and receding into the

Below: *Here the tree in the foreground helps to guide you into the shot; without it the image would be ordinary. Also note its positioning using the rule of thirds.*

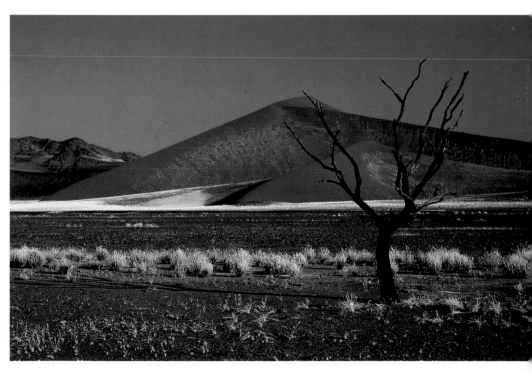

distance works well, or even rows of crops in a field that all run into the distance or up the side of a hill. Once the viewer's gaze is drawn to the distant part of the scene, it helps to have another element sitting there waiting: a building, tree or even an interesting cloud formation on the horizon.

Framing the picture

Don't be afraid to have things intruding into the shot at the top and sides. The idea is to frame your landscape with something actually in the scene; tree branches just hanging into the shot across the top edges for example. The combination of the photo's shape and the other 'framing' elements help to draw the viewer into the scene and add interest. This so-called 'frame within a frame' technique can work well, but practice and experimentation is needed to establish what works best.

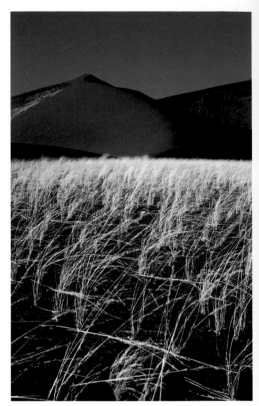

Right: *In this shot, the foreground grasses guide your eye into the shot, the ridge on the sand dune takes it in further and the deep blue sky adds dramatic colour contrast.*

Far right: *This shot of the San Juan River uses the curve of the canyon, the shape it forms and dramatic clouds to help create a stunning image. Here the rule of thirds has been broken so the interesting sky can become a key part of the scene.*

i Correct settings

Your digital camera has a finite number of pixels to employ on any image, but with landscape shots, it's vitally important to use every single one of them and to use them at the highest quality setting. This is because detail in a landscape shot can be tiny in the frame, perhaps only one or two pixels across, particularly if it's a distant part of the scene.

So select the camera's highest resolution possible. Then select the camera's highest quality mode. These usually run from 'Standard' or 'Good', through 'Better' or 'Fine' to 'High Quality' or 'Best'. Check your camera's manual

to be sure you have picked the best settings in all these departments.

White balance should be set to suit the conditions: Sun for bright sunlight, Cloudy for cloud and so on. If you're not sure, stick with the Auto setting which will be adequate in most cases.

Make sure you use a small aperture (so a high F-number such as F8, F11 or F14), which gives a broad depth of field, thus keeping everything sharp, from close by the camera to the far distance. Put the camera on a tripod or other support to keep it steady – or make sure you use a shutter speed fast enough to freeze any potential camera shake.

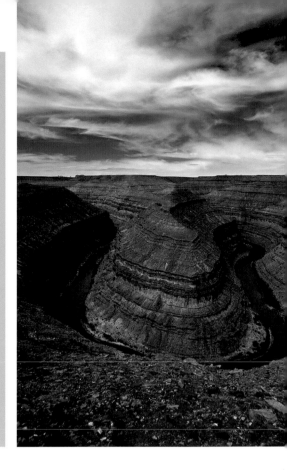

- *Get up early to capture the best of the morning light.*

- *Shoot at the highest resolution your camera has and its highest quality (compression) settings.*

- *Use small aperture settings (larger F-stop numbers) to ensure a deep depth of field.*

- *Use a shutter speed fast enough to freeze any potential camera shake.*

- *Alternatively, support your camera on a tripod or other prop. Keeping your camera rock steady is a good way to ensure sharp landscape shots.*

- *A tripod is an essential tool to help get better landscape shots; it can prevent camera shake and ensure you get horizon's level.*

Rule of thirds

The rule of thirds can make a huge difference to a landscape shot (see *Composition*). All the elements of your composition can be brought together in many ways, but by placing key elements using this rule, you can make an even stronger composition. Experimentation is important here – shots that don't work can easily be deleted. Sometimes it even helps if the rule is broken.

The right format

Just because it's a landscape shot, you don't have to use the camera in its landscape or horizontal format, with the longest edge across the top. Portrait format can work just

as well, depending on the subject. Some of the images we've used here are upright shots that would not work as well with a 'wider' perspective. You can check both options in your LCD.

Overleaf: *The upright (or portrait) format has worked well to emphasise the leading lines created by this shot of a road. The sky has been given the top third of the frame with the road filling the entire foreground. The white lines and telegraph poles help add further dynamism to the shot.*

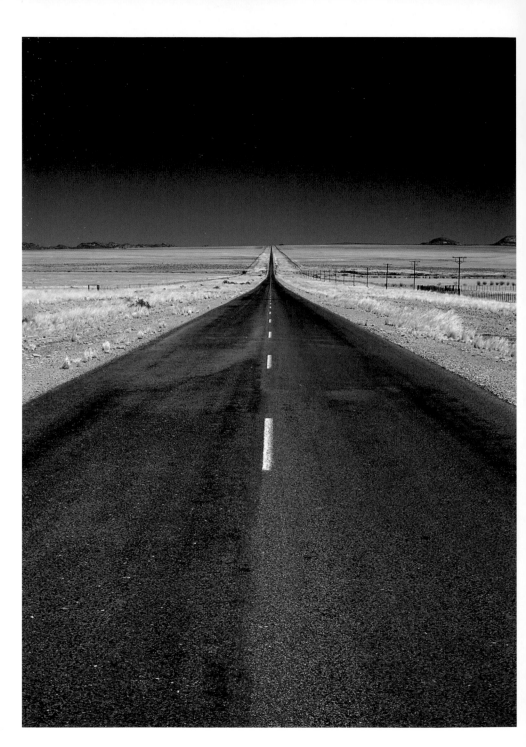

Sports and action

Capturing the action with a fast-moving subject such as sports can be a real challenge. But with a few key tips you can shoot the fastest of fleeting moments to dramatic effect.

Sports or action photography can include everything from photographing super fast sports cars, your child running at their school sports day or your dog jumping to catch a ball. In short, it's any shot of a fast-moving object which can be difficult to shoot sharply.

Helpfully, even the most basic of digital cameras has some form of 'sports' mode that can help capture these moments. But here are some additional techniques that will help you avoid blurring or even completely missing your subject.

Panning with the subject
One way to help get shots with a sharp subject and blurry background is to pan with a moving subject. This involves watching the subject in the LCD (or viewfinder) as it moves and judging the right point to capture it.

Stand with your feet firmly planted and smoothly swing the upper part of your body as the subject moves across and in front of you and, as the subject hits the point you want to take the photo, fire the shutter. Or try a series of shots, pausing and snapping as the action passes by as you swing around.

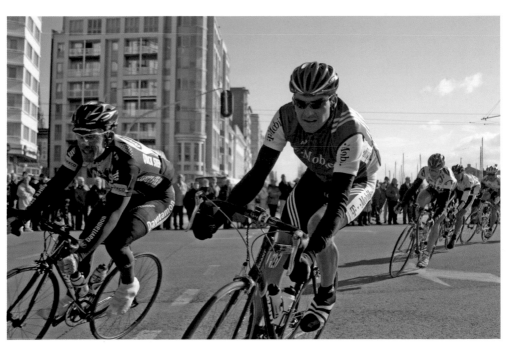

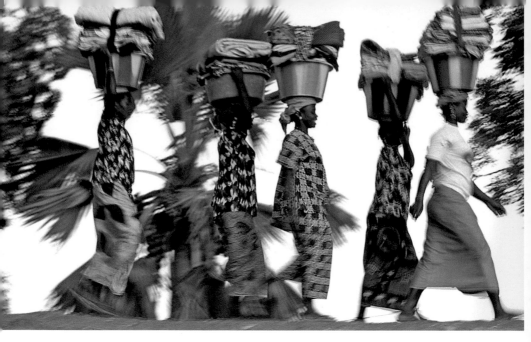

Above: *For this shot of washerwomen in Mali, a shutter speed of around 1/30th second and panning with their motion has helped give the shot a dynamic feel.*

Previous page: *In this shot, a fast shutter speed of 1/2000th second and large F3.5 aperture were used to ensure the action was completely frozen. This aperture has allowed plenty of light to get to the sensor and helped blur the background slightly.*

Shutter lag

Many digital compacts, however, are affected by shutter lag. This means that there's a short time delay between pressing the shutter release and the shutter actually firing. This is no problem for standard photos, but in action shots this delay means you risk missing the subject completely.

Basic digital cameras suffer the most from this. It's caused by the on-board computer taking time to focus, set the metering and generally get the camera primed to take the photo. More advanced cameras have faster processing and so suffer less from this problem. The best way around this with a basic model is to use a pre-focus technique.

Pre-focusing

This technique solves the problem of shutter lag because you pre-focus the camera at a predetermined point. Set the camera's focusing system to manual and focus it using the chosen point. If you don't have a manual focus setting, find a point you know the subject will pass, and half-press the shutter button to focus on that point. Then, keeping the shutter half-pressed, follow the subject, pressing the shutter the rest of the way down when the subject gets to the right pre-focused point. This will give a sharp action image with a blurred background. Use the same techniques but without panning to get a sharp subject and background.

Slow sync flash

Another idea to try is slow sync flash. Here, a slow shutter is combined with a burst of flash. The flash freezes the subject motion and the slow shutter speed keeps the background blurred. It's the same method as used in low light, but it can be equally creative in daylight.

Timing

Timing is everything, particularly the timing required to catch your subject at the right point in the action. Practice makes perfect, but whatever the subject, take plenty of photos. Set your camera to shoot continuously, which is usually around three frames per second for most consumer compacts. Some can shoot more, some less, depending on their sophistication.

If the camera has a sports mode it will do all this for you. Just keep the shutter button pressed and it will just keep on taking pictures until you let go.

What focal length?

You'll find that a longer focal length is best for capturing sports or action shots where you cannot get close to the subject. Racing tracks or stadiums are good examples – you've probably seen the banks of sports photographers at sporting events using huge telephoto lenses. You'll need a digital camera with (ideally) a 10x zoom lens, or use a D-SLR with a 250mm or longer lens.

Longer focal lengths mean slower maximum shutter speeds, particularly if it's gloomy. Watch out for camera shake, increase the sensitivity (ISO), which helps get faster shutter speeds, and open the aperture to a larger setting (a smaller F-number) such as F2.8.

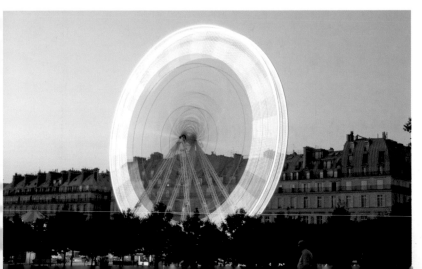

Left: *Slow shutter speeds can be used to capture light trails from cars or, as in this case, a funfair's Ferris wheel, shot with a shutter speed of around eight seconds. You'll need a tripod for this technique.*

Weddings

Getting stunning shots at a wedding can be tricky. But there are some simple steps you can take to ensure that this most important of days is beautifully and safely recorded.

Be prepared

The key to successful wedding photography is preparation and planning. You need to get organised: visit the venues beforehand, talk to the bride and groom so that they're relaxed for the photos on the day, and plan out what shots you'll need to keep everyone happy.

A professional photographer can easily rack up over 300 shots at a wedding, so if you're planning to cover the whole event, ensure you have plenty of suitable capacity memory cards available – or a way to back photos up such as a portable hard drive. Also check your camera is functioning properly, your batteries are charged and you have any necessary accessories to hand.

Group shots

Group shots can be difficult to coordinate. One way to achieve good groups is to watch what the professional photographer does and take the same shots. But you must make sure you don't get in their way or in their shot.

Big groups will need the wide-angle end of your camera's lens, then zoom into the group as it gets smaller. If you can, shoot each group with different backgrounds. Control depth of field with the apertures (F-stops) and use larger apertures to blur the background. Keep checking the shots on the LCD to ensure they work, and if not, take them again.

Candid shots

Candid shots are a great way to capture the spirit of a wedding in the way formal, posed shots don't always allow, and such informal shots are also easier to take. Catch relaxed

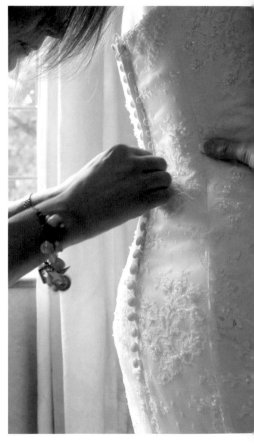

Above: *A classic 'bride getting ready' shot taken at home before the service; the sort of intimate image that helps sum up the day.*

Right: *Another idea is to shoot aspects of the bride's or groom's outfits. This shot of a bride's shoes on a windowsill using only natural light was taken while she was getting ready.*

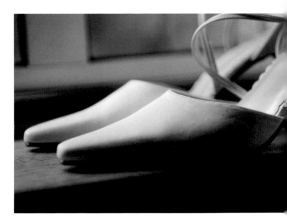

people chatting and happy figures enjoying the day. Also look for closely cropped shots of faces, and target the small animated groups that congregate at a wedding. Don't be afraid to use unusual angles or the camera's black and white mode.

Shots in the church or venue

Flash will be almost essential indoors. But it's even better if you use a support such as a tripod and slow sync flash to give an ambient exposure that will capture both the people and the atmosphere. If in a church, check whether you're allowed to shoot inside and if you can use flash. It's unlikely you'll be able to shoot during the ceremony.

Below: *Don't forget the bride and groom's more intimate shots after the group photos; this one has been taken using the camera's sepia setting.*

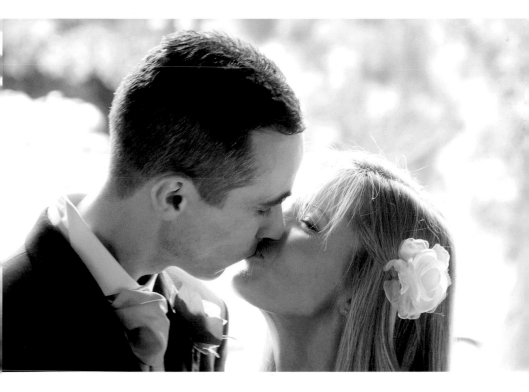

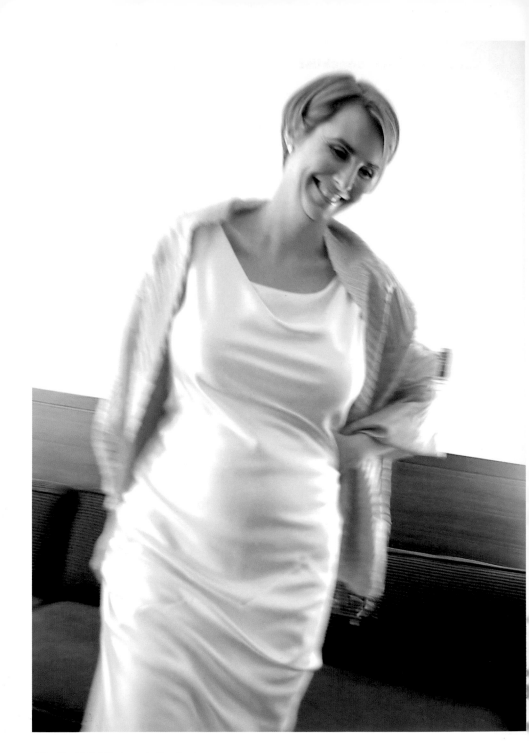

Essential shots checklist

There are a number of traditional shots you'll need to take at a wedding:

- **The bride at home:** *including preparations, and individual and group shots of the bride and bridesmaids.*

- **The groom arriving at the church or venue:** *don't forget the best man and ushers, the groom's parents and other immediate family.*

- **The bride's arrival:** *don't forget the bridesmaids, and waiting to enter the church or venue.*

- **Inside the church/venue:** *ideally a tripod shot (it'll be dark) to capture the atmosphere.*

- **Signing the register:** *the bride, the groom and a group shot with witnesses if possible.*

- **Walking down the aisle:** *including the happy couple outside the church or venue with guests swarming around and the crucial confetti-throwing.*

- **Groups:** *if you are arranging this, do the biggest groups first so that some guests can then depart to the reception, leaving more time for shots with the bride and groom. So start with big friends and family groups, then the bride and groom with the bride's family and the groom's family, followed by closer family and the bridal party, and finally intimate portraits of the bride and groom.*

- **The wedding reception,** *including the line-up, cutting the cake, and the toast with glasses raised being clinked together.*

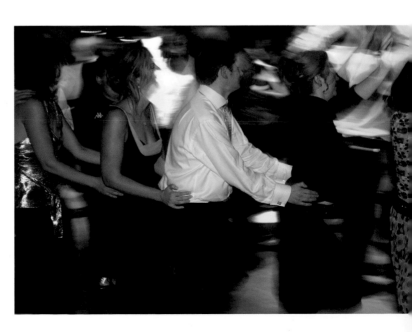

Opposite: *The black and white mode on your camera is ideal for candid shots such as this one of a demure bridesmaid. The gentle blurring is deliberate and helps give the shot a softness ideal for the subject; this was achieved by using a slow shutter speed.*

Right: *This type of slow sync candid image at the reception is fun and simple to take.*

Gardens and flowers

Gardens in bloom or individual flowers can make stunningly colourful photos. Use these ideas to make the flowers in your garden look just as beautiful as any botanical garden.

Lighting

One of the key aspects of flower photography is careful consideration of the light. Although bright, direct sunlight brings out colour, it's also very harsh and creates deep shadows. Often you'll find an overcast sky can provide the best lighting, particularly if you're shooting close-ups. Flash, while available to you, is not always ideal as it can blast so much light onto the flower that it bleaches out the detail and colour.

A great tip for controlling the available light is to use pieces of card. You can use them to shade a close-up shot from direct sunlight. White card can be used to reflect flash (if using an accessory flashgun) or to reflect available ambient light to fill in shadow. Alternatively, you can deaden 'hot spots' with black card. You can also use the card as a backdrop, helping remove a cluttered background from a shot of a single bloom, for example. Try the same shot using either white or black card to create a different backdrop in each shot.

Close-ups

The close-up techniques already discussed (see *Close-ups*) are particularly effective with flowers. You can really use the camera's macro power here. Don't just shoot the entire flower head: get even closer and shoot the detail of stamens or even just the veins in the leaves or petals, if your camera can get that close.

You'll need to fill the frame. Remember to use a small aperture (high F-stop number)

to increase depth of field and use a shutter speed that will not only stop any potential camera shake but also freeze the flower if it's windy, typically a speed at least equal to the reciprocal of the focal length in use. Don't forget those bits of card: they come in handy as a wind shade too. If you have a tripod or other camera support, use it for even more stability.

Wider vistas

As with landscapes, you need to think about composition when photographing a vista of plants: the shape of flowerbeds can be important, as can ranks of plants of the same colour. Zoom in and out of the shot to see if a smaller part of the scene looks better or offers unusual patterns that would be missed with a shot of the entire area. Move your viewpoint constantly and look for the best angle or vantage point.

Shutter speeds should be kept fast enough to stop camera shake and motion blur and at least equal to the reciprocal of the focal length in use. However, one technique is to use motion blur to your advantage, particularly if it's windy and you're shooting a field of swaying flowers or corn, for example. Set the camera on a sturdy support, and use a small aperture and slow shutter speed to catch the motion of the swaying plants. The result should be a sea of attractively swishing plants that will look like brushed cotton or a beautiful smoothed surface. Use a wider focal length to help increase drama.

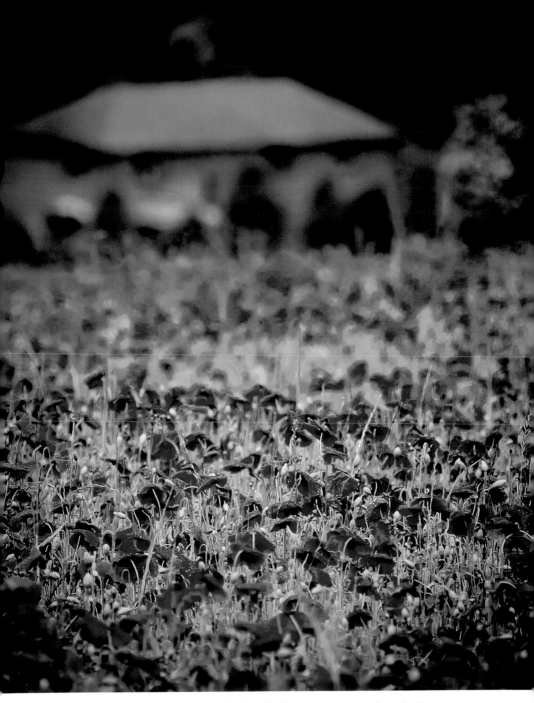

Use your zoom or telephoto lens and a big aperture (such as F/2.8) to compress perspective and add emphasis, as has been done here with this field of poppies.

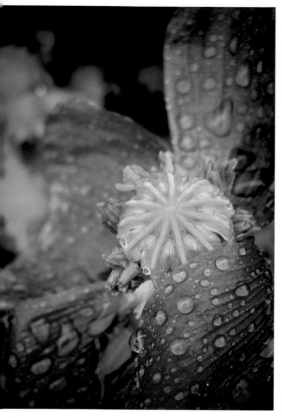

Raindrops on blooms can add fantastic detail to otherwise mundane photos.

Don't just shoot the obvious, sometimes details, such as this iron bench's frame, can make a great shot too.

Getting creative

Avoid the temptation always to stand up when shooting flowers. Changing your point of view even just by dropping to your knees can have a dramatic effect. If you want to emphasise a single plant or bloom in the foreground with a distorted perspective, lie down and use the wide-angle end of the zoom lens. Focus on the foreground flower – it must be close to the lens – and you'll have an (apparently) giant bloom or plant in a wide, distorted landscape. This is very effective if you choose your bloom wisely – a single prominent plant is better than a larger bush, for example.

Again, you can use your pieces of black and white card to help control light, along with a water spray bottle: use the spray to add a mist of water droplets to the flowers and plants. This gives an appearance of fantastic 'freshness', mimicking morning dew, and also catches the light, making even boring plants look more succulent and attractive.

Practical checklist

- The basic approach is to shoot the entire flower or flowerbed to fill the frame.

- Use a household water spray on blooms and leaves to add attractive highlights which help make the flower look crisp and fresh.

- Don't ignore other elements of gardens such as interesting fountains or buildings. Some may be worth a shot of their own or can give contrast to the plant elements of the scene.

- Hunt for the best blooms. Look for blemish-free flowers; you don't want anything with marks or brown patches.

- Set metering to centre-weighted or spot for further emphasis on certain blooms.

Filling the frame works well if there's a cluttered background. You may get a more interesting interplay of form and colour, such as in this close crop of crocuses. Note the control of DOF here too.

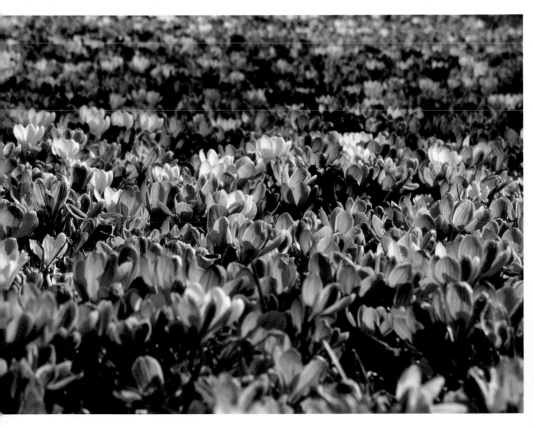

Children

Children are understandably the most popular photographic subject. So make sure you know how best to capture those childhood moments for posterity.

From newborn infant to graduate, children are in front of the lens for most of their lives. Despite this, getting great shots can be a challenge, as children rarely stand still and can get bored when you want to take a more serious or studied family portrait. Here are some ways around this.

Babies

Newborn babies offer plenty of scope for creative as well as fun shots. For instance, a close-up of a baby's hands (or feet) juxtaposed against an adult hand can make a moving image. Such shots will require a close zoom and should ideally be taken when the baby's asleep, unless they're particularly relaxed after a feed. Use natural light for a charming, softly lit image.

Other ideas include portraits with the happy mum and dad where the baby is held proudly cheek-to-cheek, and shots with the baby cradled lovingly across a parent's chest. However, avoid a full body shot while the baby is sleeping, particularly a shot from above, as this can look dull and lifeless, especially if harsh flash is used. If you want to shoot a full body image, get down to the baby's sleeping level and close in. Use soft natural light from a window and the image will look full of life, relaxed and natural.

Toddlers

When babies are starting to move around, real fun can be had. Set your camera to its sports mode if it has one, or use a fast shutter speed. Try to get in on the action:

if they're playing on the floor, lie down with them. If you want a vibrant shot, use colourful blankets and dress your subjects in bright clothes. If you use flash, watch out for dark backgrounds generated by flash fall off. However, this might be desirable in a portrait image, for example.

If there's more than one toddler, drop to one knee or lie down to get on their level. Zoom out and try to capture their group play. A slower shutter speed can help here – motion blur can make things look both active and humorous. Don't forget the camera's slow sync mode: a burst of flash can freeze the children's play, whilst the slower shutter speed captures the ambient atmosphere and some movement too.

Parties

One of the most challenging child photo opportunities is a party. Try to get a fun shot of the whole group – get the other parents involved if necessary. For slightly older children, get them all to pull a funny face in one shot, and a serious face in another. Making more of a game of the photography and showing them the results on the camera's screen often means they'll want to pose for more photos. But work as quickly as you can.

At the party table, you must of course get the candles-being-blown-out shot: use slow sync flash for the best effect. You'll also need to shoot all of the children seated

By constantly looking and waiting for the right moment you can get wonderfully wistful shots, as with this natural-light shot of a little girl.

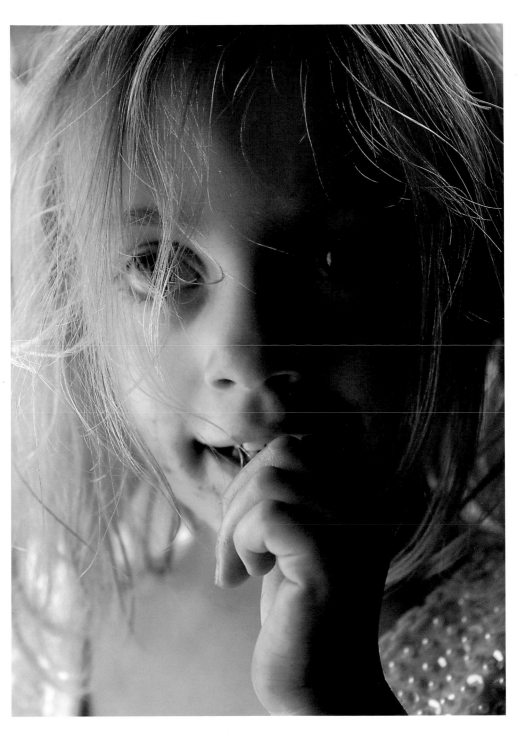

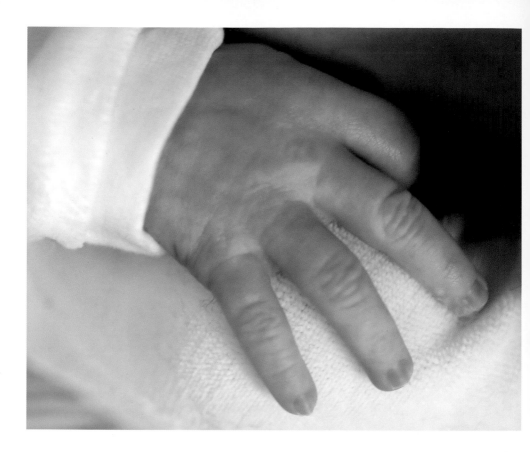

at the table, but it's usually hard to fit everyone in as it's unlikely you'll have a wide enough focal length. In this case, shoot from one end of the table and try to get the kids to lean in – ensure you get every face. If you have room, stand on a chair and shoot using the wide-angle end of your zoom lens; get someone to hold the chair and be careful.

Younger children will often not cooperate for such shots, so the best technique is to move around looking and waiting to get the 'moment', snapping as you go. Look for small groups of two or three children and you'll eventually capture all of them this way. Remember to keep the children on side by continuing to show them the pictures on the camera's LCD.

Above: *Intimate shots such as a baby's hand can work well in both colour and black and white, and also juxtaposed with a parent's hand.*

Opposite: *An unguarded moment for these children at a wedding has been captured well. The timing is great as the young bridesmaid has just realised the shot is being taken.*

Growing up

Photograph the key moments in your child's life: everything from the first tooth appearing, starting at school, being a bridesmaid or pageboy to college graduation. The photo techniques used will depend on the moment and atmosphere you want to create. Keeping a record of such momentous events can build into a wonderful album of images or a PC slide show (see *Creating slide shows*). Remember to back up all these priceless images (see *Backing-up*).

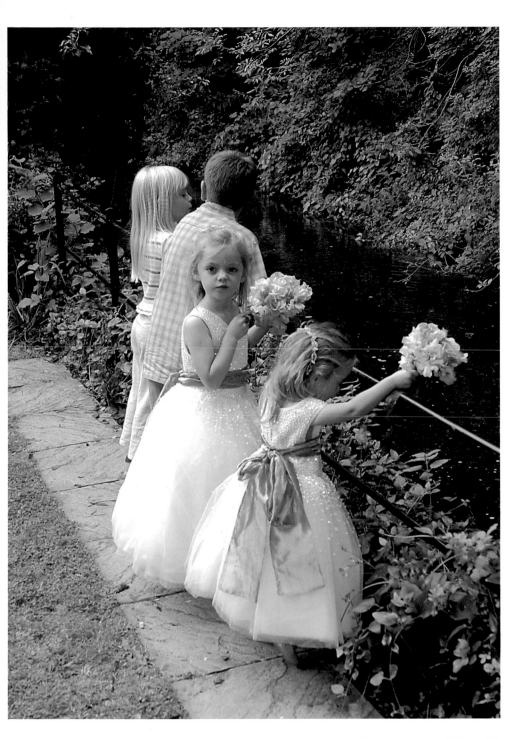

Pets and animals

Photographing animals and pets can be very tricky, but the following tips will help you get prize pictures of all different kinds of creatures.

Basic techniques

Pets can be treated just like any subject when considering the photo techniques involved. All the elements such as composition, exposure and focus must be right. Focus on the eyes, compose the shot so the animal looks 'natural' and set the camera to its portrait mode for posed-style shots. Use the sports setting if you want to get photos of a dog jumping around in the garden, for example.

Accurate exposure can be problematic, as all-white or all-black animal coats can fool the metering and under- or over-expose respectively. Check the results on the camera's LCD and adjust the exposure (lower or higher shutter speeds, for example, if you have manual control).

Flash

Like humans, pets can suffer from redeye – although in animals it's often bright greeneye! Use an off-camera flash to avoid it if you have one. If using a camera's built-in flash unit, use the redeye reduction mode and, if indoors, turn on more lights. This will help reduce the animal's pupil size, cutting down the chance of greeneye. Remember, however, that flash can startle an animal, so use natural light whenever possible.

Timing

One major source of frustration will be getting your pets to stay still once you point the lens at them. Timing is everything. You'll need to be patient and watch the animal playing, poised for *the* shot. A squeaky toy can come in useful here to get moments of alertness as they play or start to slumber.

Alternatively, recruit a helper, someone able to occupy the pet and keep it lively. However, you'll have to try to keep them out of shot to keep the photo looking natural. Move around searching for the right angle as the helper encourages the pet to sit or play as you want it to.

Zoos and safaris

Photographing animals in zoos can be difficult as the cage may get in the way. Use a large aperture (lower F-stop number) and a long zoom, and focus on animals further back in the cage. The resulting narrow depth of field means the fencing should be practically invisible in the shot.

If you're on a safari or travelling to see other animal life in the wild, the most important consideration will be your lens. You're unlikely to be able to get close to the animals you're photographing, so a long zoom is essential, the longer the better. Some of today's 10x and 12x zoom compacts are ideal for this. If you own a D-SLR, you'll need a lens with at least a 300mm focal length equivalent. In each case, framing and composition are vital (without putting yourself in danger), so look for clean backgrounds and frame-filling compositions. On safari, when shooting from a platform or Jeep, fast shutter speeds are vital to keep things steady.

For humorous shots, use a wide-angle lens setting to exaggerate the shape of an animal's face. Be sure to focus on the eyes, though.

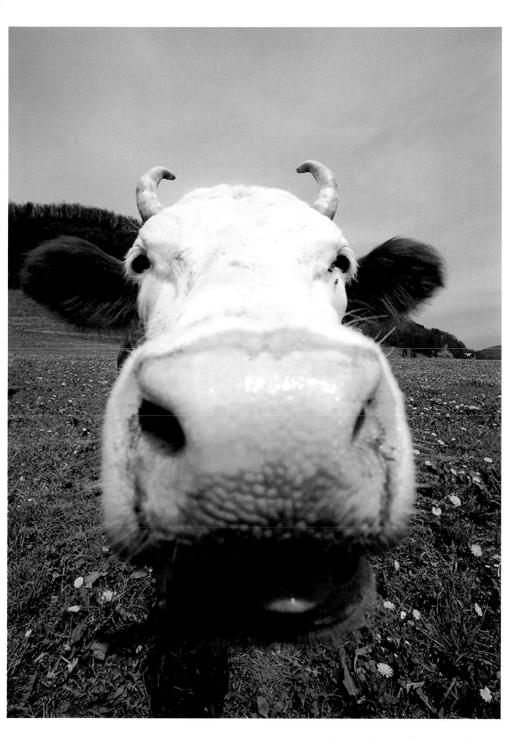

Right: *If you can't get a shot of an animal in action, go for detail or colour, as in this striking portrait of an owl at a summer fete.*

Opposite: *This shot of a cheetah was actually taken through cage bars. Using a large aperture and long focal length of 200mm gave a shallow depth of field, ensuring the cage didn't intrude into the shot.*

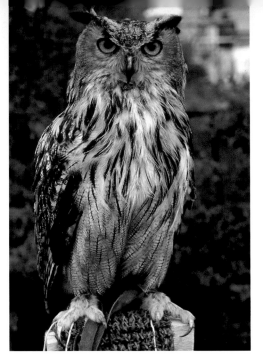

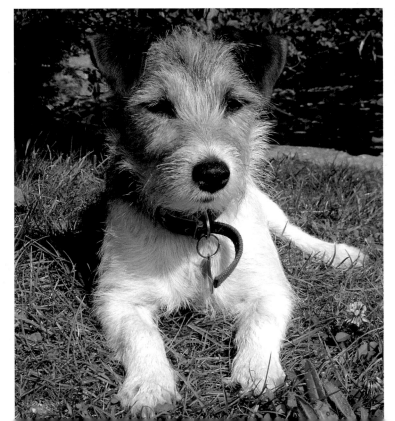

Left: *This resting but alert dog just needed a little help to prick up its ears. A quick whistle from the photographer did the trick.*

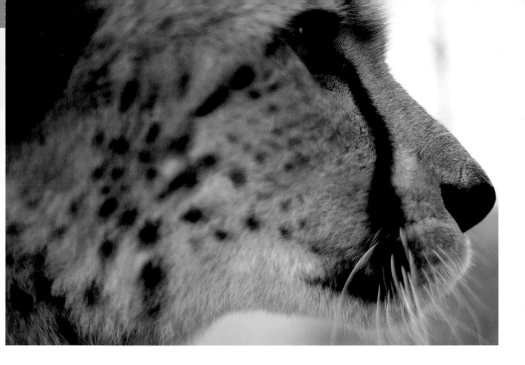

i Tips for shooting particular animals

- For **dogs and cats,** the best bet is to give the animal something to play with, such as a squeaky toy, or a bone if it's a dog. This takes their mind off the camera, but you'll have to be ready to trigger the shutter quickly.

- Shooting **fish** in a tank can be tricky as you need to avoid reflections from the glass (or water if the fish are in a pond). Avoid flash and get the lens as close to the glass or water surface as possible (you may need to switch on the camera's macro/close-up mode for small tanks). Wait for the fish to pass by the lens or to stop moving.

- For smaller pets such as **hamsters, mice or guinea pigs** getting close enough can be a problem. The best solution is to shoot them in someone's hand. Use the camera's close-up mode and fill the frame with the animal. If the animal is in a cage, use a larger aperture as the narrow depth of field will help to ensure that the cage bars aren't visible in the shot.

- For **sea life,** many digital cameras can be used underwater with a special waterproof housing, ideal when snorkelling. You'll need to get close to the subject, and the lower light underwater means a higher sensitivity setting (ISO 400 or greater) should be selected. Flash presents a problem as a phenomenon called back scatter means light is bounced back into the lens from particles in the water, ruining the picture. This can only really be avoided by waiting until there's less muck in the water or more available light.

Abstracts

Abstracts are the potentially stunning and unusual patterns in a landscape or scene, from large-scale cloud formations to the small-scale geometries of grains of sand. Our tips will help you search out the best abstract shots.

The human eye is tuned to look for patterns in everything we see. It's the reason our ancestors could 'see' constellations in the heavens: we love to find order in seemingly random things. In photography, the trick is to spot these patterns and then crop the image properly to achieve the effect you've identified. Depicting a subject with the thrust of the shot aimed at internal structure or form, rather than the thing in its entirety, can make shooting abstracts very gratifying.

Inspiration for abstracts

Abstract patterns occur in almost anything: shadows, freshly mown grass, wooden fencing, leaves on the ground, a multitude of illuminated windows in a building at night, or even people milling about a railway station. Abstracts from nature are the most common. To shoot any type of abstract successfully, you have to think about what you're seeing in terms of shapes and forms (in a similar way to how you must think in black and white when snapping mono shots). For example, a macro shot of a flower can look colourful and beautiful but also unveil an interesting cell pattern on the leaf, which then becomes a striking image in its own right.

Man-made objects can provide inspiration too. Perhaps take a tight crop on a manhole cover that shows its stippled surface and dirt or rust. Either zoom in or simply move closer to the subject and use the wide-angle end of the lens. Both approaches will provide an abstract shot with an 'industrial' feel.

Colour and abstracts

It's not just shape and form that can create an abstract. Looking closely at colours and patterns of colours will help too. An abstract can lurk anywhere within a colourful vista – markets are great examples of this, as the image of colourful shoes below shows. Perhaps an easier example to find would be a selection of ties hanging on a shop rail. Remember that colour is as important to the look of an abstract as the form of the subjects themselves.

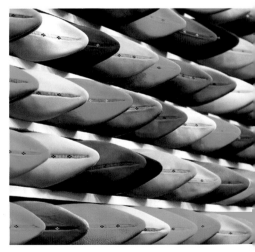

Above: *Regular patterns can help form abstracts, as can colour, but here both combine – in rows of colourful new shoes – to produce a great abstract image with strong form. Note the use of an unorthodox angle: the shoes have been photographed to exaggerate the perspective of the racks in which they lie. A flat 'straight on' shot might also work, but not as effectively as this.*

Using angles

Another tip to help create abstracts from seemingly mundane subjects is to change the angle from which you shoot. Even tilting the camera so it is composed neither landscape nor portrait but diagonally can help, and may provide a better frame within which the abstract will work. The shot below of shuttered windows provides an example of how looking for other angles, in this case looking straight up, can be used to produce unusual shapes and form in your images.

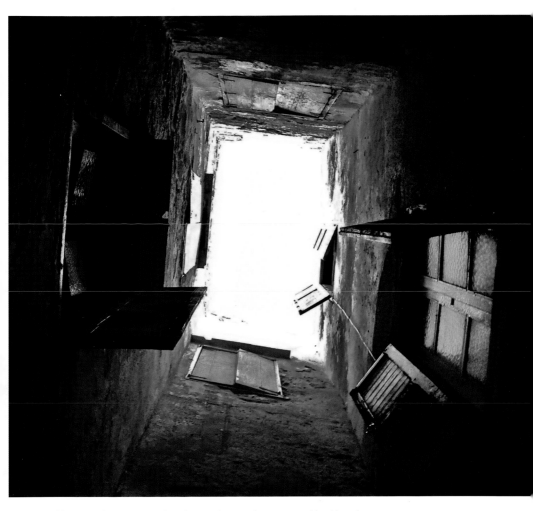

Above: *Looking around you at unusual angles can present photo opportunities. Here the shuttered windows, narrow confines of the buildings and over-exposed sky all contrive to make a pleasing 'form' abstract.*

Large-scale abstracts

If you are flying, grab the chance to shoot from a completely new perspective. The shot opposite of white clouds over the red-looking desert is a classic large-scale abstract. The clouds start the whole composition. A tight, zoomed-in crop helps exclude all but the colour of the red earth below, which is vitally important to the composition and enhances the graphic feel. Best of all, the shadows formed by the clouds add a 3D feel to the shot. But you don't have to shoot from a plane to obtain large-scale abstracts: they can exist anywhere. You just have to look for them.

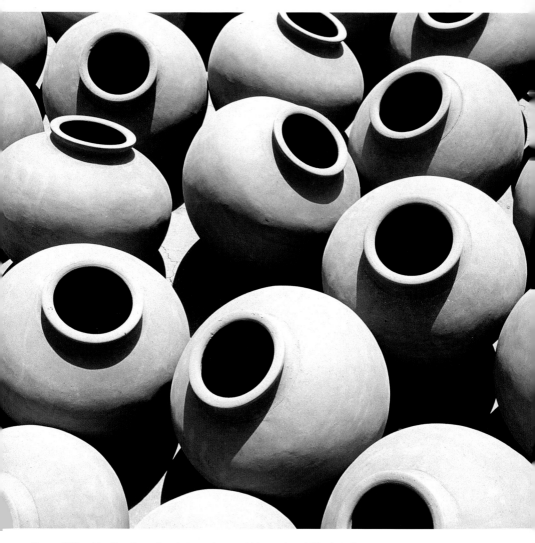

Above: *Without looking down, the photographer would have missed this shot of pots drying in the sun in India. To catch abstracts you need to look around you and really see what's there.*

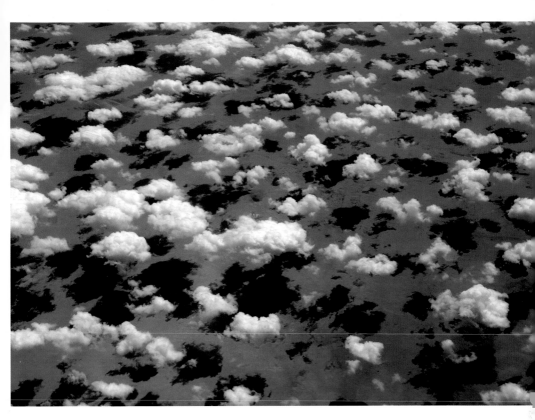

Above: *Large-scale abstracts can be found when flying, like this stunning image of clouds and their shadows floating over the red earth.*

<table>
<tr><td>**i**</td><td>## Abstracts checklist</td></tr>
</table>

- *Zoom in, zoom out, move closer and move away. A seemingly boring leaf on the ground might become something else entirely if you move in to capture the pattern of its veins, or zoom out to include all its fallen fellows on the ground.*

- *The subject you're shooting will dictate the exposure parameters you need to use, but don't be afraid to experiment. Assess the results in your LCD, then try another approach.*

- *A trick to see abstracts more easily is to look through the camera's viewfinder or its LCD to see if a shape or pattern presents itself that is not immediately apparent otherwise. Try: what emerges might just surprise you.*

- *When shooting close-up, look for the finer patterns within the subject.*

- *Think shape, shine, form, colour and scale.*

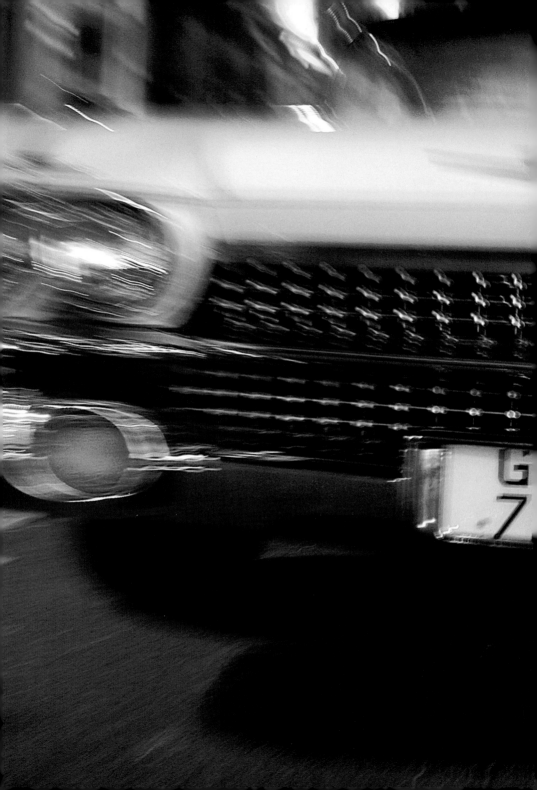

The digital
darkroom

In this section, you'll find all you need to digitally enhance photos on your PC, including:

- **How to use editing software** – finding your way around programs, using tools and menus, and saving to the different file formats

- **Basic digital techniques** – autofix, cropping, straightening, resizing, sharpening, brightening, redeye removal and converting to black and white

- **Advanced techniques** – using colour management, levels, curves, channels, cloning and healing, dodge and burn, masks and layers

- **Masterclasses** – the professional way to blur backgrounds, add movement, make panoramas, restore old prints and use special techniques such as HDR

- **Explanations** of JPEGs, TIFFs, GIFs, PICT, PDFs, filters, RGB and how to shoot in RAW

Starting to use
editing software

Image editing software allows you to manipulate your digital photos, from simple corrections to complex special effects. First we'll introduce you to finding and using the editing functions.

Image editing software in PC or app form ranges from the basic tools included with your camera to programs designed for professionals. In addition, your digital camera may have basic built-in image editing capability, accessed in playback mode. In-camera editing options may include processing a RAW file to JPEG, image cropping or effect filters, such as vignetting or highlight recovery, good for quick edits before sharing images direct from the camera.

The PC software that comes with your digital camera is more advanced and is okay for basic tasks such as resizing, modest corrections to colour or exposure for example, or RAW processing. But for the majority of editing tasks in this book, we recommend you buy an off-the-shelf program (see *Which software?*). Then you'll have a powerful tool for just about any image editing task.

Throughout the image editing topics in this book, we provide examples using Adobe's Photoshop Elements, a popular consumer-level editing package. Newer versions of Elements (and similar programs) have built-in guided step-by-steps for some tasks but, where possible, we have explained them the long way to try and encompass everyone's software. We will also look at Adobe's Lightroom software, which allows fast image edits and image organisation all from a single, easy-to-use interface. (See *Lightroom.*)

Finding your way around

Although there are lots of different image editing packages on the market, all of them use very similar tools and editing functions. They'll even have very similar workspaces, with the main tools ranged down one side (usually the left side, though you can move them around). Across the top, an 'options' bar provides ways of changing individual tool settings (such as brush sizes) and access to other menus with even more choices.

Helpful hint windows or 'wizards' are often incorporated into the software, and these will automatically pop up when needed to assist you with simple editing techniques.

Tools and functions can be accessed in a number of ways: through menus that appear (or 'drop down') when you click on them in the options bar; in a small window that pops up on the desktop; or by clicking on an icon (a small picture that indicates a function). Usually, if you hover the mouse cursor over an item for a moment (without clicking), its name will appear over the tool, so you can always check what it is.

While your software will have all or most of these menus/tools, the names and locations may differ depending on the package. Always read the manual or use the on-screen help assistant to search for a particular function.

Overleaf is a list of the key tools from the most popular software packages so that even if the names vary, you'll know which tool icon to look for.

Menus and windows you could find on your desktop

1 Options bar

This bar allows you to minimise, close or expand the workspace and any image you're working on (if it is pinned to the Organiser bar), without closing the program's tool, palette or dialogue pop ups. If you prefer to work with your image floating in the workspace, you can close or minimise the Options Bar and leave the image open or minimise or close the image and leave the full program interface open on your desktop instead.

2 Tool bar

Clicking on an icon will activate the relevant editing tool (see overleaf for a key to tool icons).

3 Organiser bar

This bar allows you to 'pin' images and organises them across it or have images float free on the workspace. It also provides access to the three editing modes of 'Quick', 'Guided' and 'Expert'.

4 Mode options drop down

The Mode Options drop down or the User Options directly above it mean you can switch between Edit, Create and Share modes, choosing to edit images or access templates and tutorials on creating projects, such as a birthday card, or share your work via email or social media sites such as Facebook and Flickr. The panel's content changes to reflect the User Mode chosen. (See also *Content panel* below.)

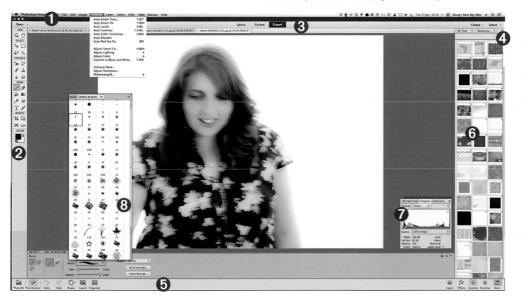

5 Program mode/options

This bar shows the currently used program mode on the right (here the Graphics filter) and the options in use, currently the Tools. The Tools or Photo bin area changes to accommodate the tools in use, as does the Content panel area.

6 Content panel

This panel changes to reflect the mode you're working in. Here, in the Edit mode, it shows a variety of backgrounds you could choose between to enhance an image or photo project such as a birthday card.

7 A window or 'pop up'

These pop up on your screen to provide choices when their associated function is selected, often from a menu. In this example, an options box accessed from the levels menu has popped up.

8 Tool options or Photo bin

The tool options provides a sort of one-stop shop for various options depending on the tool in use (the options for the paint brush tool are shown here). The Photo bin, layout options and photo library organiser are also located here. The Photo bin holds a list of the images you have open in the software.

Tools explained

Marquee tools
Used to outline a selection in an image for copying or cutting.

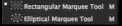

Lasso tools
Used to surround specific objects in an image in order to select them for cutting or copying, for example.

Crop/ recompose tools
Crop allows you to define an area in an image so that you can permanently 'crop' away the rest. Recompose lets you resize, crop or recompose a shot, protecting or removing elements to produce a more balanced image.

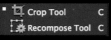

Healing Brush/ Spot Healing Brush
Samples pixels from one area and copies them using the texture of the pixels from a selected area to 'heal' marks such as spots in a portrait shot, for example.

Eraser
Used to remove/ erase pixels from an area in an image.

Shape tools
These draw custom shapes onto an image on a separate layer or layers.

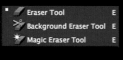

Blur/Smudge tools
Tools that allow you to blur, sharpen or smudge pixels.

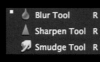

Clone tool (or Rubber Stamp)
Allows the copying of pixels from one area to be pasted over another area.

Brush and Pencil tool
Selecting this tool activates the brush currently active in the program, or you can select the pencil tool.

Dodge, Burn and Sponge tool
Lets you mimic traditional darkroom techniques to Dodge (lighten), Burn (darken) and add or subtract colour with the Sponge Tool.

Colour Samplers
A pipette-style icon for a tool that lets you 'sample' colour from pixels for use elsewhere in an image or layer.

Redeye Removal tool
This allows the quick removal of redeye from portraits.

Move Tool
Allows you to pick up and move elements within an image or on layers in a document being edited.

Content Aware Move tool

Allows you to move an element in an image and the software fills in the hole in the background based on the 'content' of the background image pixels, making it possible to recompose a shot after the image was taken.

Straighten tool
Allows you to 'draw' a line across a sloping horizon and the software will automatically straighten it for you.

Hand tool

This tool allows you to move an image around in an open window if, say, you've magnified the image and want to see an adjacent area without altering the magnification factor.

Magic Wand tool
Allows you to quickly select (or make a selection of) all the pixels of a similar colour to the ones clicked on.

Gradients tool
Allows you to apply predefined gradients across an image or layer.

Zoom Tool
Magnifies an area of the image you're working on.

Paint Bucket tool

The paint bucket allows you to fill (or 'pour') a chosen colour into large areas of an image (or selections) without the need to 'paint' it in by hand.

Smart Brush tool
This tool lets you apply different preset adjustments to an image/part of an image you choose from its pop up menu when activated.

Type tools
These tools allow you to apply text onto an image or layer.

Horizontal type tool
Vertical type tool
Horizontal type mask tool
Vertical type mask tool
Text on selection tool
Text on custom path tool

(a) (c)

(d) (b)

Foreground Color (a)
This allows you to define the colour of the foreground in a layer.

Background Color (b)
Clicking this lets you define the background colour.

Exchange Colors tool (c)
Works with both the Foreground and Background Colours (above) to swap quickly between the two.

Default Color Settings (d)
Clicking this resets the colour of the foreground and background to their respective black and white positions.

Saving your photos

If you adjust images on your PC and don't want to lose your work, you need to save those changes. There are various ways to do this – here's how to pick the best one for any situation.

Save/Save As

You have two main saving options: 'save' and 'save as'. The first overwrites the existing data with your changes – in other words, you lose what was there before and it gets replaced with the new, edited data.

The second option lets you save the image as a new file with a new name of your choice. In this way, you preserve the original file as it was and create another image file that has had the changes applied. This is ideal should you make a mistake, as you can go back to the original file and work on it again and 'save as' again.

While the latter option means you double up on files – you'll end up with two files: one edited and saved, and the original left untouched – it also allows you to retain the original files for future use and for archiving (see *Backing-up*). So now let's look at the most common file formats available for you to use in most image editing programs.

File formats

Digital images are created by your digital camera using a range of special data structures – or formats – that allow them to be 'seen' by a variety of programs on a PC. Each format has advantages and disadvantages that may mean you prefer one type over another, depending on what you want to do with the finished image.

Each time you save an image, you need to decide which file format to use. Some formats save the image using compression, which is a special computer algorithm that crunches your images down to fit into a smaller memory space.

Some compression algorithms remove data to do this and are called 'lossy' formats: data is 'lost' in order to 'squeeze' (or compress) the file. Other formats offer compression without losing data or creating artefacts, and these are called 'lossless' formats. The amount of compression is nowhere near as high as with 'lossy' formats, but you'll still be able to reduce the file's size by around 50%.

JPEG or JPG format

JPEG (denoted by the '.JPEG' suffix or sometimes '.JPG', depending on the camera, program or PC you use) is a lossy format and can be compressed down to around 10% of the original file size with slight loss of quality. If a file is saved using JPEG compression, the JPEG format looks for similar pixels and removes those that are not needed; then it makes a 'best guess' to put them back again when the file is opened, say on a PC screen. It is for this reason that small errors in the compression algorithm can cause a drop in quality, as occasionally it gets those 'guesses' wrong. This compression process can also create JPEG artefacts – small blocks of unwanted pixels in the image.

You can save JPEGs at settings between 1 and 10, with one being the lowest quality (most compressed) setting and 10 offering the highest quality, least compressed file. A setting of five or six usually provides the ideal balance between file size and quality for most uses.

TIFF format

TIFF (denoted by the '.TIFF' or '.TIF' suffix) is a 'lossless' format and the best file format to choose if you need to maintain the image's quality, memory space is not an issue, and you don't want to compress the file as heavily as you might with a JPEG. TIFF stores information about colour and dimensions as a 'tag' appended to the file (hence the name: Tagged Image File Format) and is the standard file format to use for saving high quality images ready for printing, for example.

Photoshop file format

Photoshop is an image editing software package that uses a file format denoted by the suffix '.PSD'. It has become so popular that it is practically a 'standard' file type and therefore extremely common. It is able to support enhanced colour information (better even than TIFFs) and holds other image edit specific information. Some non-Photoshop software packages use this file type even though it may be called something else in those programs. It creates large-sized files.

Photoshop
Alias PIX
BMP
CompuServe GIF
Photo Project Format
Photoshop EPS
IFF Format
✓ JPEG
PCX
Photoshop PDF
Photoshop 2.0
Photoshop Raw
PICT File
PICT Resource
Pixar
PNG
Scitex CT
Targa
TIFF

GIF format

Another compressed format for images uses the suffix '.GIF' and was originally designed for Internet applications such as web graphics. It uses a very limited set of colours (just 256) and is ideal for graphic images with large expanses of even colour. Photographs saved in GIF format lose a great deal of colour information and any smooth gradations between shades of the same colour. This can make the image look 'stepped'.

RAW format

RAW files are created in the camera without any in-camera processing affecting the data. (see *Shooting in RAW*). They provide all the information captured by the camera's sensor. You can process the images later on a PC and access all the unprocessed information within the image file. You will need special software to be able to edit RAW photos: this is usually supplied with the camera.

PICT format

This is a file type developed for use on Apple Macintosh computers, designed primarily for on-screen-only images with a limited resolution. It offers a way to see an image with very basic software, so even some text programs will be able to see a PICT file, although they cannot be used to edit it.

PNG format

Another lossless compression format, PNG (suffix '.PNG') is built for use over the Internet and is therefore ideal for web images. It supports information on colour, greyscale and true-colour images and is designed to be a more advanced substitute for the GIF file format.

A typical save menu in image editing software indicating the various file formats in which you can choose to save the image. JPEG is highlighted, while TIFF is at the bottom of the list.

When to use each format

- **TIFF:** *Lossless compression with best quality for images that are to be printed.*

- **JPEG or JPG:** *Lossy compression format, ideal where quality needs to be retained but memory space is at a premium or for Internet use when a better quality is required.*

- **PSD:** *The generic file format used by the popular Photoshop editing programs, again for high quality usage.*

- **GIF:** *Lossless file format designed for web graphics. Not for printed photographs.*

- **PNG:** *Offers lossless compression and is ideal for Internet use; similar to 'GIF' but better quality.*

- **RAW:** *RAW images are composed of the raw data as captured by the camera sensor. Most, if not all, digital SLRs have this option, as do many of the more advanced 'enthusiast' compact digital cameras. Most current image editing packages can edit RAW files; alternatively, use the software that comes with the camera.*

- **PICT:** *An Apple Macintosh-specific format designed for saving on-screen images with a limited resolution.*

- **PDF:** *A cross-platform file format readable on most computers and ideal for newsletters, posters or letters containing images, graphics and text.*

PDF format

The Portable Document Format (suffix '.PDF') is a file type that is used by Adobe Acrobat. As its name suggests, though, the document can be looked at anywhere. You need to have Adobe Acrobat Reader software to do so, but it should be included free with your computer operating system. You cannot edit the document with 'Reader'.

PDF is ideal for use in documents such as newsletters or other designed jobs that will be printed, like posters, because it retains information about the images, typography, graphics, text and layout all together within the document.

BMP format

BMP or Bitmap image file is a device-independent file of great simplicity. It's widely compatible and can be losslessly compressed. Great for sharing images with someone who will work on the files when you don't know what software they will be using.

EPS format

EPS or Encapsulated Postscript is a standard format for files including images, text, drawings and layouts for documents and pages. It's used mainly for designing documents and pages in, for example, newsletters, magazines or leaflets.

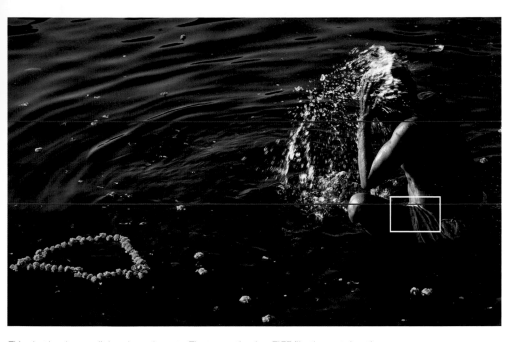

This shot has been split into three elements. The top section is a TIFF file, the central portion
a high quality JPEG and the bottom third a very low quality JPEG. The enlarged area shown
below reveals the blocky JPEG artefacts caused by the JPEG compression from the area
indicated in the rectangle above. The high quality JPEG has almost no visible problems at all.
Also note the way the colours have blocked together in the water below the man washing.

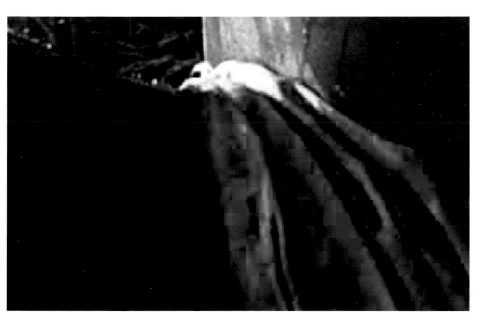

Auto and **quick fix**

Image editing packages provide easy-to-use tools that allow you to make fast edits to images at the click of a mouse. Here's how to make the best of these 'auto' or 'quick fix' tools.

A quick fix is exactly that: a fast and easy way to adjust common problems, such as low contrast or under- or over-exposure in an image, simply by using a couple of clicks of your mouse. Some packages call it 'auto fix' or 'smart fix' because the program itself analyses the image, looks for problems that either make the image dull or colourless and then adjusts the settings to compensate.

Each editing package works in a similar way and, whichever software you use, the auto fix has a similar effect – improving the image. The function is usually found in a drop-down menu; in Adobe Photoshop Elements it is in the top menu bar under 'Enhance'.

With the image you want to be fixed open in the program, highlight the auto fix option and the program will go to work. If your software has other settings such as auto levels, auto contrast and auto colour correction, each operates in the same automatic way, applying corrections according to their titles. If one produces an unsatisfactory result, try one of the others. The auto fix, however (as it works across all the image variables at once), will usually be sufficient for most minor image corrections.

Some packages allow you to adjust the amount of correction that is applied as you go. This is ideal if, after applying an auto fix, you think it has overdone the 'fix'.

Other programs have a preview screen that provides a before-and-after window (as the example below illustrates) to show how the edit will affect the image. This allows you to adjust the amount of auto fix applied by judging its effect 'live' on screen.

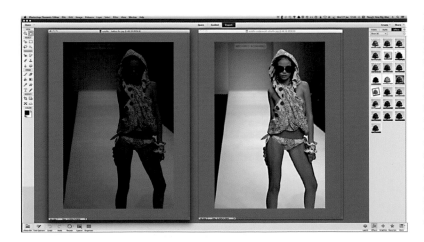

This 'before' and 'after' screen shot shows the effect a quick fix has had on a very under-exposed image (left). The colour and exposure have been fixed enough to save the shot (right). Other new automated or 'quick' fix tools include (depending on the software you use) auto smart tone (to quickly fix skewed colours), auto colour correction and, in some cases, automated redeye fix too.

Fixing colour casts

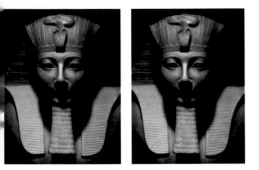

In this shot taken indoors in a museum, the display's lighting has created an unnatural orange colour cast that has completely hidden the true colours of the statue. Using an auto fix, the program has analysed the shot and completely removed the orange colour cast, without affecting the dark background, thus revealing the true, more neutral, bluish colour of the statue.

Fixing low contrast

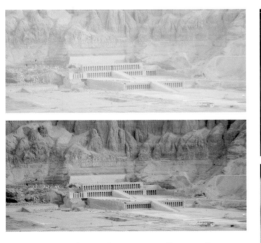

In images such as the top one here, where there's little contrast (contrast is simply the difference between the blackest and whitest areas in a shot), the whites are muted, the blacks look brown or grey and detail is pretty

much invisible. An auto contrast fix can work wonders here. In the second shot, the auto contrast fix has checked the image for the brightest and darkest parts and fixed them. It has boosted the colours as well, making the shot look brighter and more natural.

Fixing exposure problems

Under- and over-exposure can be adjusted in auto fix too. Under-exposure is caused when the camera has not recorded enough light to produce a bright, colourful image; over-exposure is the opposite. Using auto fix will help brighten or darken an image. The cake shot shown below was under-exposed, but with auto fix it has been brightened and the colour has been enhanced.

A problem with correcting exposure issues, however, is that the auto fix can sometimes overdo the processing. This means you may lose detail in some areas of a shot and colours may be adversely affected. You may need to judge the amount of auto fix you apply if this is the case.

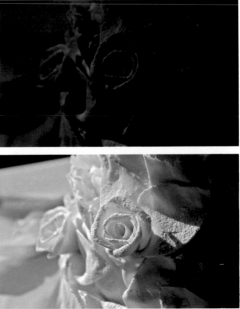

Cropping

There's no need to worry if an image isn't framed as you'd like. The cropping function of your imaging software is a great way to remove unnecessary details from a scene or to add emphasis to a shot.

Cropping an image can be done at the beginning of the photography process, when you take the snap, or later on when you edit the images on PC. The process you go through when taking a picture – zooming in, for example – is a form of cropping. It simply means cutting away parts of the scene in order to improve a photo or to remove aspects you don't want. All image editing programs contain tools to crop images.

Removing unwanted detail
As the images on the facing page and below show, cropping can dramatically improve a photo. Just as the snap below was taken, the photographer caught a disembodied arm protruding into the bottom right of the shot. This is a very distracting intrusion indeed. Cropping, as shown in the image right, has removed this and helps to emphasise the viewer's attention on the main 'action' in the finished photograph opposite.

Using the crop command
By clicking on the crop icon, the cursor changes to the cropping tool. You then click the mouse button, hold it down and drag the cursor across the image to mark out the area you want to crop around.

If you don't get it right first time, don't worry. The hatched line that will have appeared, denoting your currently selected crop area – everything outside of which is deleted – has a series of small, box-like 'handles' halfway along each edge and at the corners. They can be clicked and dragged to a new position to fine-tune the crop or even rotate the cropped area.

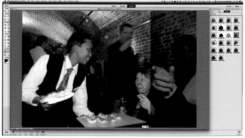

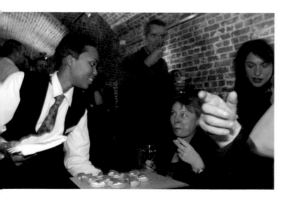

Above: *Cropping removes this distraction.*

Left: *The intrusive disembodied arm.*

Top opposite: *The finished photograph.*

Once you are happy with your selection, double click inside the crop area indicated by the hatched line and the unwanted, 'cropped away' parts of the image, indicated with a shaded area, will be deleted, completing your crop. Remember to save the image once you've finished.

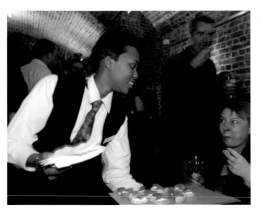

Pixels and memory considerations

Cropping not only removes unwanted parts of an image but, as it is permanently deleting areas of the shot, it is also removing pixels. The number of pixels in an image directly affects the file size, so when you remove them by cropping, you also reduce the file size of the image. A 50% crop of an image will reduce the file size by up to three quarters. While this saves on computer memory, it also has implications for printing, as the larger the file size and the more pixels you have, the larger the print can be (see *Printing* for more details).

So always consider what you want to do with an image later if the intended crop is to be a dramatic one. This is another reason why it is always better to shoot images at the digital camera's maximum resolution – you will always have the optimal number of pixels to play with for more dramatic cropping edits.

Creative cropping

Cropping can also be used to change the emphasis of a shot, alter its format or to zoom in on a smaller area of interest. This can improve its creative merit. Here's an example of a shot cropped to create extra emphasis on the model and her extraordinary fingernails. Removing the background also helps balance the photo.

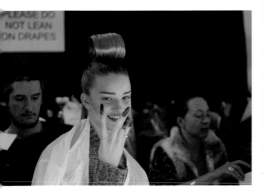

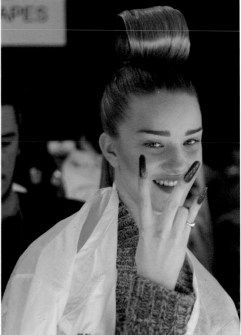

Straightening

Probably the most common problem for any photo is the sloping horizon effect. Luckily, with image editing it's easy to rectify.

Sloping or lopsided images are caused when the camera is not held sufficiently level, which can happen very easily. The safest way to avoid this is to use a tripod or to make sure that the camera is level before you press the shutter button. However, setting up a tripod is not always practical, and often you may not even realise that your picture is not level until later when you look at the image on a PC.

There's a simple image editing function that can quickly correct a sloping horizon. Straightening the horizon is particularly important in landscape images that need to be printed at larger scales, say for framing and mounting on the wall.

This straightening function does crop out a little of the original image but not enough to cause major problems. Here's how to do it.

Step 1:
Open the image to be straightened and activate the 'grid' overlay pattern, in this case using the **View > Grid** command. A grid of lines and squares will overlay the image; this will not affect the image as the grid sits over the picture.

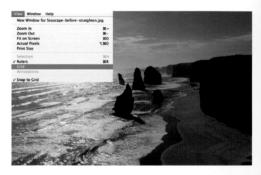

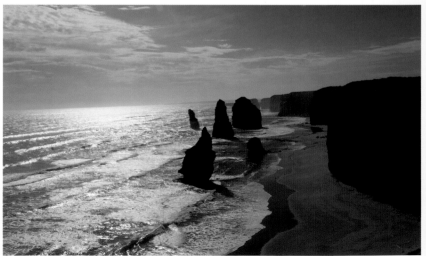

This image has an unnatural sloping horizon which needs to be straightened.

Step 2:

Using the grid of lines and squares as a guide, choose the **Image > Rotate > Free Rotate Layer** command. Depending on the software, a box may appear asking you to make a 'layer': click the 'OK' button. The image is now transformed into a movable image layer called something like 'layer o'. You'll see a new box appear around the image with handles similar to those used to crop an image.

Hover the mouse cursor over a corner handle and little arrows appear, indicating that you can rotate the image in either direction.

Step 3:

The technique's the same as for cropping an image: you click and hold on a corner handle but this time rotate the image until the horizon is aligned correctly with the overlying grid.

Once you're satisfied the horizon's straight, double click inside the image and the transformation will be complete. You will see, however, areas around the edge of the straightened image where cropping is required to tidy up the edge. Simply use the previous topic's crop technique to complete the image edit and then you're done. Now save your image.

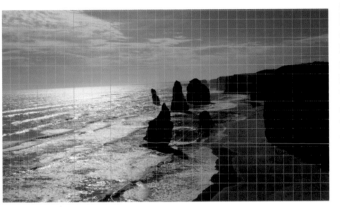

The final straightened image, without the sloping horizon.

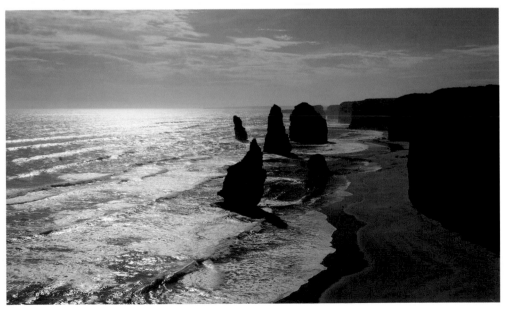

Resizing

It's very simple to change the resolution, dimensions or file size of an image. Here's how and why to resize your photos.

Whether you need to reduce the resolution and file size of an image for use with email or the Internet, or you want to enlarge the file in order to print the image at a size that its current resolution would not otherwise allow, there is a simple method to achieve your goal: the 'resize' command.

Resampling

When you resize an image you can change its output size without altering its physical, pixel or file size. Or you can 'resample' the image, which actually changes the dimensions of the pixels as the image is resized, and therefore its file size will alter too. Resampling is necessary in some circumstances, but to be avoided in others. Let's look at some examples to explain what's involved.

Making images smaller

Here's how to resize an image which is only needed at a small size, for use on a website, for example. Resampling will reduce the file size, but won't be detrimental to the quality of the final, smaller image.

Step 1:
To make an image smaller, open the image you wish to reduce in size and use the **Image > Resize > Image Size** command, which brings up a new dialogue box indicating the current size of the photo. Specifically, it presents information on the pixel dimensions, the document's size in centimetres and the current resolution, and the resample check box as shown here.

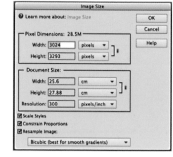

Step 2:
To reduce the resolution from 300 pixels to screen resolution, 72 pixels per inch (ppi), click the 'resample' check box and the 'constrain proportions' check box which ensures the aspect (height-to-width) ratio of the shot will not change, then type '72' into the 'resolution' box.

Notice how when you click in the resample box, the 'pixel dimensions' box becomes editable. Click OK to make the change. The image will shrink on screen to its new size. Use the **File > Save As** save command and give the new, smaller image a new name, otherwise it will overwrite the original file and you'll lose it.

Making images bigger

Here's how to increase the size of an image so that it can be printed at a larger size. This can be done with resampling, thus increasing the size of the file, or without resampling, leaving the file size unchanged.

If resampling, the software will use interpolation, which is the name given to a calculation that adds pixels based on those that are already there. Unfortunately, interpolation can cause a softening or blurring of your image as the program 'guesses' what pixels to add.

Step 1:
Open the image you want to enlarge and use the **Image > Resize > Image Size** command to bring up the image size dialogue box.

As discussed, there are two strategies that can now be used to make the image bigger: with resampling, which changes the file size, or without resampling.

Step 2:
To resample and make an image bigger, check the 'resample' and 'constrain proportions' boxes, and type the required dimensions into the width or height boxes. Typing in one affects the other, and the pixel dimensions will change as well as the file size, which will increase dramatically. To keep the quality, don't enlarge an image with the resampling set to more than double its start size.

Step 3:
Enlarging without resampling is achieved by typing the required dimensions into the height or width boxes but leaving the resample check box clear. The file size and pixel dimensions remain unchanged, but the 'document size resolution' has

now reduced. To keep print quality high, don't let this drop below around 180ppi. Use the **File > Save As** command, resaving the shot without overwriting the original image.

Resizing example
These three images below reveal the effect resizing with resampling has on both the pixel dimensions and the file size. The largest image has 2048x7032 pixels with a file size of 18MB, ideal for printing at over A4. The middle image has 1536x1024 pixels and a file size of 4.5MB, okay for smaller print sizes. The smallest image has just 640x427 pixels and only a 800KB file size, ideal for email.

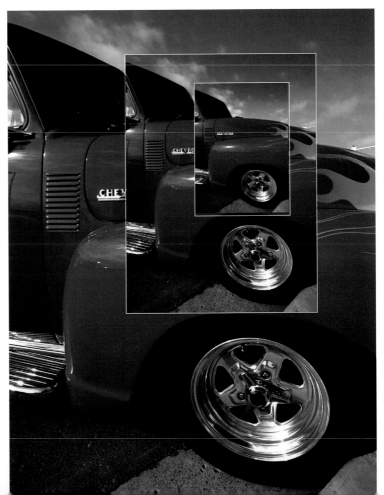

Sharpening

If you have a soft image or a shot that's not quite focused and think it's ruined, think again. Your editing software can sharpen the image quickly and easily.

Occasionally, the very digitising process involved in creating images introduces 'softness', which appears as a slight lack of focus. All digital cameras have built-in settings to process this softness away, but when you add camera shake or the camera not focusing properly, the pictures can look even less sharp.

All image editing packages have functions designed to help sharpen digital images, called 'filters'. Sharpen filters have a variety of modes, but one filter stands out as the best tool in the sharpening armoury: the 'unsharp mask'.

Using unsharp mask to sharpen

The unsharp mask filter is generally the best to use for sharpening, as it can be finely tuned to each image. It works by increasing the contrast between adjacent pixels: the higher the contrast at these points, the better the unsharp mask works. Because these points usually represent an 'edge' in an image, the overall effect is to sharpen the shot.

But the settings you use will depend on the image's content; a portrait may require completely different unsharp mask settings to, say, a shot of a building. Here's an example that will make this clearer.

Step 1:
File > Open the image to be sharpened and then navigate to the unsharp tool via the **Enhance > Unsharp Mask** menu. A new dialogue box appears with a preview window and three 'sliders', which can each be dragged to a desired point.

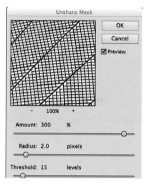

Step 2:
The first parameter to set is the 'radius'. It controls the width around the pixels it sharpens (similar to a halo effect). Entering a radius of 1 tells the software to 'look' outwards one pixel as it evaluates each pixel. The higher the radius number, the bigger the halo of sharpening around each evaluated pixel.

Step 3:
The next setting to adjust is the 'amount'. Think of this as controlling the 'volume' of the unsharp mask as it determines the strength of the sharpening effect. A small radius setting will need a higher amount than a bigger radius setting to produce the same visual sharpening effect.

Step 4:
Last but not least comes the 'threshold' control, which acts like a noise reduction setting by instructing the software to ignore certain differences between pixels as it sharpens, helping prevent over-sharpening in areas such as skin tones in a portrait, for example. Move all three sliders to get the best sharpening effect for the shot you have on screen and then **File > Save** (or **Save As**) when you're done.

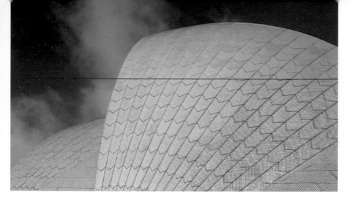

This shot shows before (top part) and after the sharpening effect. The detail in the roof has been revealed without adversely affecting the rest of the image.

Settings for best results

As a rule of thumb, start by using an amount setting of 200 to 300%, then a threshold of zero and a radius setting to match the photo's content, typically between 0.5 and 2. Overdoing the radius will generate white lines (the halos become visible) around everything with an 'edge' in the shot. You rarely if ever need a radius of more than 3, for example.

To sharpen the image above, which lacked sharpness primarily in the roof detail, the amount needed was 222, a radius of just 1 was set and a threshold of 5 used, primarily to reduce noise artefacts that appeared in the blue sky.

Other sharpen filters

There are other sharpen filters that can be applied to your images for slightly different approaches to sharpening. Let's have a look at the main ones.

Auto Sharpen

This tool automatically analyses the image and applies sharpening. It is quite sensitive but the effect can sometimes be too subtle or too strong, depending on the subject. If so, you can revert back to the Unsharp Mask as detailed previously, or use the following tool.

Sharpen

The sharpen filter can be used to increase apparent focus but needs to be used sensitively. It is best applied to smaller parts of a shot rather than the entire image, as it can actually be detrimental to some types of image.

Adjust Sharpness

The adjust sharpness tool is found by clicking **Enhance > Adjust Sharpness**. A dialogue box appears with two sliders, one for Amount and one for Radius, which work in the same way as in the unsharp mask box.

You also get a few new tools. A drop-down menu allows you to adjust sharpness affecting Gaussian Blur (any even or smooth blurring), Lens Blur (softness introduced by camera optics) and Motion Blur (caused by camera shake or subject blur). A check box allows you to further refine the edges of the area being sharpened, while an Angle adjustment allows you to tweak the angle at which the sharpening effect is applied to the pixel on which it is working.

A certain amount of trial and error is often needed to get the required effect.

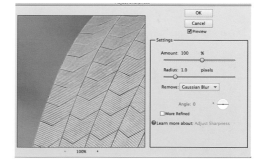

Brightening and darkening photos

Some photos are too dark or light to be adjusted using a quick fix. But don't despair: the photo can still be rescued.

Images can come out 'too dark' or 'too light' due to under- or over-exposure, meaning they have detail missing in their shadow or highlight areas: the pixels have just gone completely white or completely black. These problems can be improved by brightening or darkening the problem areas to reveal the detail. This is usually very successful for shadow areas. Highlight areas can also be improved to a lesser degree.

Brightening an image
Depending on your software, you'll have a menu offering a control for highlights and shadows and/or a levels adjustment control. We deal with levels, a more advanced method of adjusting lighting and colour, later in the topic *Levels*. Let's stick with the 'shadow' and 'highlight' controls here.

Step 1:
File > Open the image that needs to be lightened. In your image editing package, choose **Enhance > Adjust Lighting > Shadow/Highlights** or equivalent from the dropdown menu.

This before (bottom section) and after picture shows how a 50% adjustment to the lighten shadows slider has lifted fine skin detail out of the shadowed elephant that was completely missing in the original shot.

Step 2:
Drag any of the three lighten shadows, darken highlights or midtone contrast adjustable sliders (or enter a numeric value into the relevant boxes) until you're happy with the result. In our example (below), an adjustment of 50% was applied to lighten shadows. Ensure you check any preview box to preview the effect and accurately assess the adjustments before they're applied.

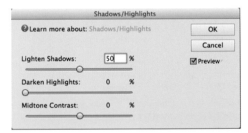

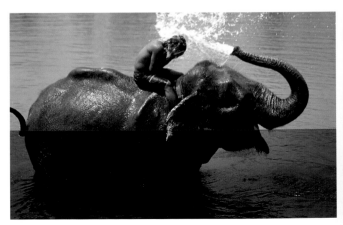

Step 3:
Click OK once you're happy, then save your photo and you're done.

Darkening an image

A helpful technique for bringing in details on highlights, such as fine cloud details.

Step 1:
As before, **File > Open** the image that needs editing to make it darker. In your image editing package, choose **Enhance > Adjust Lighting > Shadow/Highlights** or equivalent from the menu.

Step 2:
Drag the darken highlights and, if required, the midtone contrast sliders (or enter a numeric value into the relevant boxes) until you're happy with the result. Below, a setting of 50% to the darken highlights adjustment was required and the effect on the contrast meant an additional adjustment to the midtone contrast was needed, in this case plus 10%. Once again, check the preview box to preview the effect and accurately assess the adjustments as they're applied.

Step 3:
Click OK once you're happy, then save your photo and you're done.

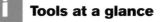

i Tools at a glance

- **Lighten shadows:** *Brightens all the dark areas in a photo, revealing more of the detail hidden within but still captured by the digital camera.*

- **Darken highlights:** *This darkens the lighter areas in a shot and can reveal more detail contained within the brighter areas of a scene. Bear in mind that any pure white areas won't have more detail, so will remain untouched by this setting.*

- **Midtone contrast:** *This control lets you adjust the midtones (greys, for example) in a picture if, after you've adjusted the highlights or shadows, the contrast doesn't look right.*

- **Brightness/contrast tool:** *This controls the brightness and contrast of all the pixels in an image, rather than specific areas.*

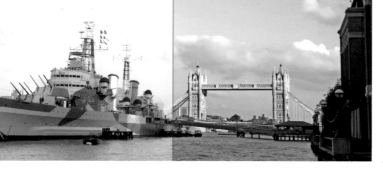

In this shot, the image was over-exposed; as a result, all the highlight detail has gone from the clouds and colour has been leached too. Using the darken highlights and midtone contrast correction has recovered most, if not all, the detail and colour previously not visible.

Removing **redeye**

We've all had pictures of our friends and family ruined by the dreaded redeye. But even if your camera can't prevent it, you can still edit it out.

Redeye is a common problem with today's small digital compact cameras, which even with their redeye reduction modes (see box) can still produce shots marred by that demonic look.

If you have a shot with redeye, don't worry: most editing software packages have a simple-to-use tool for removing or reducing the effect, saving an otherwise ruined photo.

Step 1:
File > Open the image that needs redeye removing. Using the zoom or magnify tool, magnify the eyes of the subject suffering redeye by clicking and dragging around the

Preventing redeye

Redeye is caused when light from a camera flash is reflected from the back of the eye (the retina) into the lens. The closer together the camera's lens and flash, the more likely it is your photos will suffer from redeye. Redeye is red because the blood vessels in the eye colour the reflected light, producing the effect you see in your photos.

It becomes most prevalent in low light when the subject's pupil is bigger and in children, whose eyes and pupils tend to be naturally bigger all the time. It's a common problem simply because of the small size of most modern digital compacts. Their tiny size means the flash and lens are always quite close together, hence the reason practically all digital cameras have a redeye reduction mode.

To help prevent or reduce the redeye effect, always make sure the redeye reduction mode is on when shooting with flash and/or in low light. The redeye mode will either fire a burst of quick flashes or project a beam of light towards the subject before the shutter fires. This has the effect of helping reduce the iris's size, thus reducing the pupil size and so reducing the redeye effect in the final shot.

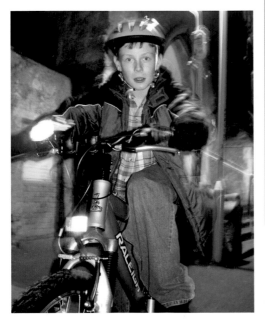

This slow sync shot taken at night has a dramatic redeye problem. Let's see how we can fix it.

eyes with the magnify tool. This will enlarge that portion of the photo sufficiently to work on. Or, with the image open click on the **Enhance > Auto Redeye Fix** menu option (if your software has it) to apply the fix automatically. If not ...

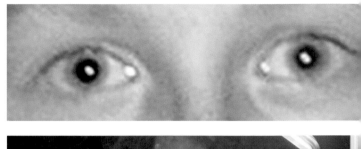

Step 2:

Click on the 'redeye removal' tool and in the same way you clicked and dragged the image to magnify it, click and drag the redeye tool around each eye separately. The software will 'look' at the red pixels and replace them with a series of dark grey pixels (also preserving any catch lights in the eyes – as shown above) producing a natural-looking pupil colour.

Step 3:

Repeat steps one and two above for each person suffering the effect in the shot until all the redeye is removed.

Step 4:

Save your photo and you're done.

If your software has an automatic redeye reduction mode, try it as it may work faster. You can always follow this step-by-step if not.

The same slow sync flash photo after the redeye reduction tool has been used. It has produced a natural-looking effect, keeping the catch lights and rescuing an otherwise unusable picture.

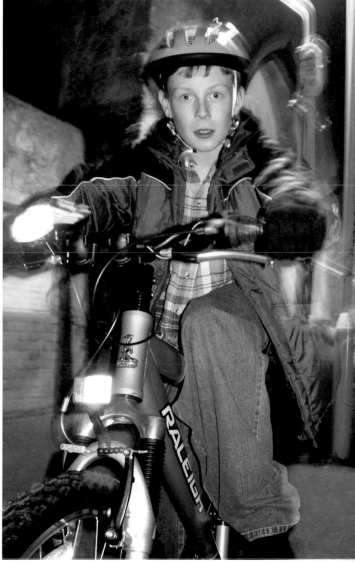

Creating **black and white**

You can easily create black and white photos from colour shots – ideal if you want to make a dramatic change of emphasis in an image.

Removing the colour from a perfectly good image may seem a little odd, but it is a useful device when a shot has not worked the way you intended in colour. There may be distracting colours in a portrait image, or the contrast, texture and shapes in the photo may strike you as something that could be better treated in black and white or 'mono'. Some images have such muted colours that it may be possible to derive more impact from a mono version than the original colour image.

Subtle colour to black and white

Step 1:
File > Open the image that you'd like to convert to black and white. Use the **Enhance > Adjust Color > Remove Color** command, or use your software's equivalent – it may be called 'desaturate'.

Once the 'remove colour' command is activated, all the colours in the original image's pixels are given equal red, green and blue (RGB) values but lightness is not changed. This actually gives you the black and white effect. But it's possible the resulting image can have a lack of contrast. Without definition between blacks and whites it looks almost too grey.

Step 2:
If the image does lack contrast try a quick fix (or smart fix or auto fix, depending on your software) to improve it. Follow the steps in auto and quick fix. Or try auto smart tone, if your software has this feature. A new window pops up with a grid overlay with dark/light and most/least contrast in opposite corners. Move a 'controller' around the grid with your mouse, to achieve the desired balance.

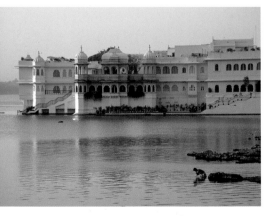

This photo of a lake in India has such subtle hues and tones that it is an ideal shot to use this technique on.

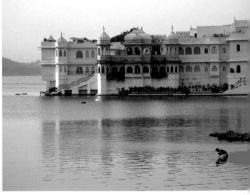

The finished image works well in black and white thanks to the graphic-looking nature of the subject matter.

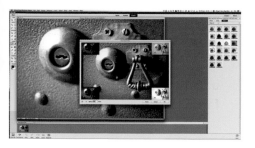

Step 3:
File › **Save** your image with a new name.

Strong colour to black and white

Other types of image, such as the one on the right, have deep shadow and stronger contrast – features which also lend themselves to a mono treatment. Here, the dark background and lighter skin tones would be a great graphic contrast in a mono shot.

Step 1:
File › **Open** the image that needs converting to black and white. Use the **Enhance › Adjust Color › Remove Color** command as before. With the remove colour command activated, all the colours in the original image are changed to black and white once more. However, because of the dark background and lighter skin, the emphasis on the woman needs to be improved.

Step 2:
Because this image has stronger areas of contrast than the previous shot, a quick fix won't help: it would just try to equalise the dark and light areas, ruining the shot.

This time use your software's **Enhance › Auto Color Correction** command or equivalent. This looks at the (now grey) pixels. These all have equal RGB values, but with untouched 'lightness' parameters, so this command boosts the brightness of less grey pixels. This adds punch without damaging the blacker parts of the shot. As before, you can use the auto smart tone tool if you want to fine-tune or experiment further.

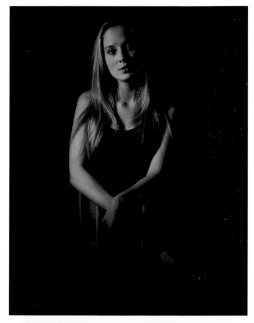

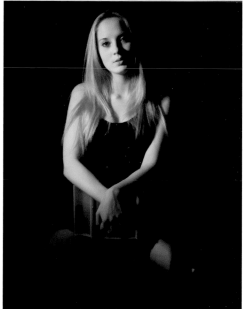

Step 3:
File › **Save As** your image and give it a new name so that you don't overwrite the original colour shot.

Colour management

The way a colour is displayed on a PC's screen can vary dramatically when printed by an inkjet printer. Here's how to ensure the colours you see when you take a photo are the colours you get on screen and in the printed photo.

Digital cameras, computer screens and digital imaging devices, including scanners and printers, have their own specific way of 'seeing' and representing colours. These are called colour profiles, and in order to reproduce colours consistently across all of your digital devices, you'll need to ensure that they all use the same profile. This is the essence of colour management.

RGB and CMYK colours

In the digital domain, colour can be represented in one of two ways. The first, on a PC screen, for example, uses red, green and blue (RGB) pixels which combine to create all the colours of the rainbow. The second is via coloured inks from printers that use a basic set of four colours: cyan, magenta, yellow and black, often abbreviated as CMYK. These four colours are used to represent the RGB colours, which are converted by your printer when printing your photos.

Getting accurate screen colour

Helpfully, most digital cameras and devices have industry standard colour management systems built into them. However, it's important that you can see them properly on screen, particularly when you want to manipulate colours using editing software (as we'll discuss in the following topics of this book).

So the first thing to do is to calibrate your PC's screen so that it uses the correct colour settings. This ensures it has the correct brightness and that its colour balance is set

properly. The set-up process is judged by eye and is best carried out with as dark a background as possible for optimal accuracy. Consult your manual or on-screen instructions about how to do this accurately – most PCs will have a handy software wizard to guide you through the process. Once completed, you're prompted to save the information as a profile, which other programs, such as image editing software, can use to ensure colour is properly displayed.

You'll probably find that the colour accuracy of your monitor is almost spot-on out of the box. However, it is worth checking, as so much of your later colour work will be based on this.

Colour gamut

The colour gamut is the name given to the range of colours available on a specific device, such as a digital camera, PC screen or inkjet printer. The larger or 'wider' the gamut, the more colours the device has at its disposal. This is usually represented by a diagram or graph which shows all of the colours visible to the eye (the total gamut) and those colours within the gamut that can actually be used by the device, indicated with a triangle inside the graph's colour range – as shown top right.

Typically, printers have a range of colours smaller than those available to your digital camera or even your PC screen. This is because greens and blues reproduce poorly on paper, as do purples and oranges. However, with your screen calibrated correctly

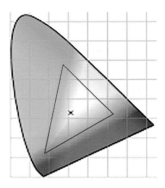

embed this into your images. This is a good idea as Adobe RGB is an industry standard setting that can be used on your PC too and, as we've seen, has a large colour gamut.

To check the colour management in your software, go to the colour preferences or colour settings control panel and ensure the program can use Adobe (or Full) RGB. Switch on the setting as shown below (in this case **Always Optimise for Printing** and its associated Adobe RGB profile).

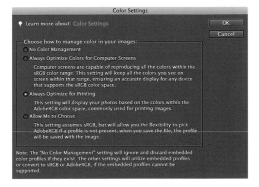

*This is a typical colour set-up screen with **Always Optimise for Printing** checked, ensuring all images have their colour profiles preserved or adjusted to Adobe RGB, the setting with the largest colour gamut.*

you'll be able to get a good idea of what a finished print might look like before printing, and you'll be amazed at how lifelike it can look despite these apparent drawbacks.

In the set-up or preferences of all of your connected devices, such as printers or image editing software, ensure they all use the same colour settings, i.e. the same colour profile. One profile known as 'Adobe RGB' (sometimes called 'Full RGB') is particularly good because it has a larger gamut than many other image profiles, meaning it has more colours to utilise and is therefore ideal for digital images. Or use any profiles you have previously saved if you're happy with the results they produce.

Another common profile is called 'sRGB', which uses fewer colours than Adobe RGB, for example, and is typical of colour profiles used on the Internet and in many digital cameras.

Colour settings in your software

The image editing software you use will have a colour settings section that will always either preserve or convert the images you open in it to a specified colour profile, one that ensures standard colour control across all devices.

Some digital cameras even allow you to save a specific colour profile into an image. Adobe RGB is one such profile and your camera will have a menu that allows you to

Colour: at a glance

- *Use the same colour profiles across all devices, ideally Adobe RGB (sometimes called 'Full RGB'), the best setting for printing digital images.*

- *Use sRGB for images used on the Internet.*

- *Calibrate your monitor and always recalibrate it if you move its location or you change any ambient lighting arrangements around your workstation.*

Adjusting colours

It's easy to change and improve the colours of your images digitally.

All image editing software on the market provides for the control and adjustment of colour. Some of the more professional image editing packages will even provide you with individual controls for each element of colour. Some colour tools allow you to completely replace one colour with another, which can give dramatic effects.

For now, let's concentrate on getting the existing colour as accurately rendered as we can.

Controlling colour balance

Colour balance is simply the term used to describe the overall tones and hues in an image. The colour balance control can be used to make global changes to any image to help make the balance more natural, ideal for fast removal of odd colour casts.

Depending on your software, you'll have tools for controlling 'hue', 'saturation' and 'colour intensity'. Some packages will have a method of removing colour casts and most will have a tool which shows how variations of colour would affect your images.

Removing colour casts
Step 1:
File > Open the image you wish to adjust and use your software's colour adjustment tools to bring up the colour control dialogue boxes, in this case the remove colour cast dialogue box, by clicking **Enhance > Adjust Color > Remove Color Cast**. Now click the 'pipette' icon that appears on grey, completely white or completely black areas of the shot, neutralising colour casts by ensuring everything

This shot of a model with her digital camera has an odd, orange colour cast on the skin that needs to be removed to make a more flattering shot.

black, white or grey is actually black, white or grey. Trial and error may be required.

Adjusting hue and saturation

If the colour cast tool doesn't achieve the desired result then the next weapon to use is the adjust hue/saturation tool in the same menu we just use

Step 1:
The hue/saturation tool offers a powerful suite of colour control options. A drop-down menu offers various individual colour range settings, such as reds, greens, cyans and yellows, or a 'master' control (as shown above) that affects all the colours at once by moving the hue, saturation and lightness sliders.

Step 2:
Move the hue, saturation and lightness sliders. This affects the colour range displayed in the

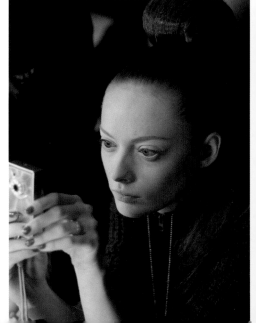

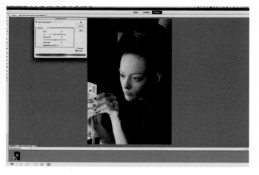

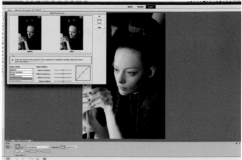

image. Subtle movements of each slider are all that's required to remove any colour cast – or add a colour cast, should you wish to. Or try the auto colour correction tool if your software has it. This can work really well on general images but is not always successful in images with more complex colour problems, such as those shot in mixed or very harsh lighting conditions.

Adjusting using colour variations

To compare the effect of your changes with the original image, use the 'colour variations' tool (top right).

Step 1:

The colour variations tool allows you to make fine adjustments to an image by selecting the brightness values you want to adjust. You have a series of buttons for midtones, shadows, highlights and saturation, depending on where you want the change to be applied in the shot. Large thumbnails of the image represent the 'before' and 'after' versions.

Step 2:

The 'intensity' slider can be moved to fine-tune any effect. By clicking one of the smaller thumbnail images once the slider's been moved (each small thumbnail previews the change), the change is applied to the larger, 'after' thumbnail, as above. Specific software programs may vary a little in the layout of the controls, but the process is the same.

The finished shot with the skin tones edited back to a more normal colour. Whichever of the methods is used, the application of colour control can make a big difference to your photos.

Adjusting using colour curves

Some software has this tool (shown above left) instead of the colour variations tool.

Step 1:

The adjust colour curves tool has a set of predefined adjustments you can select, such as darken highlights or increase contrast. Pick a predefined setting that best suits the effect you're after.

Step 2:

If the desired effect needs further adjustment, fine-tune using the four sliders for highlights, shadows, midtone brightness and contrast.

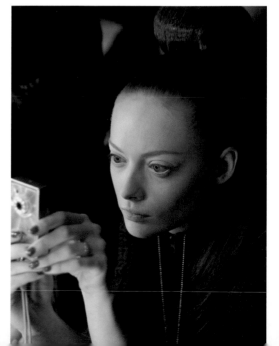

Levels

Want to manipulate colour but with improved control over brightness? Use 'levels' to achieve this.

Using levels is another powerful way to control colour. It offers greater control over brightness than the colour balance tool; each colour can be adjusted separately and the settings can also be saved for you to use on other photos in many software packages.

Levels uses histograms (shown below and represented by the black curve shape within the graph) to represent the colour values in a shot. A histogram is a simplified graphic representation of the pixels in an image, graphing the colour intensity at each level, hence the name of this tool. In other words, it shows you the amount of colour in the image from the darkest pixels to the whitest and it allows you to manipulate the coloured pixels in order to improve colour rendition, brightness and contrast.

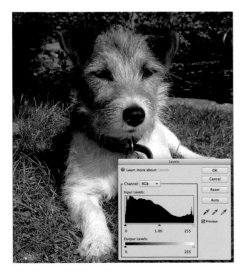

Using levels control

The levels control is accessed via your image editing program's **Enhance > Levels** or **Adjust Lighting > Levels** menus. When activated, a dialogue box presents you with a histogram representing the colour values, a drop-down menu for the colour channels and small triangle sliders: one each for black, grey and white.

The aim of the levels control is to move the triangular sliders under the histogram to align them with the graphed pixels in the display. In this way, the colour is optimised across the spread of pixels.

The 'channel' drop-down menu chooses the colour that will be adjusted, while the sliders can be moved freely to make changes in each colour, the changes affecting only the colour selected. Alternatively, the global RGB channel can be selected so that all three colours are edited together. Also, the two black and white sliders affect the overall darker and lighter value pixels of the colours being worked on, thus adjusting image contrast.

The top-left image on the opposite page shows how the pixels in the red channel have crowded into one end of the histogram – towards the right, 'brighter' side. By moving the black slider and aligning it with the first pixels in the histogram, the red in the image deepens. Moving the white slider in the other direction would remove red from the shot.

Other levels controls

Alternate controls include an 'auto' button, which automatically makes adjustments for you in a similar way to a quick fix. And there are three small pipette icons: one each for

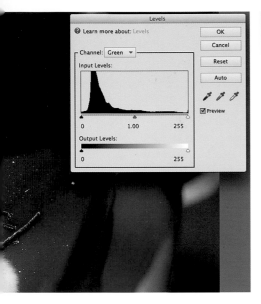

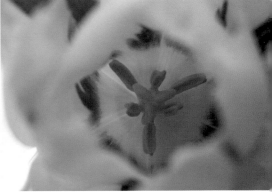

In this shot, the colour is muted and contrast is quite low, making the flower shot look very drab. This is where the levels control comes in.

black, grey and white. By selecting these pipettes and clicking in those areas in the image that are supposed to be black, grey or white, the levels control will try to make the image more neutral, making whites whiter and blacks blacker, for example. This is another useful tool for removing colour casts.

Controlling colour and brightness
Step 1:
File > Open the image you wish to edit using levels: the first step is to assess the histogram and check the preview tick box so that the changes you make can be seen before they're fixed into the shot.

Step 2:
Click the channel drop-down menu and select each red, green and blue colour in turn – adjust each as you go, as described above.

Step 3:
If the histogram reveals that the pixels do not reach both ends of the graph at any point, move the relevant – endmost – slider(s) to align them with the pixels in each colour

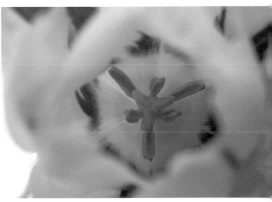

The finished image. Adjusting the levels has boosted the natural colour – but not excessively – and sorted the contrast too.

channel. Note the colour changes and then tweak the sliders as needed. Only adjust the grey slider to neutralise any colour casts (or add them!) and to adjust the midtone colour levels – if required.

Step 4:
Once you're happy with the result (which will depend on each individual image), click OK and the changes will be applied. **File > Save** (or **Save As**) the image to finish.

Cloning and healing

Stuck with unsightly blemishes or unwanted objects in a scene? Cloning or healing can easily remove them.

Almost everyone has taken a photo where the subject has a tree or other odd object in the background apparently growing out of their head, or the subject of a portrait might have an unsightly spot or blemish. The 'clone' and 'healing' tools are perfect for removing these unwanted pixels from a digital photo.

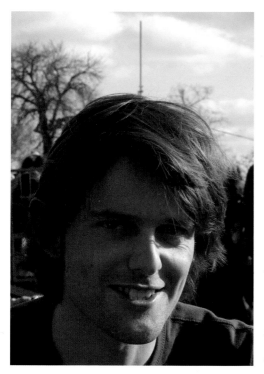

This informal portrait was taken quickly and it was not until later, reviewing the images on screen, that the antenna in the distance became apparent, 'growing' from the subject's head. In order to save this otherwise perfectly fine shot, cloning must be used.

Using cloning and healing

Cloning works by creating a pixel-by-pixel copy of a part of an image, which is then applied to another area of the same image; healing works in almost the same way in terms of applying the edit, but in this case it assesses the pixels to be adjusted, matching the colour, tonality and texture to preserve the 'look' of the area as you apply the 'healing' effect. In this case, we are going to use 'cloning' to take pixels from the sky above and around the subject to cover the pixels forming the antenna sticking out of the subject's head. 'Healing' is used in a similar way as described below for 'cloning', and is often used on spots, wrinkles and other blemishes on skin within portraits.

Step 1:
File > Open the image and zoom into the area to be worked upon using the magnify tool, leaving enough space around the part that must be cloned away to provide fresh pixels to clone over it.

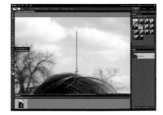

Step 2:
Click on the clone tool button. The cursor will change to a small circle: effectively it has become a 'brush', which can clone pixels.

Step 3:
Pick a brush with a soft edge and size it to suit the object you're removing.

Step 4:

To use the clone tool, hold the control key (or alt key on Macs) and click an area adjacent to the part of the image to be removed that has similar pixels, suitable for the background. This step selects the new pixels you'll use to cover the offending object in the shot.

Step 5:

Now click and drag the clone brush over the pixels to be removed. You'll notice the pixels from where you control/alt-clicked earlier are now being copied over the pixels you want to cover up.

A small cross indicates the pixel pick-up point as you progress. In order to ensure the pixels being cloned are as similar as possible to those being covered, frequently reselect the clone area with similar pixels to those from the background. It's worth noting some software now automatically samples the pixels used to clone, so you can just paint away the offending pixels.

Step 6:

Repeat Step 5 until you've completely cloned away the offending part of the scene. The more fiddly the bit to be cloned away, the longer it will take. Zoom in closer if you

need to in order to get a more detailed view (you'll need a smaller brush size too). Check the 'aligned' check box to ensure the clone point is always parallel with the brush point, particularly when cloning linear subjects, as is the case in this example.

Step 7:

Once you're happy with the final result, **File ›** **Save** (or **Save As**) the image.

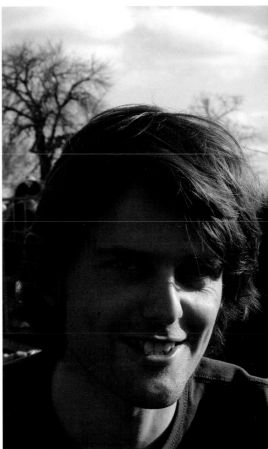

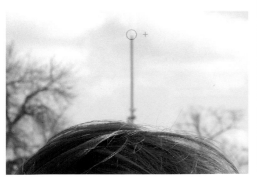

The clone brush and clone pick-up cursor appear each time you click and drag over the area being cloned away. Frequent reselection of the clone point may be needed, depending on the fiddlinesss of the image parts that need to be removed.

The finished picture now has the offending mast completely cloned away using the surrounding sky and cloud pixels to seamlessly cover it up. Practice will help you judge how pixels are cloned and help hone your technique.

Dodge and **burn**

Want to darken or lighten small sections of an image? Here's how.

Traditional film photography darkroom techniques included 'dodging' and 'burning', in which the printer of the photograph was able to allow more light into some parts of a print (the so-called 'burning in') to make them darker or hold light back ('dodging') from reaching the print, making them lighter. In essence, dodging and burning simply means you're controlling local areas of light and dark.

This has been translated to the digital domain and it is a fantastic technique to help get the tones in smaller areas just right. It can be used to brighten shadows to reveal detail in a shaded face, or to add deeper tones to, say, a landscape, where you might want to emphasise a stormy, brooding sky by deepening the tones or colours of clouds. This can all be achieved without affecting the photo as a whole.

The technique can be applied to black and white shots or to colour images. All that matters is that you can lift shadows if need be (dodging) or deepen them (burning). Here's how to do it.

Using dodge and burn

The image we are working on requires two things: shadows lifted from the faces of the subjects; and a deepening of the background shadow to de-emphasise the distracting image content. We don't want to affect the whole shot, just

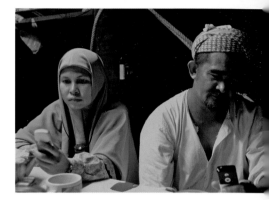

Above: *This shot has deep shadows in the background and on the man's face on the right. Lifting the facial shadows but darkening some of the background distractions without affecting the rest of the image will keep its contemplative atmosphere and help direct the viewer's eye to the two subjects.*

the faces and deeper background shadows, so dodging and burning is perfect here.

Step 1:
File > Open your image and select the dodge tool. Pick a soft-edged brush (in this case of 65 pixels) ready to start dodging.

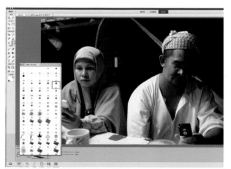

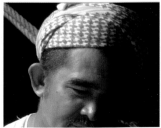

Once you've zoomed in, you can work to lighten the darker areas.

Step 2:

Now zoom into the shadow area on which you want to work. The dodge and burn tools can be set to work on a specific range of pixels: shadows, midtones or highlights. In this case, with the dodge tool and the midtones selected, start with an exposure of around 25%, selected from the adjacent exposure menu.

Step 3:

Click and paint with the dodge tool over the shadow area you want to lighten, just a small brushstroke at a time.

Step 4:

To deepen shadows, switch to the burn tool by clicking on its icon and continue to click and paint over the required pixels. The pixels being painted will begin to darken.

Step 5:

Repeat the processes of Step 3 and Step 4, going over each area, dodging shadows on faces and, as in this case, burning unwanted background detail away by deepening the shadows. Keep going until you're satisfied.

ⓘ Dodge and burn colour

The process of dodging and burning colour images is essentially the same as that for black and white: lightening and darkening localised areas of an image. However, such work can sometimes make image noise more evident, so you have to be careful. Switching from midtones to shadow and highlight modes can help, but experimentation is needed to see which works best on different images. Again, you need to use both dodge and burn tools sensitively or risk overdoing it. As with most image editing techniques, less is often so much more.

You'll need to change brush sizes and the zoom ratio depending on how fiddly the task gets. The more 'zoomed in' you are, the smaller the brush required and vice versa.

Step 6:

File > Save (or **Save As**) your image once you're happy and you're done.

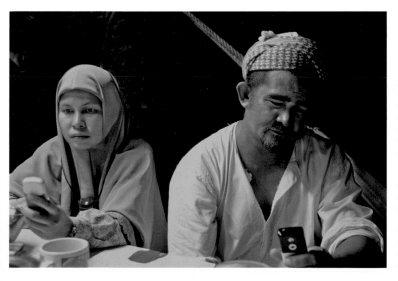

Left: *The finished shot has lightened the man's face and deepened the background shadow to help hide distracting elements such as the plug socket on the pillar and items behind the woman's left side. The rope's been darkened too, but it's important that realism is maintained. The lady's face has been dodged, brightening the eyes, as has her cowl, in order to help make her stand out.*

Layers

Don't risk losing your original shots when editing. Here's how to make dramatic changes without affecting your original pixels.

Layers are powerful tools available in higher-end editing packages and it's a good idea to get into the habit of always using them whenever you're image editing. While they make the edited image's file size bigger, they allow you to completely change an image. You might want to add text to a shot, add a new element from another photo, change the colours of a specific part, or add a pattern, all without affecting the rest of the image. By using layers, you can do almost any edit imaginable and yet not affect the original underlying pixels.

You can think of layers as transparent sheets of glass stacked one on top of another and onto each of which you can 'paint' elements. Because the layers are transparent, you can see through them to what's below.

The bottom layer in the stack is labelled 'background', but each new layer you make can be given a name of your choice so that it is always recognisable. These layers can be worked on independently, allowing you to experiment with an effect to see if you like it. Once you've finished, the layers can be merged together to give you your finished, edited image.

Although we've not dealt with layers until now, all the image editing tasks we cover in this book can be carried out on layers.

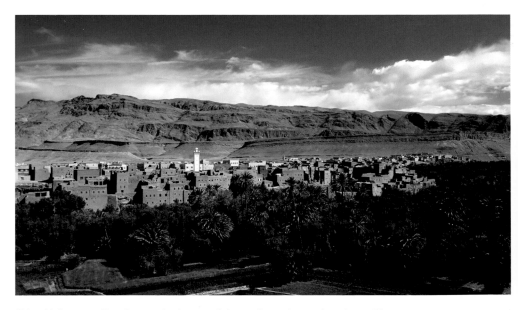

Using this image, we'll apply a couple of easy-to-do layer edits, sorting out the colours with levels, changing the colours and then adding text.

Basic adjustment layer

To keep the first one simple, we'll use a simple 'levels adjustment layer' to correct colour, saturation and brightness in an image.

Step 1:

File > Open your image and navigate to the **Levels Adjustment Layer** via the **Layer > Adjustment Layer > Levels** command.

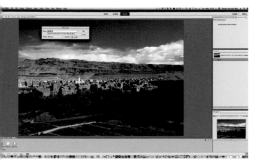

Step 2:

A levels dialogue box will appear, and a new layer icon will appear in the layers palette. The new layer is named by you; below it is the original image layer called 'background'.

Step 3:

Adjust the levels for the image in the normal way – as dealt with in *Levels*. If you click on the eye icon to hide the new layer, you'll notice the image switch back to its pre-levels state. The underlying pixels have not been touched by this levels edit.

Step 4:

Once you have the levels right for the image click OK. Now you can merge the layers if required. Use the **Layers > Merge Layers** (or **Flatten Image**) command. Notice in the layers palette how the two layers become one, simply called 'background' again.

Step 5:

File > Save (or **Save As**) your image.

Fundamental changes

This time using layers, we'll make a more dramatic change and completely alter the colour of the sky.

Step 1:

File > Open your image and, just as in Step 1 of the basic adjustment layer, adjust the levels for the image on an adjustment layer first. Once done, merge the result to give a new, correctly adjusted background layer.

Step 2:

Create another new layer, this time an exact copy of the original via the **Layer > Duplicate Layer** command. A dialogue box will appear asking you to name the new layer 'background copy'. Click OK. You now have a duplicate of the original image (after the adjustment layer has been applied) above it in the layers palette.

Step 3:

Use the **Enhance > Adjust Color > Replace Color** menu to bring up the replace colour dialogue box. Using the colour selection tool, click on the sky in the image to select that colour (blue here). If necessary, switch to the 'add to selection' tool (typically a pipette with a '+' symbol) and keep adding to the sky selection. If you pick too much, use the 'remove from selection' (a pipette with a '–' symbol) tool.

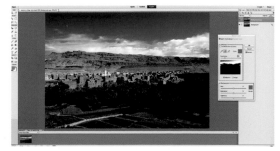

The **replace colour** *dialogue box has selection tools (the three pipettes at the top) and a large black and white preview to help you check your selections.*

Step 4:

Using the replacement section of the replace colour dialogue box, click in the result box. A new colour selection window appears. Pick any colour you like. In our case, it was bright green! Watch the sky change to the colour you selected. Once you're happy with the effect, click the OK button. Note that the change has only been applied to the new background copy layer. Click the icon for the background copy layer and you'll see the newly changed sky colour vanish as the layer is turned off.

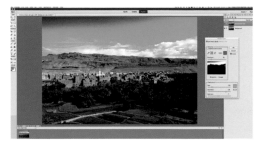

The bottom section of the **replace colour** *dialogue box houses the* **replacement** *colour selection tools. Using the* **hue**, **saturation** *and* **lightness** *sliders, you can fine-tune the colours selected.*

Step 5:

If you're happy, you can either **File > Save** (or **Save As**) the image with the layers intact or merge the layers using the **Layers > Merge Layers** (or **Flatten Image**) command and then **File > Save** (or **Save As**), permanently embedding the new coloured sky into the image.

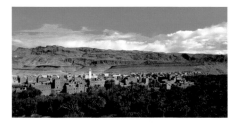

The finished image with the sky colour replaced, but on an editable layer which means the underlying original image pixels are untouched by this extreme effect.

Adding text with layers

On some images, say for a home-made birthday card, you might want to add text and, with layers, you can do it quickly without damaging the original pixels.

Step 1:

As before, **File > Open** the image onto which you will add text (we've used the same shot here). Go through the levels adjustment on a layer again and **Layer > Merge Layer** it with the background layer if you want to embed the levels changes into the photo.

Step 2:

Use the **Layer > New > Layer** command to create a new layer: this time name it 'text layer'.

Step 3:

Click on the 'horizontal type' tool. Select a reasonably large type size (depending on your image) and a typeface from the selection offered (in this case a typeface of Arial black at 72 point size).

Step 4:

Now type your chosen text onto the 'text layer'. Once typed, you can alter the typeface and size by first highlighting the text and selecting any new parameters. If you want to move the text about, click on the 'move' tool and then click on the text. By clicking and dragging it about, you can change its position as required.

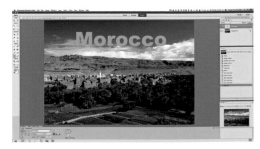

Step 5:

To give further impact, you can warp text and change its colour; the tools to do this appear across the bottom of the software's desktop and become active when you click the relevant type tools. For colour, click on the 'set text colour' button and a menu of colours will appear for you to choose from. To warp the text (to fit a shape in the picture, say, or to simply add more interest to the final image), click the 'warp text' tool that sits next to the 'set text colour' button. Pick a shape from the menu that appears, such as 'arch', and it will change the text shape immediately.

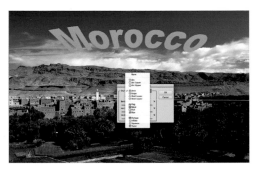

Step 6:

If warping the text changes its position so much that it is outside the image area, use the move processes in Step 4 (above) to get it positioned correctly again.

Step 7:

Either **File > Save** (or **Save As**) to preserve the layers for future editing or **Layers > Merge Layers** (or **Merge Down**) the layers to create a single background layer and then **File > Save** (or **Save As**) as required.

The latest Elements software has a new feature called the 'text on shape' tool. This automatically creates a text layer and lets you choose a predefined, scalable shape, such as a butterfly or heart, which you can then type text onto as an outline. This gives you even greater creative potential.

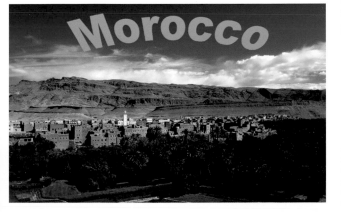

The finished image with text applied and distorted into an arch. There are plenty of effects and typefaces to choose from to suit your needs, and with patience and practice these techniques can be used to great creative effect.

Masks

Want to protect sections of your image, whilst radically editing others? Masking areas will keep them unaffected by any changes you make.

Y ou can use masks to paint on effects to selected areas or paint away unwanted parts of an image. Using masks on a layer means you can use an edit or effect without affecting underlying pixels.

Using masks

If you want to change a large element in a photo, such as replacing the sky in one shot with the sky area pixels from another, masks come into their own. You can cover or reveal portions of two images to create a composite of both.

The shot of the mosque below has a bland sky so it would be good to add more colour, ideally matching the blue of the woman's clothing. You can use any two shots to do this, but the more simple the sky and foreground outlines on the second shot, the easier it will be.

Step 1:
File > Open both the images you're going to use, call one the 'sky' image, and the other the 'ground' image. If you haven't already done so, and they need it, apply a levels adjustment layer to both shots (as described in *Layers*) and merge the images.

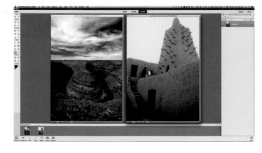

The two images side by side ready for compositing.

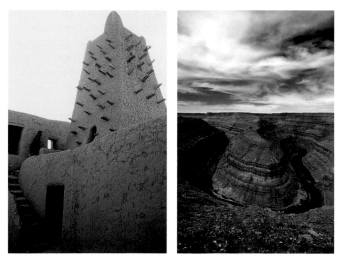

Step 2:
Create a copy of the ground image (called the 'background' layer) in the layers palette with the **Layer > New Layer Via Copy** command (the 'background copy' layer may also be called 'layer 1', depending on the software you use).

Step 3:
Using the magic wand tool (used to select all pixels of a similar colour with a single click – it looks just like a small wand), click on the sky in layer 1. The layer will highlight to show

it's the active layer. This will select the sky pixels, which must be deleted in order for the image pixels from the desired sky shot eventually to show through. Select the selection paintbrush tool and activate mask mode (shown here accessed via a small drop-down menu to the right of the brush tool) and the non-sky area will change to a red mask, protecting it.

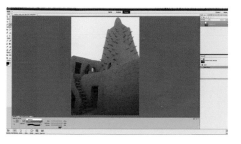

Step 4:

If any of your selected sky in the ground image has not been properly selected using the magic wand tool, click on the brush tool (it looks just like a small paintbrush icon). Check you're in selection mode (via the small pop-down menu at the bottom of the work space) and paint more selection into the area NOT already selected by the magic wand tool, in this case, the window in the wall. This new selection area will also become part of the mask. Paint more selection into the areas which need it with an appropriate brush size and zooming as required. Remember, if you make a mistake and paint in too much selection, switch back to mask mode and paint back in the mask again. Keep going until you're happy.

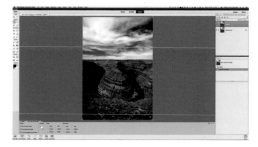

Step 5:

Feather the selected sky area by about 2 pixels with the **Select > Feather** command, shown here. Feathering helps smooth hard edges, blurring them slightly to limit abrupt joins of different pixels, making a more natural-looking fit.

Step 6:

Hit delete to remove the sky (and other selected areas) from the ground image.

Step 7:

Select the sky image and using the rectangular marquee tool, click and drag across the entire image to select its pixels. Use the **Edit > Copy** command to copy the selected sky image. Close the sky image.

Step 8:

Click on the ground image and then click the background layer in the layers palette. Using the **Edit > Paste** command, apply the copied sky image pixels over the ground image. Depending on your software, a new 'layer 2' is automatically created containing the copied sky pixels, overlaying the ground image. You can check this in the layers palette. The new sky is now composed with the transparent layer 1 and you have added your new sky.

Step 9:

Click on the relevant layer if any aspect of the image requires further fine-tuning. The finished image would usually have three layers: a 'background' (untouched), then 'layer 2' (containing the sky image), and on

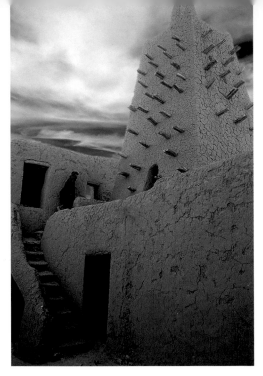

The final image will have a single background layer after merging and will have the new colourful sky pixels in place of the old, bland sky pixels. With practice, you'll be able to use this technique with multiple layers to edit in – or out – almost anything in a shot and without permanently changing the original image's pixels.

top the masked 'layer 1'. Its mask protects and covers the unwanted parts of the sky image. Once you're satisfied, use the **Layer > Merge Layers** command and **File > Save** (or **Save As**) your new image.

Painting onto layers

Another technique to use for a more creative or arty effect is to paint a mask onto a layer to protect one part of an image from a filter effect, for example. Here's how to do it.

Step 1:
File > Open your image and do the levels tasks again if you need to. Then, using the **Layer > Layer Via Copy** command, create a new copy layer as we did in the first task above. It will be called 'layer 1'.

Step 2:
Now use the **Layer > New Layer** command to make another layer (name it 'paint' layer in the dialogue box that appears, shown below), and make sure you select the selection brush switch to mask mode (as we did in the previous topic at Step 4) and a soft edge paintbrush selected from the paintbrush selection pop-down menu.

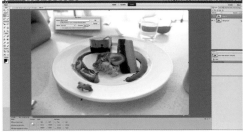

Step 3:
Paint shapes over the image on layer 1 (simple squiggly lines over the food were added – see below) and a red mask will be painted on, representing protected areas of the image – those that will NOT be affected by future edits. (You can also invert the mask in the **Select > Inverse** command, which means the areas not painted over will be masked and protected instead.)

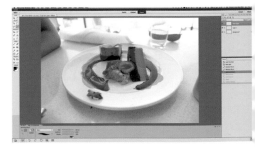

Step 4:
Once you've painted your mask onto the paint layer, click on layer 1 (the background copy) to make it active and use the **Filter >**

Distort > Ripple command to apply the filter (you can use any filter you wish, though). Then, apply the **Filter > Sketch > Chalk & Charcoal** filter (or any other filter of your choice that's suitable for your image) to strip the colour away and add another texture effect. Note how your painted mask area has been left untouched, as below.

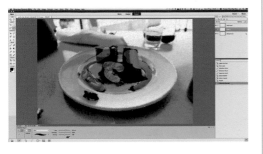

Step 5:

Once you're happy with the effect, you need to de-select the mask/selection layer by clicking on any other selection tool (such as the rectangular marquee tool) and clicking inside the image. Then use the **Layer > Merge Visible** command to merge the layers, then **File > Save** (or **Save As**).

i Masking tips

- **Feathering:** *Feathering allows you to soften edges (it makes them fuzzy-looking) for a more realistic joining effect. You can define the number of pixels around the selection that will be feathered: the larger the number, the more pixels outward from the selection will be made fuzzier.*

- **Selections and Masks:** *Selections are the area you've defined in a layer using a selection tool such as the magic wand or selection brush. You can add to a selection by painting onto the layer in mask mode. By switching back and forth, you can ...*

- **Add and Subtract a Mask:** *If you paint too much of a selection onto a layer in selection mode, you can remove it by switching to mask mode and painting it back in again. Careful use of the right brush size and zooming allows very accurate masks to be made, even around complex features such as tree branches and hair.*

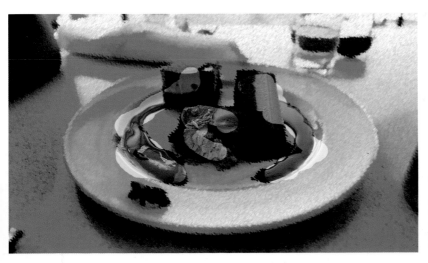

The final effect leaves colour in the protected masked areas and the effects of the filters you've applied everywhere else.

Blurring backgrounds

This professional technique allows you to emphasise your subject by reducing the impact of the background.

Adding 'blur' to a shot allows you to lessen the impact of a distracting background. This is similar to the effect of a shallow depth of field. For example, in the shot below, we want to reduce the detail in the background (the umbrella, table and chairs), creating emphasis on the person in the foreground.

Step 1:
File > Open the image to be worked upon, perform a 'quick fix/auto levels' if required and then create a duplicate layer. Use the **Layer > Duplicate Layer** command and rename it something you'll remember. Working on this layer protects the original pixels while you're editing.

Step 2:
Working on the newly created layer, select the selection brush and in mask mode, paint

a red mask around the subject, which should look something like this.

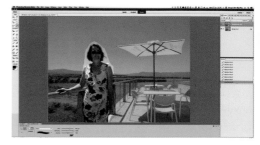

Step 3:
Choose a 'soft' brush in a size small enough to paint more mask carefully around the subject, right up to the edges. This additional step means that the initial selection does not have to be very accurate – you can adjust it as necessary.

Step 4:
If you make a mistake while painting, switch between the add or subtract mask tools, shown below in mask mode to the left of the brush and mask mode menu. Paint the selection away (subtract) if you overlap the main subject, or paint it back again (add) if you subtract too much. Adjust the brush size as you progress

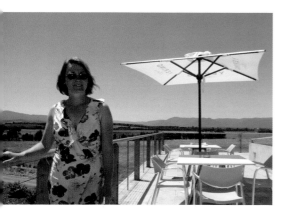

This is an otherwise good image that would benefit from emphasising the figure in the foreground.

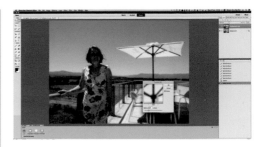

- *Remember to feather the selections to make the edges blend more naturally.*

- *Adding to or removing elements from selections can be achieved using masks.*

- *Step the level of blur. More blur should be applied to the parts of a scene in the distance.*

- *If your software has it, use the Depth of Field tool for even faster edits.*

and ensure that the mask does not cover anything in the foreground or in front of your subject. In this case, we made sure that the fence cables and the post, level with the person, were also masked to help make the effect look more natural.

Step 5:

Use the **Select > Feather** command and feather the selection by around 2 in the dialogue box that appears. This helps blend the edges of the selection, making it look natural. Or, for more powerful refinement, use the **Select > Refine Edge** tool to help improve the selection. Now, invert your selection using **Select > Inverse**. This selects the background

(rather than the main subject you've been painting round with the mask).

Step 6:

Now, apply the blur effect (mimicking a large aperture lens) using the **Filter > Blur > Gaussian Blur** command. Select a level between 3 and 5, judging the effect in the preview. You can experiment to see what seems most natural. You'll notice everything except the masked subject (above, right) is now blurred. Click OK.

Step 7:

If the blur has invaded the main subject, which is not supposed to be blurred, use the **Select > Modify > Contract** command and select 1 pixel in the dialogue box that appears. This will pull the blur back very slightly (by 1 pixel) from the selected area.

Step 8:

Once you're happy with the final effect, you can flatten the layers (**Layer > Merge Layers** or **Flatten Image**) and **File > Save** (or **Save As**).

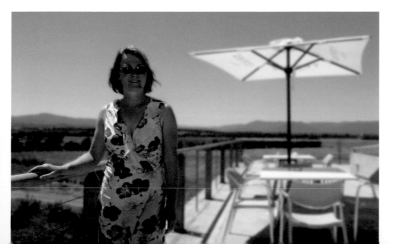

The finished image with emphasis placed on the person in the foreground by blurring the background.

Adding **movement**

This Masterclass shows how to add the appearance of movement to a photograph.

Occasionally a photo can be improved by adding 'artistic' blur, for example, adding motion blur to emphasise the feeling of speed in an event.

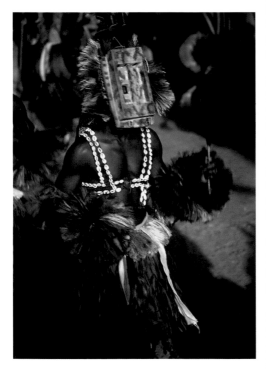

This shot of a dancer has some natural blur in the background, but to make it even more dynamic, motion blur is going to be added to the main figure in the foreground. This technique can be used on multiple elements in a shot if you repeat the following process for each element.

Step 1:
File > Open the image you'll be adding motion blur to, and create a duplicate layer with **Layer > Duplicate Layer.** Rename it something you'll remember and, working on this layer, apply 'quick fix/auto levels' if your image requires it. (From now on, let's assume that you'll already have done this where necessary on each image.)

Step 2:
We need to place each part of the scene that will have motion added onto a separate layer. Use the rectangular marquee tool to draw a rectangular selection around the subject(s) to have motion added.

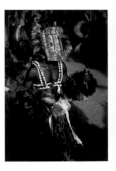

Step 3:
Switch to the magic wand tool; press the alt (option) key, which allows you to remove from the rectangular selection you've already made.

Keep alt (option) clicking until the selection is right. If you have a fiddly selection to make that the magic wand cannot help with, you'll need to use a mask to add to the selection. Select the selection brush in the tools palette and switch to mask mode, painting in more mask as needed. Switch back to selection mode once you're done.

Step 4:
Now choose **Layer > New > Layer Via Cut,** which will become the 'blur layer'. Go through steps two, three and four for each element of

your original image (the background layer) that you want to apply blur to. Each will become a separate layer. Note that your background layer will have a 'hole' where each element of the image has been selected and put onto a new layer.

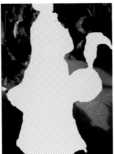

Step 5:

Before we add the motion blur we must use the clone tool to fill in any holes in the background layer that were left by selecting the elements for the addition of blur. Click on the background layer to make it active, use the **Layer › New › Layer** (name it something memorable, such as 'fill in holes' layer) and click OK. Select the clone tool and check the 'sample all layers' check box at the foot of the work area beneath the brush drop-down menu.

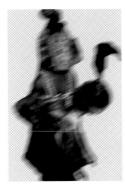

Step 6:

Turn off the blur layer, and using the clone tool click in the new 'fill in holes' layer. Alt (option) click on the background areas (not the holes!) and using the selected pixels, paint in the holes. With the 'sample all layers' control active, it will copy pixels from the background layer to the new layer and fill in the holes. Make frequent 'alt clicks' in different areas to make sure you don't get any repeat marks from the cloning process. Keep going until the holes are filled in and to check this, make all the layers active and ensure you're happy.

Step 7:

Click on the blur layer (or each layer in turn if you have more than one) to which you'll add blur and choose **Filter › Blur › Motion Blur.**

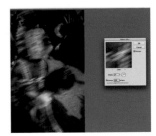

In the dialogue box select an angle for the blur that more or less follows the direction your subject's facing, and a 'distance' for the pixel blur, in this case of 27 degrees and 100 pixels respectively.

Step 8:

Once you're happy, click OK, **Layer › Merge Layers** and finally **File › Save** (or **Save As**).

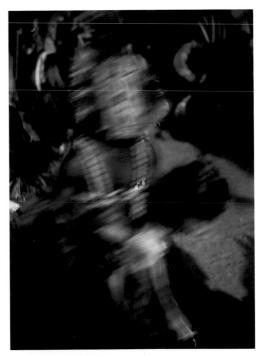

The finished image with motion blur applied has a more dynamic look, giving more life to the main subject of the photograph.

Content Aware Move

The latest versions of editing software use clever content aware tools that let you improve a photo by moving elements around in the shot afterwards, back at home on your PC. Here's how …

Sometimes, when you hurry a shot, or there's not enough time to get the composition exactly as you'd like, you can end up with an image that could be superb but isn't quite as good as you'd have liked. Using the latest software tools, with their 'content aware' processing features, you can now move elements of a shot around to help improve the composition.

Moving content around

In the image below, the striking main sunflower is too far to the left and there is a distracting building, blurred by the narrow depth of field, in the centre of the shot. Let's see how to fix an image with these issues.

Step 1:
File › Open the image you want to edit and choose the Content Aware Move tool from the tool bar on the left (in Elements it looks like two intertwining arrows). The cursor will change to a small cross icon.

Step 2:
Draw around the element in the shot that you want to move. This is called the selection – be careful not to draw the selection too close to the actual object you wish to move because the software needs to 'look' around the selection area to 'learn' which pixels to put back in its place after it has moved. Once you have drawn around the entire element to be moved, the line will turn into a crawling dotted line and the cursor will change back to the intertwined arrows with a small pointer.

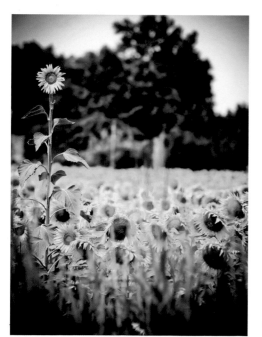

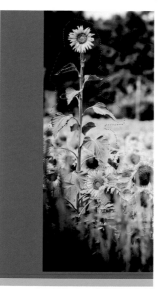

This shot shows the selected sunflower ready to be moved to its new location in the centre of the image.

Step 3:

Click and hold with your mouse inside the selected area, then move the selection to its new location. When that's done, click on the image outside the selection. The software will start processing the move, by blending the selection into its new surroundings and filling in the empty space left by its move.

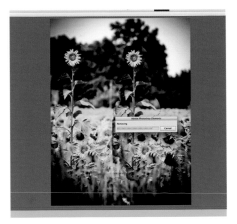

Tips for moving content

- *If the elements you wish to move are small, select the magnify tool and enlarge the part of the shot you want to work on so it is easier to edit.*

- *Experiment with the Healing slider control to increase or decrease the amount of healing applied.*

- *Some trial and error is needed to get the moved elements just right.*

- *Depending on your software, the Content Aware Move may need to be performed within its Expert or Guided Editing mode.*

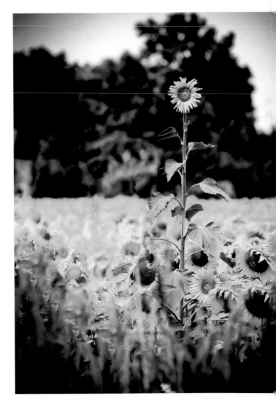

Step 4:

The Healing slider at the bottom of the screen is used to fine-tune the amount of blending and healing that goes into the newly empty space and the new surroundings for the moved selection. Slide the Healing slider left for less or right for more healing processing.

Step 5:

After the move, there may be a few things that need tidying up. In this example, there were a few jagged bits of sunflower left behind and a vertical stem too close to the sunflower in its new position. The clone tool and spot healing brush sorted them out in a few minutes, making everything look natural.

Step 6:

Once you're happy you can **File > Save** (or **Save As**) your image and you're done.

The finished image with the sunflower moved across into its new place.

Making **panoramas**

Separate images can be stitched together to create a seamless panoramic image.

Whilst some digital cameras can create panoramic images automatically, their quality can be compromised by the camera's processing. However, image editing software programs have special panorama-making tools to join photos together. It's relatively easy to get a good result, providing you shoot images from the same position (ideally from a tripod), with the same focal length, and pay attention to the exposure values so that the brightness is as even as possible throughout. You can remove any minor differences with editing software.

Step 1:
Use the **Enhance › Photomerge › Photomerge Panorama** command to launch the photomerge system. Your package may have a different path or name for this function (something like **File › Automation Tools › Photomerge**), but the process is otherwise the same for most software packages. A dialogue box appears asking you to browse to find your images. Navigate to them and highlight those that will be used for the panorama. Click OK and

they'll import into the software. Depending on your software, you can click the following check boxes: Blend Images Together, which will help create a more natural fit; the Vignette Removal, which can sort darkened corners in the original images; and Geometric Distortion Correction, which is great for straightening any buildings in the scene.

Step 2:
The software either automatically starts to build the panorama, or you can move the images manually into the correct order. Then the software will 'stitch' them together, which can take a few minutes depending on the number of images. The stitched images will appear as a wide, thin image. If the software (or you) have made any alignment mistakes, use the move tool to adjust the images until they are properly aligned.

Step 3:
If some elements still don't fit perfectly, don't worry. You can either go back and reprocess the images again (simply don't save your most recent work), switching off the Vignette

The finished image, consisting of separate images stitched together to create a long panoramic image.

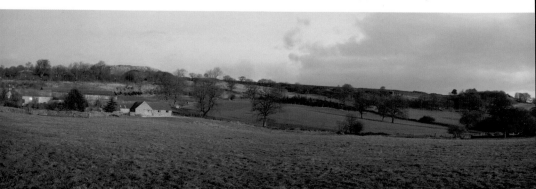

Removal and/or Geometric Distortion controls, or use a different setting from the options available when you launch the Photomerge Panorama processing. If your software has it, click the 'advanced blending' check box to preview the result and you'll see where any poor exposure areas are corrected.

Step 4:
Once 'merging' is complete, zoom into the image and check the images have blended properly. If not, use a combination of the clone tool (to remove unwanted elements) and the healing brush (for repairing areas without defined joins) to repair any small elements that don't quite fit or look natural.

Step 5:
Once you're happy with the fit, you can either use the crop tool to remove any uneven edges around the panorama or use the clean edges tool, which pops up once the Photomerge has done its stuff and automatically fills the edges with details from the image. This may also need a little tidying up with the clone or healing tool. If you are manually cropping ragged edges, try to keep as much of the image as you can and when you're happy, double-click within the crop area to crop away the unwanted ragged edges.

Step 6:
Use the **Layer > Flatten** command to remove unwanted layers and then the **Layer > New Adjustment Layer > Levels** command and carry out general levels or auto levels (just like a quick fix) on the image to help even out any other exposure and colour problems. Once you're finished use **Layer > Merge Layers** (or **Layer > Flatten Image**) to get rid of the unwanted layers, and finally, save the finished panorama.

Restoring old prints

Precious old photos don't need to be lost to dirt or scratches – you can repair them with some basic software techniques.

Scanning and editing techniques make it easy to restore damaged, scratched or dirty photographs. First off, you need to scan the original to bring it into your PC in a digital format (see *Scanning your photos*). The image can then be manipulated just like any of your digital photographs.

Step 1:
File > Open the image, create a duplicate layer with the **Layer > Duplicate Layer** command and rename it something you'll remember. Do a quick fix/auto levels at this stage if your image requires it.

Step 2:
Apply a dust removal filter using the **Filter > Noise > Dust & Scratches** command, but be careful as this can reduce sharpness. Use it only to remove small defects.

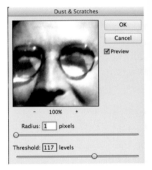

Check the effect, monitoring changes to the radius and threshold parameters – or adjust the sliders – checking the results as you go. When you're happy, click OK.

Step 3:
With the topmost layer active in the layers palette, create a new layer with the **Layer > New Layer** command and rename the layer something you'll remember, here 'clone/heal layer'. Note that this layer sits atop the first 'dust and scratches layer' and the original background layer.

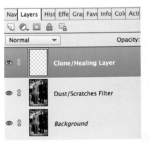

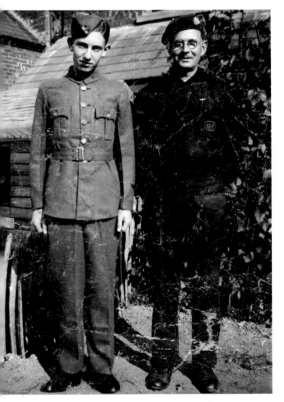

This old scanned negative of my grandad and uncle suffers from the ravages of time: it is covered in scratches and specks of dust.

Step 4:

Select the clone tool from the tools palette, ensuring you tick the 'sample all layers' box at the foot of the work space. Magnify an area to work on and select a soft brush from the brush menu, ensuring it is slightly larger than the dust marks you're going to remove, or you can use the spot healing brush if available.

NB: If using the spot healing brush, the software selects the cloned pixels for you.

Step 5:

Sample the pixels you want to clone by placing the cursor over a clean area close to a mark you wish to remove. Hold down the option key (or alt on a Mac keyboard) and click with the mouse. Release the option (alt) key and click on the dust mark. Cloned pixels from the area you selected will be painted over the top of the mark.

Step 6:

Repeat this process to repair all the blemishes on the image, but remember to sample pixels from fresh areas near to the marks you want to remove. Keep going and continue to paint until the image has been cleaned up. This can take some time, depending on the state of your images. Any mistakes made while cloning can be undone quickly with **Control > Z** (or **Command > Z** on Macs).

Step 7:

Once you've finished cloning/healing and you're happy with the finished and repaired effect, you should flatten the layers (**Layer > Flatten Image**) and save your image with **File > Save** (or **Save As**).

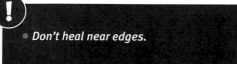

!
• *Don't heal near edges.*

✔

- *Use the clone tool to sample pixels from one part of the image and place (or 'clone') them elsewhere.*

- *Repeated sampling will be required, and remember to sample from similar areas to help ensure the cloned effect looks natural.*

- *If your software has it, try the 'Guided' mode 'restore old photo', which has a step-by-step process to achieve the edits described here. Bear in mind, however, that it won't use layers (that you can edit) and may not offer the same flexibility that you get if you do it the long way.*

The finished, cleaned image. All blemishes have been diminished or removed, enough for a respectable-size print to be made with ease.

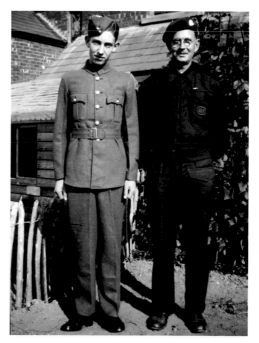

Shooting **HDR**

One of the most impressive and popular techniques in digital photography is High Dynamic Range (HDR) photography. So, what is it, how can you shoot it and how can you create the look in Photoshop Elements?

Shooting HDR-style images

An HDR image is a single image created from a set of two or more photos taken at a range of exposures from very under-exposed (darker) to very over-exposed (lighter). The images are combined in software to produce a final photo with an otherwise impossibly wide (or high) 'dynamic range'. HDR photos have stunning detail and dramatic colours which are extremely difficult to create any other way.

Typically, a digital camera can only expose either highlight or shadow details, but not both simultaneously. However, by following this camera technique and processing the images, you can combine a range of shots to create a photo with stunning detail and dynamic colour.

Camera set-up for taking an HDR sequence

First you'll need a tripod and self-timer or remote release, because it is vital that the camera remains as steady as possible for each image to achieve a sharp final photo.

To create a set of HDR-capable images, you need to use exposure bracketing. This is the term for taking an image at a correct exposure, then 'bracketing' around it, by over-exposing another image and under-exposing a third image.

If your camera has an Auto Exposure Bracketing (AEB) setting, you can use it to take a bracketed sequence of exposures of a correctly metered shot, another under-exposed by -2 stops and a third over-exposed

by +2 stops. Depending on your camera, you may be able to do between three and nine exposures in AEB. Check your camera's manual to locate your AEB mode.

The more exposures you can do the better, because you get more light from each of the lighter or darker parts of the scene that you expose for. However, be warned, taking more shots increases the risk of blurring, either due to camera movement (use a remote release or the camera's self-timer to reduce this risk) or the wind moving trees, clouds or parts of the subject. Both will make the final combined shot soft and less impactful.

The easiest way to shoot a sequence of images such as these is in manual mode. Set the camera's metering to Matrix or Evaluative, which measures the light from the entire scene; set the white balance to the correct setting (daylight mode for sunny days and so on); set the aperture setting to a small aperture, around F/11 or F/16, which will ensure everything is sharp; and set the ISO (the sensitivity) to a low setting such as ISO 100 or 200 to minimise image noise.

Then, you will be able to take your photos adjusting ONLY the shutter speed to brighten and darken the scene as required. Your camera should show you (either in the viewfinder, on the display, or both) the amount of under- or over-exposure being used. As a general rule bracket to one or two stops over and under the correct metered exposure. Take the 'normal' shot first, then the under-exposure shot(s) and finally the over-exposed image(s).

Processing the photo sequence to HDR

Photoshop Elements lacks a true HDR processing mode, but you can use its automated Photomerge Exposure tool to mimic the HDR look.

Step 1:
File > Open the sequence of images you want to apply the HDR effect to and make sure they are all selected in the Photo Bin at the bottom of PE's workspace (hold the Command or Control key and click each other with your mouse). You'll see that they look rather flat and lifeless on their own.

Step 2:
Click on the **Enhance > Photomerge > Photomerge Exposure** mode and the software will start working.

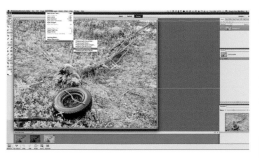

Step 3:
Leave the program in its default automated **Smart Blending** mode and use the three sliders of Highlight, Shadows and Saturation to adjust each respective setting to a level that you want. This will depend on the effect you want to achieve boosting colour,

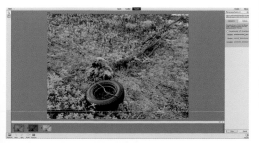

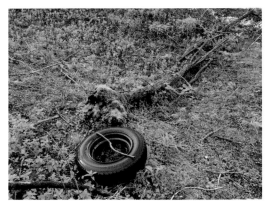

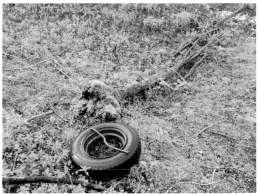

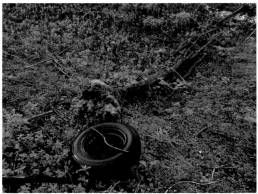

The three images taken for this project, showing (from top to bottom) a normal exposure, an under-exposure and an over-exposure. All were taken using AEB mode on tripod with the self timer.

highlights or shadow details until you're happy. If you select the Simple Blending mode, the software will do the 'slider' bit above for you. However, the effect tends to be less dramatic. Switch to Manual mode and you do all the work from aligning images to adjusting the way each individual element looks. I find the automated Smart Blending does a great job, but by all means, have a play.

Step 4:
Click **Done** and the program will build the output image based on your settings above.

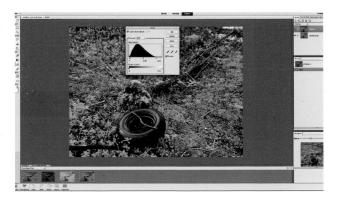

Step 5:
Go to **Enhance > Adjust Lighting > Levels** and adjust the black and white adjustment and bring them in towards the main part of the histogram (as shown left) in the dialogue that appears, to help add even more HDR-style impact, and click **OK**.

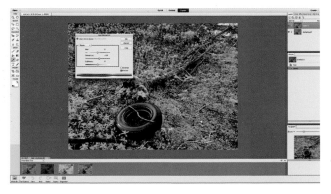

Step 6:
If it needs it, go to **Enhance > Adjust Colour > Hue/Saturation** tool and tweak the colours up a bit to add even more punch. Click **OK**.

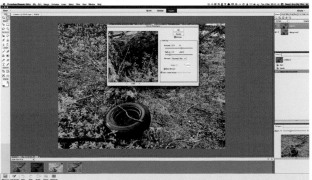

Step 7:
Go to **Enhance > Adjust Sharpness**, click the **More Refined** check box in the dialogue that appears and choose an **Amount** and **Radius** that adds sharpness without creating an unnatural effect. This helps get all the detail to really "pop". Click **OK**.

Step 8:
And now you should have a vibrantly coloured, extremely sharp image with detail across the highlights and shadows. If you're happy then go to **File > Save** (or **Save As**) and you're done.

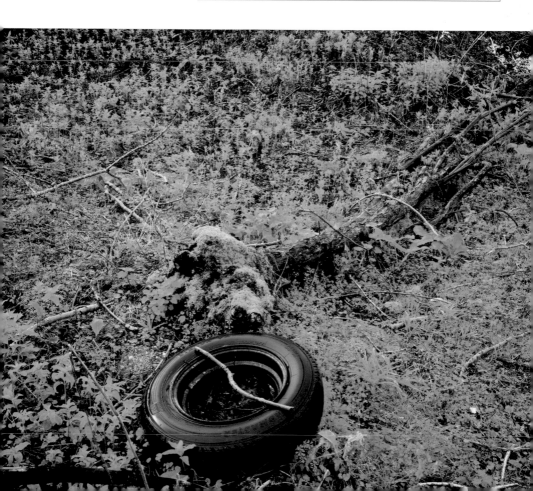

Shooting in **RAW**

As your photography progresses, you may want to move on to shooting RAW. Capturing images in RAW gives you the digital equivalent of a film negative, and the ability to process the image in your editing software to a much greater degree than you can with JPEGs.

When you take a photo, your camera creates the image and will (typically) compress each shot using the JPEG file format. (JPEG stands for Joint Photographic Expert Group, an organisation set up to govern and control the 'standards' for image compression.) JPEG compression is used across digital cameras along with the TIFF format (on some models), which we will discuss in a moment.

When you take a JPEG image, the file is compressed by the JPEG algorithm, which in simple terms works by removing similar pixel data, such as blue pixels in a shot with lots of sky, to help make extra room on your memory card. Those compressed pixels are put back again (using what is effectively a best guess) by the JPEG algorithm when you open the photo up again on, say, a computer.

The amount of compression can be varied: the settings on a digital camera are typically something like Good, Better, Best, each a step up in quality using lower levels of compression, applied alongside other processes such as white balance adjustment, sharpness, saturation and colour tweaks and other filters or effects you may have 'asked' the camera to apply to each shot.

In summary, JPEGs are images processed by the camera according to the settings you have asked to be applied at the time of shooting.

So what about RAW? First you need to check if your camera can shoot RAW, as not all of them can. The higher end models (compacts as well as D-SLRs) will usually have a mode that will allow you to shoot in RAW or simultaneously shoot a RAW image and JPEG duplicate at the same time.

What is RAW?

A RAW image file is simply an image with none of the above processing applied. When you take a shot in RAW, it is left completely alone: no compression is applied, no tweaks to colour or adjustments to sharpness. So why shoot RAW?

The reason why many professional photographers do so is that a RAW image contains far more data than a compressed JPEG. Typical 12MP cameras will produce a JPEG image file of about 4.3MB when set to top quality. The same camera, shooting RAW, will produce an image file of around 30MB, containing almost seven times the data and it is this information that makes RAW files so powerful. It means you can use editing software, such as Photoshop Elements or proprietary software supplied with the camera, to lift the full range of data out of the image and use it to improve the final shot on screen or as a print.

The RAW advantage

Working with RAW files in photo editing software (see overleaf) offers advantages in key areas:

Camera set-up for RAW and compression

- **To change the type of compression,** *go to the quality and/or image size settings in the menu. There should be a range of compression settings to choose from: some camera makers use Good, Better, Best, others have Basic, Normal and Fine. Image size settings change the number of pixels used in a shot so these often have names such as Large, Medium and Small. Combine both quality and image size settings (as is possible in many cameras) and you can create images at varying resolutions and quality (compression) settings.*

- **To set your camera for shooting RAW** *(if it has the ability), go to the quality and/or image size menu and choose the RAW option, or the RAW + JPEG option (or similar name) if you want to shoot both JPEG and RAW.*

- **TIFF files** *are a way of compressing images without losing any information (called lossless compression). JPEG compression is said to be a 'lossy' compression, as data is removed (or lost) to squeeze the file size down: the more compression you apply, the lower the quality of the image. However, you can only compress TIFFs to around 50% maximum and so these files retain vital image information but still allow you to compress an image. It can be a useful middle ground between shooting RAW and JPEG.*

- **DNG** *(Digital Negative) is another image format offered by some digital cameras, such as Pentax D-SLRs. It is analogous to RAW and offers the same flexibility but is in a format that is widely recognised as a 'standard' so it does not require the proprietary RAW processing software often needed for shooting in a specific manufacturer's RAW mode. As an example, a Nikon RAW file (called NEF) will not be compatible with Canon's CR2 RAW software and vice versa.*

- You can extract more details, particularly in highlights and shadows.

- You can adjust almost every image parameter post-shoot, such as white balance, colour and sharpness, giving you the ability effectively to re-photograph a scene with different settings.

- You can also process a RAW image file in various ways, such as colour or black and white, thus creating different versions and all without affecting the underlying pixels of the image.

A real-world example of where it offers advantages for me is when shooting weddings. Here, the bride's dress is usually white or very bright and the groom's suit is normally very dark, making it hard to capture all the fine detail if shooting using JPEG alone. RAW allows me to enhance the image later in software to ensure the finer details of the wedding dress and the groom's suit are rendered properly.

Processing RAW files using software

The latest version (or update) of Photoshop Elements (PE) contains a RAW processing plug-in that enables it to process RAW files without additional software from the camera's manufacturer. If you have RAW images to process, here's how to do it.

Step 1:

Launch your software and open the RAW image you want to work on. The program should recognise the RAW file and launch the RAW processing window. If it doesn't, use the **File > Open in Camera RAW** command, or similar depending on your software.

Step 2:

In the RAW processing screen that appears you have a broad choice of tools to make adjustments to the RAW file (before it opens in the usual software interface). These include some basics (on the right), such as white balance, colour, clarity and vibrance, shadow and highlight detail (to lighten or darken them respectively), exposure, and other fine-tuning adjustments such as sharpening, detail and noise reduction adjustments. Or you can just click 'Auto' to see how the program does things.

Across the top of the RAW processing screen you'll find other editing tools for even greater RAW image finessing, including a fine-tune for the white balance via a pipette tool (that allows you to select down to individual pixels), cropping and straightening, and there's even a redeye removal tool as well.

Across the bottom of the RAW screen there's an option to open the image at 16-bit/channel or 8-bit/channel colour levels. The main difference here is the number of colours it is possible to reproduce. At 8-bit,

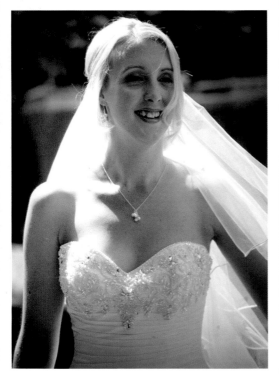

The original image without any RAW processing enhancements. Typical of an unprocessed RAW file, it is very flat and lifeless looking and detail has been lost in the veil.

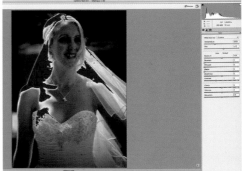

This image shows the RAW plug-in processing screen, with adjustment sliders on the right and a tool bar for cropping and white balance fine-tuning across the top. Note how the user interface shows the highlight areas of the image where detail has been lost by colouring them red (mostly the veil here). If details have been lost in the shadow areas they are coloured blue.

you can get 16.8 million colours. Switch to 16-bit and it's possible to achieve an amazing 281 trillion colours! Not all software programs can deal with this type of 16-bit file, and neither can many printers (home, high-street or otherwise). There's certainly no need for 16-bit files on screen, but if top-quality, full-colour fidelity is what you need, and you have the means to reproduce it, 16-bit offers that capability.

Step 3:

When you have made the adjustments suitable to your specific subject and image, you can click **Open Image**. The RAW file image, with your adjustments applied, will open inside the program's usual interface for further adjustment, if required. Or you can simply click **Done**, and the file will be saved with your edits. Alternatively you could choose to click **Save Image** and then you can save the image with various options, from RAW to DNG, with the compression and quality settings you choose but without further edits than those applied at this RAW stage.

Step 4:

Assuming you don't need to make any more adjustments, you can now **File > Save As** to save the image to a JPEG (or another file type) and in this way, the RAW file is still retained and available for re-processing as, say, a black and white image. You repeat the processes above, doing a new **File > Save As** each time to create a variety of versions of the same image, if you choose to.

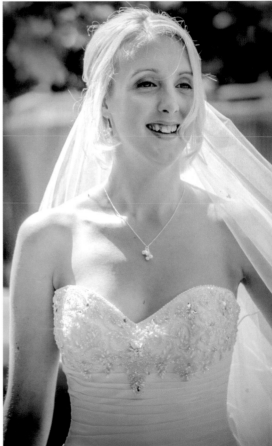

The finished image with colour, shadow and highlights restored, brightness improved and, at the same time, detail recovered, and sharpness and contrast also boosted.

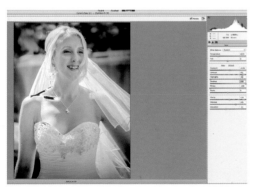

This is the RAW plug-in interface after adjustments have been made. Note how, even though the image is brighter, the red over-exposed areas in the veil, which lacked detail, are much reduced, bringing the detail back into the image.

Making art: painted effects

Turning a digital image into a 'painting' can give it a new lease of life.

With astute use of filters and masks, it's possible to create vivid digital imitations of painting styles, ideal for hanging on the wall or as unique-looking presents. In this example we'll create a look similar to the painting effect used by Impressionist artists such as Claude Monet, in which colour, light and form are emphasised.

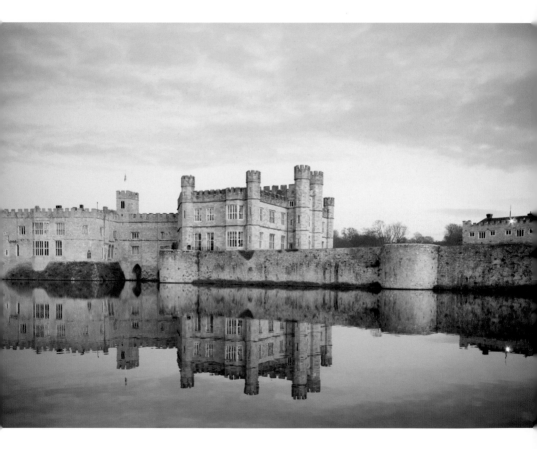

This is a beautiful image of Leeds Castle, Kent, and one that is ideal as the basis for an art-style edit. It needs a slight crop, top and bottom, to focus more on the castle, but apart from that, we can get started.

Step 1:
File > Open the image and using **Layer > New > Layer Via Copy**, create a new layer upon which we'll apply the first edits. Call it 'watercolour' and then change its blending mode to luminosity. Crop the image if necessary to close in on the detail. A slight crop was applied here to make the castle larger in the frame.

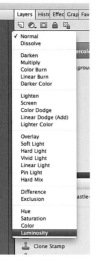

Step 2:
Use the **Filter > Artistic > Watercolor** command and select levels of 8, 0 and 2 in the brush detail, shadow intensity and texture sliders respectively. Click OK to apply the edits.

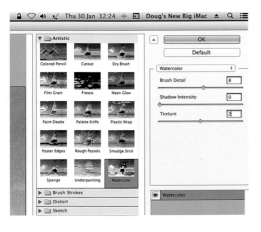

Step 3:
To duplicate the background layer ready for a new effect, click on it to make it active in the layers palette and use the **Layer > Duplicate Layer** command. You'll get a new background copy layer. Click OK. Using

the layers palette options at the top, set the opacity to 50% (making the layer more transparent) and set the blend mode to 'lighten'. Move this layer (by clicking, holding and dragging it) to the top of the stack of layers in the layers palette. You'll see the darkest parts of the previous watercolour effects brighten.

Step 4:
With the new 'background copy layer' active, use the **Filter > Artistic > Fresco** command. Set the parameters to 1, 8 and 1 in the respective brush size, brush detail and texture boxes (or use the sliders to suit your image).

Step 5:
Now use **Layer > Flatten Image** to remove the layers. Then draw a selection around the main image using either the rectangular or polygonal lasso tool (depending on your software) and switch to mask mode. A red mask border will appear. Select a large (200 pixels should do it) textured brush and paint around the border as shown below.

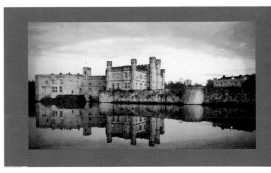

Step 6:
Switch back to selection mode, and use **Select > Feather** to a level of 2 or 3, and click OK. Now use **Select > Inverse** and hit delete, making a nice soft edge, and deselect the selection by clicking anywhere inside the image with the rectangular marquee tool active.

Step 7:
Now use **Layer > New > Layer Via Copy** and with the rectangular marquee tool, make a selection around the whole image. Switch to the selection brush and then mask mode. **Use Filter > Artistic > Rough Pastels** in canvas mode and click OK.

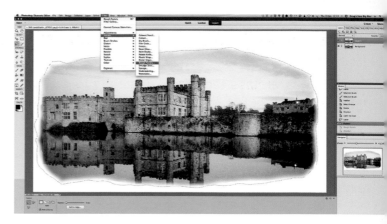

Step 8:
Use a levels layer to brighten things a bit more if needed, adjusted to suit your photo as necesssary, and then use the **Layer > Flatten** (or **Merge**) command to make one final layer. Finally, **File > Save** (or **Save As**) your image.

The finished image, with the artistic brushes and layer effects building together to form an Impressionist-style image with a softened border.

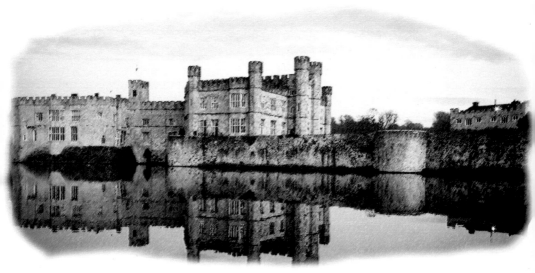

Making art: poster effects

With this Masterclass technique, it's easy to create a pop art poster that Warhol would have been proud of from any of your images.

Editing software can be used very effectively to give a portrait image a poster look. Here we'll create an example in the style made famous by Andy Warhol to show how easy it is to add a new spin to the 'traditional' portrait.

The starting image can be any portrait but ideally one with lots of contrast. As this image does not have that much contrast, we'll need to adjust this first and then proceed with the rest of the process.

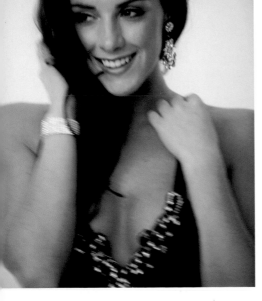

Step 1:
File › Open the image and using the **Layer › New Adjustment Layer › Levels** feature, click and drag the black point and white point sliders towards the centre of the histogram. Brighten the image if needed by sliding the central (grey point) triangle towards the black point slider. **Layer › Flatten** the image.

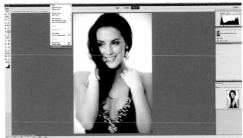

Step 2:
Next, just like Warhol's technique, we must reduce the number of colours in the image to give us those big blocks of colour. To do this, use the software's 'posterise' feature. Create a new layer (**Layer › New Layer Via Copy**) and use the **Filter › Adjust › Posterize** command. Call it 'posterise layer' or something that's

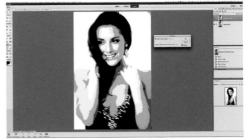

memorable. In the dialogue box that appears, the smaller the number chosen, the fewer the colours that will remain in the final image. Use four levels of colour (or whatever best fits your image). Assess this by checking the effect of your changes in the preview box.

Step 3:

Now we must increase the canvas size. Think of your image as being stuck onto a canvas the same size as the image. We must increase this canvas size in order to fit more than one image on to it. Use the **Image > Resize > Canvas Size** command and double the width and length, ensuring the 'anchor point' is central as shown below. Click OK.

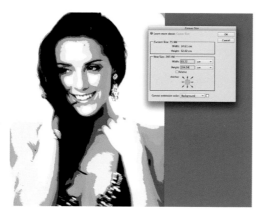

Step 4:

With the posterise layer active, use the **Layer > New Layer Via Copy** three times to produce

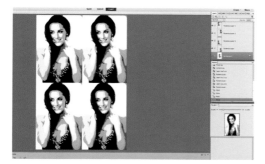

four versions of the same image, including the first layer. Name each one and turn the background layer off. Using the move tool, click on each layer and position its image within the new, larger canvas. Make sure there are no gaps between the four images. Use the crop tool to trim the image if necessary.

Step 5:

Now you can make the colour adjustments to each layer. Use the **Enhance > Adjust Color > Adjust Hue/Saturation** command and create a unique colour combination for each layer using the hue and saturation sliders in the dialogue box. Click on the layer you want to work on to make it active and keep experimenting with each layer until you're happy with the results. Use the levels control to brighten (or darken) the layers as necessary.

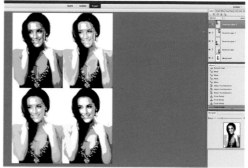

Step 6:

If you're happy with the results, all that remains is to **Layer > Merge Visible** (or **Flatten**) the image, discarding the 'hidden' background layer (if your software asks to do this) and then **File > Save** (or **Save As**). If your software has the feature, use the Create Pop Art tool to create a similar effect, but it's worth bearing in mind, this 'manual' method allows more fine control.

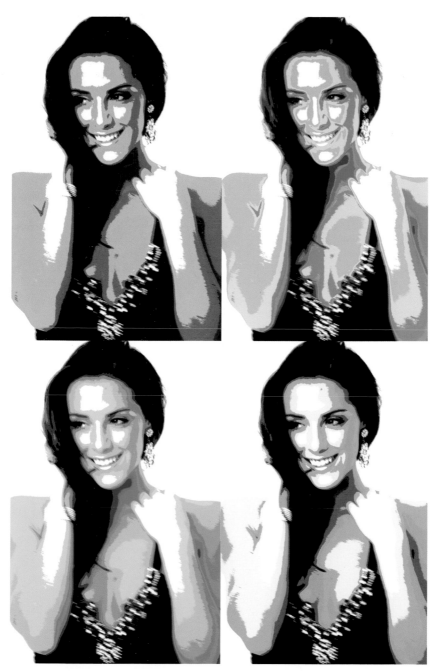

The finished image has all four layers merged into one and each image has its own colour palette, creating a bright, colourful 'Warhol-style' poster.

Lightroom

Lightroom is a simple yet powerful image editing and organisation program that makes editing images as easy as clicking a mouse.

Lightroom (LR), up to version 5 at the time of writing, is a single piece of software that allows you to organise, edit and share your images all from one interface. Images and other media such as video are stored and organised within a database that LR calls a catalogue. Using LR catalogues means you can edit an image in a similar way to using layers in Photoshop Elements (PE): the original image remains unchanged, with the catalogue holding all the edit information. This makes LR fast and easy to use – an ideal hub for all your images.

Lightroom's interface

The main Lightroom window is called the 'Library' module and comprises three key areas:

The viewing area sits right in the middle and allows quick browsing of thumbnails of the images in the catalogue. Click on an image and it will fill the centre of the window for closer examination.

An information panel to the right reveals detailed information about the image selected within the middle window.

The navigator is to the left and below it a list of LR's catalogues, as well as all folders available (on your PC's hard disk, for example), including those already added to LR and the publish services area.

- *It's better to have one large catalogue with everything in, rather than lots of smaller catalogues where things can become cluttered and easily lost.*

- *You can quickly preview the effect a filter edit will have in Develop module in the navigator by hovering your mouse over the filter you want to preview; its effect is revealed in the navigator panel.*

- *Ranking your images prior to editing them, for example, with (up to) five stars or with coloured flags (such as red or green), makes choosing the best photos faster and more logical when you come to editing or sharing them.*

- *Work logically across LR's interface. Start in Library, move to Develop, Map, Book; then go to Slideshow Print and finally Web.*

- *Any adjustments you make to an image can be saved as a Preset, so if you adjust something and like it, create a Preset of that adjustment and in the future you can quickly apply it to any image you wish at the click of the relevant Preset button.*

Lightroom main tools and features

1 Publish services

The publish services panel in the LR Library module allows you to export a collection of photos to your hard drive, or any connected external hard drive. It can be used to export images to a tablet or smartphone and there's built-in integration with social media including Facebook, Behance and Flickr.

2 Catalog

Where your images can be found within the catalogue.

3 Library filter

Used to search images by attribute, image ranking (number of stars), text or metadata, such as the time it was shot or if flash was used.

4 Picture information panels

Panels showing details of each photo selected in the thumbnail view or enlarged into the main Library window.

5 Quick develop

The quick develop tool in LR's Library module lets you do fast global image editing, such as image colour tweaks and tone changes to a single image or a group of images without leaving the Library module. Ideal if the image(s) just need a minor fix rather than more detailed work.

6 Image bin

A scrollable list of images in the current folder.

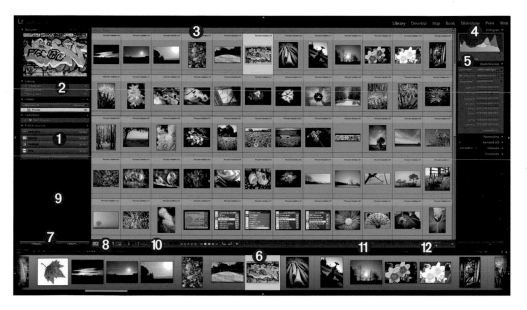

7 Import/export buttons

Buttons that allow you to import or export images into or out of the catalogue.

8 Screen modes

Buttons that change the screen options and the way the thumbnails are presented.

9 Picture folders

An alphabetical list of all your images and folders of images within the open catalogue appears here.

10 Sort

A button to sort your images by time (as shown here) or by name.

11 Image ranking

A method of ranking images by stars or coloured 'flags' to help you sort the wheat from the chaff.

12 Resize thumbnail slider

A slider that allows you to enlarge or shrink the size of the thumbnails being viewed.

Lightroom 5: The main modules

We have already looked at the Lightroom (LR) Library module on the previous pages. Library module is used to organise and preview your images, slide shows, videos, print tasks or websites you may be building. It's the first port of call when you launch the program and lets you import and sort images by ranking them using colour labels or stars and to apply quick edits if more detailed work is not required. But what do the other modules do? Let's take a look at them.

The **Develop module** allows you to apply edits and effects filters to your images either one at a time or in a batch. The module is split into three main areas. The image being edited is in the middle, while the main filters and effects that can be applied are ranged down the left side (called presets). If you want to add a global edit, for example, make a colour image black and white, then you can choose one of these presets. Hover your mouse over a preset, preview the effect in the thumbnail in the top left corner and, if you like it, click the preset and it is applied to the image. On the right side are the main tools for more detailed manual edits, including various brushes (such as cloning and healing), colour tools, and exposure and image parameter adjustments, such as white balance, sharpness, exposure and saturation. All these edits can be done at the click of a button or by moving a slider for more or less of the required effect.

The **Map module** uses reverse geocoded GPS data from your images (if shot on a smartphone or GPS-enabled camera). The GPS location data is sent anonymously to Google, and then, when you switch to the Map module, the location of any images with GPS data are indicated by a small orange pin on the map. If there is more than one image taken at the same location, the pin contains a number indicating how many images were taken there. Clicking on the pin reveals the photos in a small scrollable pop-up screen and running across the bottom of the Map module.

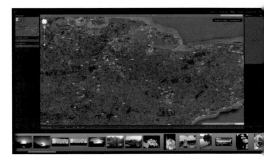

The **Book module** allows you to pick images from your library and build a photobook-style album and get it printed, all from within the LR interface. You pick your images from collections on the left side and use the preset layouts (or create new layouts of your own) on the right side, choosing the number of images per page, whether you want to add

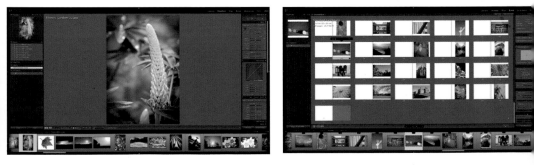

text, zoom or fit images and so on. Once your book is complete, you can export it to Blurb (in the UK), a photobook printer or export it as a PDF (to take and print anywhere you wish, or to share, or save it as a JPEG file as well).

The **Slideshow module** works in a similar way to the Book module in that you can build a slide show of your images and videos in your library, and then export them to share on-line or as HDTV slide shows to play on compatible TVs or on your computer, tablet or smartphone. You can add sound and effects, intro screens and end credits. As with all LR modules, there are built-in presets to get you started but you can adapt and change them to create your own or download them from the Internet too.

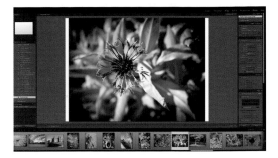

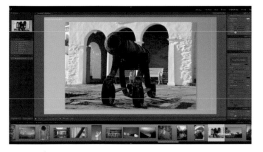

The **Print module** provides a set of predefined templates from which you can print your images, reached from the left-hand side of the module's screen. You can print contact sheets at the click of a template preset or a standard set of prints, from 6x4 to large formats. You can manually create (or change) the preset layout options using the tools on the right side of the interface, from the printed image dimensions to adding borders or logos and copyright information. Output can be sent to your printer directly or you can print as a JPEG file from the template you've created, making it portable for printing elsewhere.

LR's **Web module** provides a set of website templates ranged down the left side of the screen, with any user-created templates housed below. Websites can be built quickly, by picking the collection of images from your library and clicking on a template. LR builds a web gallery and you can preview it in your web browser by clicking the Preview in Browser button at the bottom left.

A choice of five layout 'styles' can be selected at the top right or you can search for more by clicking the 'Find More Galleries Online...' button. Key information can be adjusted too, such as the website's name, description and colours, or you could add identity plates should you be making a site for your company, for example.

Again LR does all the hard work, generating the HTML or Flash processing, leaving you to upload the site to the Internet (assuming you already have a web host) or export it to your computer to upload later.

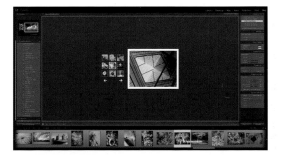

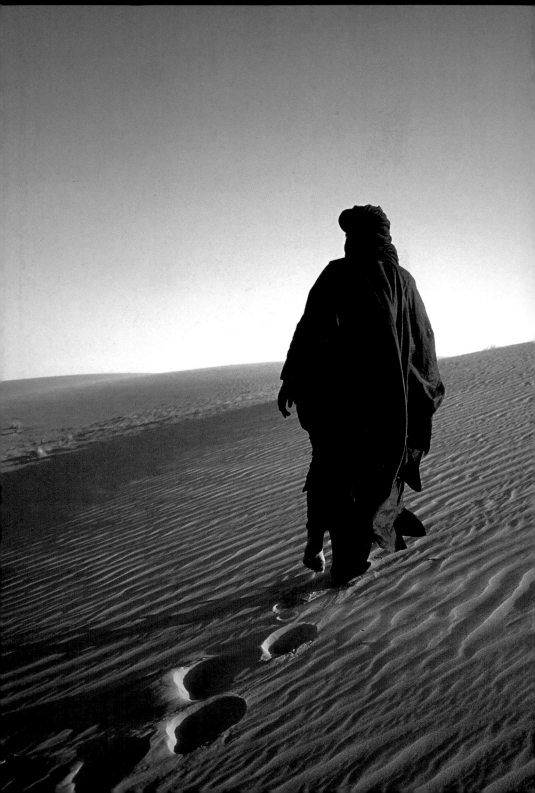

Output

In this section, you'll find all you need to know about how and where to output your pictures, including:

- **Printing** – how to get the best results

- **On-line** – email or build a website of your pictures

- **Backing-up** – send your files to secure storage

- **Slide shows** – display a picture collection on-screen or on TV

- **Scanning** – output your old prints into the digital realm

- **Making money** – with an on-line or traditional portfolio

Backing-up

If you keep all your images on your PC, one computer problem could wipe out your entire picture collection. Here's how to keep it safe.

Saving your images onto additional storage should be an automatic task. You should consider all your data as vulnerable and ensure you back-up regularly.

Software packages are available, often bundled with external hard disks or as part of your computer's operating system (OS), which allow for fast and easy automated back-ups.

A typical back-up window. It shows when, where and what items have been selected for backing-up. Some files are designated for daily back-ups, while others will be backed-up on a weekly or monthly basis. You can check the status of back-ups by checking the back-up logs, ensuring everything is saved properly.

It is vital to keep your data well organised on your computer when using any back-up strategy. Save files with relevant and logical names or by date (or both) so you know where everything is.

Manual back-ups

Manually copying your data, without the aid of software, is the simplest way to make a back-up, either to another hard drive or PC or to a disc.

You can back up manually or with a schedule to CDs, DVDs and Blu-ray discs, as long as you have a CD/DVD/Blu-ray writer. The biggest difference from using built-in back-up is that you'll need to be on hand to change the discs if they fill up before all the data is written to them. A CD holds 700MB of data, a DVD can store 4.7GB, while a Blu-ray can hold more than 50GB, so use a writable disc with enough space or be on hand to swap discs as they fill up.

Built-in back-up

All computers, both PCs and Macs, come with a back-up system within their OS, although Windows XP Home Edition is a bit more complex and requires you to install back-up software from the discs that came with your PC. Windows 7 and Vista use Backup and Restore (see below) and Mac's Time Machine is a very straightforward system. Windows 8 offers an even easier way to back up, called File History. Turn it on manually the first time you use it and then, after that, it automatically backs up your files every hour, as long as you have an external hard drive connected to the computer.

Windows Backup and Restore

Backup and Restore creates copies of your most important data. It can choose what to back up automatically, or you can select the folders, files and drives, or even DVDs to use yourself. You can schedule back-ups to suit you and then let it do its stuff.

Step 1:
To back up your files, open 'backup and restore' by clicking the 'start' button, then **Control Panel > System and Maintenance > Backup and Restore**.

Step 2:

Next, do one of the following:

1. If you've never used Windows Backup before, click 'set up backup' and follow the back-up wizard that appears.

2. If you've created a back-up before, simply wait for your regularly scheduled back-up to occur, or manually create a new back-up by clicking 'backup now'.

To Create a New, Full Back-up

Once you've created your back-up, Windows Backup will then add new or changed information to your subsequent back-ups. If saving your back-ups on an external hard drive or network location, Windows Backup will automatically create a new, full back-up for you when needed.

If saving your back-ups on CDs or DVDs, you'll need to stay around to make sure you

---

ℹ Back-up hints

● *Back-ups should be performed on a regular basis. The frequency depends upon the maximum acceptable (to you) amount of work that would be lost in the event of a catastrophe!*

● *Various simple back-up software packages can be downloaded from the Internet, but these tend to be time-limited (usually lasting about 30 days) so you get to try before you buy. Once the trial period is over, you'll be left without a back-up process again unless you're ready to pay.*

● *You may find any external hard disk you buy comes complete with a back-up utility of its own that can save you money. Use it if you don't have anything else, as they are normally robust enough for most 'home' uses.*

ℹ Back-up to external hard disk

Probably the most common way to back-up your data is to use a high-capacity external hard disk. This is because with such a disk you can set up a back-up protocol that happens automatically – so you don't have to remember to do it! And because you don't have to intervene to change disks (as with a CD or DVD back-up) it is very convenient. One drawback is that the external hard disk can crash, so you may still need another strategy to back-up its data.

---

can change them as they fill up. If you can't find an existing back-up disc, or if you want to create a new back-up of all of the files on your computer, you can create a new full back-up. Here's how to do it:

Open 'backup and restore' by clicking the 'start' button, then click **Control Panel › System and Maintenance › Backup and Restore**. In the left dialogue box that appears, click 'create new full backup'. It's worth noting that you will only see this option if your back-up is being saved on CDs or DVDs.

Off-site back-up and the 'Cloud'

The best back-up solution is an off-site back-up (your data's safe even if your house burns down), so here's information on two ways to do it.

1. Buy an on-line service – CrashPlan (shown overleaf) is a good example. It charges monthly fees for its software, which continually backs up your data when your PC is on. Data is stored on CrashPlan's computers, so should the worst happen, you can restore your data over the Internet or via 'seed' discs; you can add multiple computers to the system too, and your data is encrypted, so it cannot be recovered by anyone other than you.

CrashPlan (and similar systems) offer a free back-up option, allowing you to share a friend or family member's spare disc space over the Internet; they back-up to your spare disc space and vice versa.

2. Buy on-line storage. On-line storage is another good off-site back-up solution, such as MozyHome, Rackspace or DropBox. Each provides a modest amount (typically around 2GB) of inexpensive or free storage and you pay a yearly or monthly fee for more space if required. You use a folder on your PC for the data to be backed up, which synchronises with their computer servers. One benefit with this option is that your data is available anywhere with an Internet connection and you can 'sync up' multiple devices.

Network Attached Storage

Network Attached Storage (NAS) is an external hard disk connected to your network (wirelessly or via an Ethernet cable) to which you can transfer your data. It's always available to all your PCs too. You can use it as a back-up or simply as additional external storage.

Remember ...

There are a few other pointers to keep in mind to help you with your backing-up routines:

- Use an off-site back-up for critical data: then even if the worst happens, your critical data is safely stored elsewhere. This is great for a small business or anyone working from home.

- Always check with your Internet service provider (ISP) about offsite back-ups as it might include its own 'Cloud' back-up provision as part of its service.

- Remember to check with your ISP whether there are data transfer limits (or so-called bandwidth). Some Internet services have

i

Scheduled back-ups

'Set a schedule and stick to it' is the maxim you should always use for all backing-up. If you're disciplined enough and you can remember all the steps to a good back-up, say once each week, then great. If not, use a scheduled back-up (see Backing up with Windows earlier in this chapter).

If using other back-up software, follow the steps to set up a back-up schedule in that software's wizard, or read the software manual if it lacks a wizard.

maximum data limits above which you will have to pay an extra charge; on-line back-up services can use a large slice of your data quota because they run continually in the background.

- Consider NAS drives if you have more than one PC (or device) connected to a WiFi network at home or plugged into your Internet router. It saves on space and money as you need only buy one larger NAS disk, rather than multiple additional storage for each PC you have.

The CrashPlan back-up system is just one of many 'Cloud' or on-line back-up services available, making secure off-site back-up fast and convenient. The interface shows the items being backed-up, where they are stored and their progress.

Printing and scanning

You can print stunning images from your digital photos and from scanned prints, slides or negatives. Here's how.

As well as printing out digital photos at home on a photo-quality printer, if you have a scanner you can also make new prints from negatives, slides or even old prints.

Printing your photos at home

Obviously this requires you to have your own printer. If you don't have one but want the convenience of printing at home, you'll find all the buying advice you need in the topic *Which printer?* Let's get started with a few printer basics.

First make sure the printer's software (or driver) is installed on your computer. This should happen automatically when you first set up your printer. **File > Open** the image to print in your image editing software and go to **File > Print**. Pick the paper and print size you need and click the print button. A new dialogue box will appear which allows you to change the printer settings. Ensure you have the correct paper type

(many inkjets do this automatically) and colour options in the drop-down menus. You can preview your print job. Set the print resolution and hit print again – the print job will start.

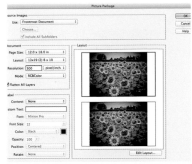

The image size box allows adjustment of the output resolution (the document size) without altering the pixel dimensions.

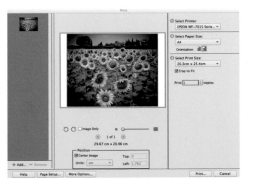

The print preview allows paper and print size selection; the software does all the working-out for your chosen settings.

A picture package dialogue box. This lets you select the number of images to be printed together on a single sheet of paper. Clicking on one of the image thumbnails lets you browse to another image if you want a variety of images to be printed together.

Printing on-line

On-line photo printing is very popular, with dedicated photo-printing websites easily accessed from all over the globe. Using them is fairly straightforward and inexpensive; you either email in your images or upload them via the website. You pay on-line with either a debit or credit card; some sites accept PayPal payments too, if you have a PayPal account. The photos are sent to you in the post. Make sure you use a service that is based in your country, though!

Ideally you'll need a broadband Internet connection (otherwise uploads will take too long). Such sites usually have virtual photo album functionality, where you can upload images and store them on-line – although there may be a charge for this. Incidentally, this on-line storage may offer you a neat off-site back-up, since you could upload all your images if you wanted to. Then you can email links to the images for friends and family to view.

Printing in shops

There are many retail outlets where you can take your memory card to print out images quickly and cheaply, in the same way you used to drop off your films. Some shops have print kiosks where you insert the memory card and follow on-screen prompts to select and print the photos yourself.

However, whether you use a kiosk or an over-the-counter service, remember one thing: if you print everything on the memory card but don't have a back-up (say a CD of the images) then you will lose all the original images forever if your card is later reformatted in your camera. So always have a CD made *and* get prints if you don't have a computer at home. That way, you can take the CD into the shop for more prints and you never have to worry about losing images.

Using the right paper

There are many types of paper (or media) available for inkjet printers, and they come in a range of sizes (A4 or A3, for example) or on rolls.

Using the right paper is essential – you cannot get a photo-quality print on plain paper, for example. On photo paper, the paper and ink work together to give the best possible effect and to help make the print last a long time. Here's a quick run-down of what to look for and when to use each type.

- **Plain Media:** Use plain paper only for printing letters or basic graphics and text, not for photographs.

- **Photo Media:** Photo paper comes in glossy and matt finishes and is the best paper to use for photo-quality output as it is designed to make the most of every droplet of ink and to boost colour.

- **Transfer (or T-Shirt) Media:** A speciality media for printing images that can then be transferred, to a T-shirt, for example, using a hot iron.

- **High Resolution Media:** Ideal for graphics and text (say a display banner) where perfectly smooth edges to text and colours are essential for a good impression.

- **Transparency Media:** Transparent media designed for presentations using overhead projectors, for example.

- **Speciality Media:** There are many types of textured or special finish papers available that can add a canvas look and feel to a print, ideal for framing or 'art' shots.

- **Speciality Inks:** You can also buy special inks such as dedicated black-and-white inks to get neutral black-and-white prints without odd colour casts.

Get the best from your printer

To ensure perfect prints (or the print output you're expecting!) follow these tips.

- Make sure the paper selection in the printer set-up dialogue box matches the paper you're printing on. If you choose plain paper but load photo-quality paper, the printed result will be very poor. However, many new printers automatically detect the paper and set the printer accordingly, unless you override it in the printer set-up box.

- Inkjets can print at very high-resolution settings that are slow to print and can use a lot of expensive ink. To save ink (and time), use the lowest print resolution that's acceptable for the job at hand. A few test prints may be needed to ascertain these settings. Make a note of them for each paper type or print job (or save the settings for reuse if your software allows), and then you won't have to experiment each time.

- You can alter the print size without changing the image's dimensions (see also **Resizing**) by altering its resolution in the **Image › Size** dialogue box. A resolution of 300dpi is best, but don't go below 180dpi or the print quality will be poor. The lower the output dpi, the larger the print will become, which you can check in the print preview window prior to printing.

- Some image editing software can automatically create picture packages, ideal if you want more than one copy of a photo. The program does all the resizing and other changes so you can print many images on one sheet of paper. This can be great when you want a contact sheet of lots of photos to review off-screen.

Get the best from your scanner

It is important to scan at a setting adequate for the intended output. In other words, if you want to make an A4 photo print, you'll need to scan the original at a setting that provides enough information for a good print at that size. Getting this right saves time and memory space as it is easy to create scanned images of hundreds of megabytes if you're not careful. These will take ages to scan and there will be far more image data than you need to make the print. The optimal resolution to scan at for print is 300ppi; 72ppi is sufficient for on-screen display. Here's a quick guide to the (approximate) file sizes you should make for various tasks.

Scans for inkjet photo printing
- For A3 (or larger) prints: 25MB (at least and with compatible printers)
- For A4 prints: 18MB
- For 10x8-inch prints: 10MB
- For 4x6-inch prints: 8MB
- For 3x5-inch prints: 5MB

Scans for email and Internet use
- For use on screen/web only: 480x320 pixels, around 0.5MB
- For email to print out: 960x640 pixels, around 1MB
- It's worth noting, many email programs can automatically resize larger images if you add them as attachments. Refer to your email program's help feature to check.

Creating **slide shows**

A great way to display your photo collection is as a slide show on-screen or even on your TV.

Creating a slide show is simple with easy-to-use slide show creation software. Once created, you can show it on the Internet or on your TV, or save it to a CD or DVD. There's a wide range of such software available. A quick Internet search reveals hundreds of websites with slide show software (some free to use, some demo versions and some shareware). Most packages provide Hollywood-style effects and transitions and even allow you to add music.

Building the slide show

Although Apple's iMovie software has been used here for illustration purposes, the slide show creation process is essentially the same for most slide show packages (though you will need to check the documentation that comes with your software for the exact process you'll need to use). Once you know what to do, you can begin.

Step 1:

Having launched your software, you will need to create a slide show project. You can pick a theme to use (in this case Photo Album) and click on the **Create** button to get things rolling.

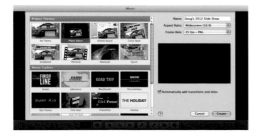

Step 2:

Go the folder or disc holding your slide show images and drag and drop your pictures into the work space (shown at top left in the image below). Keep dragging them into the work space until you have them all in situ and ready.

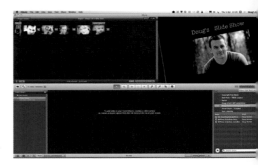

Step 3:

Add transitions, music, special effects, text and other fun effects, which are accessed from the menu at the bottom right of the screen. Musical tracks can be added simply by dragging the relevant music track from your collection of MP3 files into the same photo work space where your images are placed. Some packages may require you to add audio separately to the images, however.

Step 4:

Once you've done the adjustments and added all the images, music, transitions and effects that your slide show requires, preview it to make sure it looks exactly how you want by clicking the **Preview** button.

```
File  Edit  Clip  View  Text  Sha
  New Project...                    ⌘N
  New Folder...
  New Event
  Duplicate Project
  Import from Camera...             ⌘I
  Import                             ▶
  Project Properties...             ⌘J
  Project Theme...                 ⇧⌘J
  Convert to Project
  Finalize Project
  Move to Trash                    ⌘⌫
  Move Rejected Clips to Trash
  Space Saver...
  Consolidate Media...
  Merge Events...
  Split Event Before Selected Clip
  Adjust Clip Date and Time...
  Analyze Video                      ▶
  Optimize Video                     ▶
  Page Setup...                    ⇧⌘P
  Print Project...                  ⌘P
```

Step 5:

When you're happy with
it, you can get the slide
show ready for export
and viewing. In iMovie,
you click the **Finalise**
button from within the file
menu (shown), but your
software may just ask
you to 'export' it. Then all
the images and music are
processed and prepared to
create the final slide show.

Step 6:

Once (in this case) finalised,
the slide show is ready to
view and share. In iMovie,
and most other slide show
packages, you can send the
slide show to YouTube or
Facebook. Alternatively, you
can either send it to be burnt
to disc or simply export it
ready to burn later.

```
Share  Window  Help
  Media Browser...
  iTunes...
  iDVD...
  MobileMe Gallery...
  YouTube...
  Facebook...
  Vimeo...
  CNN iReport...
  Podcast Producer...
  Export Movie...              ⌘E
  Export using QuickTime...
  Export Final Cut XML...
  Remove from                   ▶
```

Step 7:

Finally, the export dialogue here shows that the
slide show will be exported as a 720P HD movie to
the Movies folder on to the computer's hard drive.

Export and save your slide show

Some slide show programs
allow you to burn directly
from the software in which
you built the show. Follow the
on-screen guide (or wizard)
once you hit the burn button
or similar control, such as an
'export to disc' command. It
will send your assembled slide
show data to the burner.

Alternatively, the show needs
to be exported and then burnt
to disc separately after it's been
created.

Adding the photo files

Some slide show programs allow
you to add the original image
files to the disc in addition to
the slide show versions of the
image. This is a great way of
giving family members their own
copy of the images, useful if
they wish to make some prints
for example. You must have
room on the disc to be able to
do this, however, and if you
have a large show, it's unlikely
that it will all fit on a CD. Use a
DVD instead.

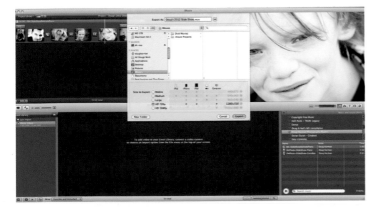

Emailing photos

Email is one of the fastest ways to get your latest shots to friends and family. Here are a few tips to make it work better for you and them.

To get your photos ready for emailing to friends and family, the most important consideration is the image's file size. Not everyone has broadband Internet access so sending large files by email may just jam up their system and make it expensive for them to download the pictures.

As some recipients may want to print the photos, while others just like to look at the images on screen, you can adapt the image sizes you send accordingly.

Many email programs can now resize images automatically – check your system to see how it is implemented.

Resize the images

As we've already seen in the *Resizing* topic earlier in the book, it's a straightforward process to resize the images ready for email. Let's begin by looking at the 'start' size for an image you might want to share via email.

Checking image size

To check the picture's dimensions, open the image and use the **Image › Resize Image** command. In this case, the shot to be emailed is a 15MB file at 300ppi with 27x13cm dimensions. This is far too large to email.

Emailing for screen viewing

To resize this image to both a reasonable size in terms of viewing the image, and also a file size small enough for emailing, first check the 'resize' button in the resize

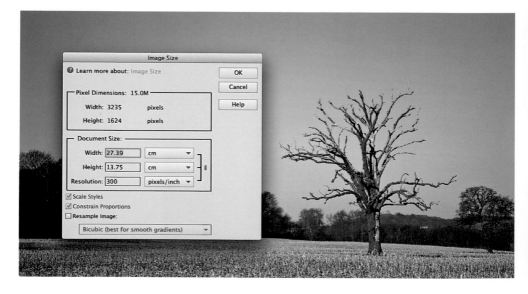

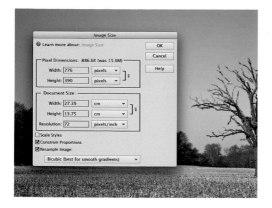

image dialogue box. Change the 300ppi setting to 72ppi (as above), the default resolution for computer screen viewing. Now the file size has plummeted to only 886KB and the pixel dimensions have dropped to 776x390 pixels. However, the document size is untouched.

Finally, **File > Save As** the image using a JPEG compression level of about 5 in the dialogue box that appears. This will provide a small email file without harsh compression, preserving image quality.

Emailing for printing

With the same image as an example, go through the exact same process but this time, instead of changing the ppi figure, adjust the pixel dimensions. An image set

to around 900 pixels on its longest edge (and left at 300ppi) will provide an image that has enough data for a decent 6x4-inch photo print and yet it will produce a file small enough to email. If you wanted to resize slightly larger for a bigger print, adjust the pixel dimensions higher or type in the size you want in the document size boxes, keeping an eye on the pixel dimension's file size so it does not get too large to send by email.

The 1.22MB file this has created (below left) must be saved using the **File > Save As** routine again, but this time you can adjust the JPEG compression in order to suit the Internet connection speed at the recipient's end. If they're using a dial-up modem, use a JPEG setting of around 2, but if they have broadband then a setting of 7 should suffice. Of course, you can successfully email the unaltered image if required with broadband connections, assuming it's not hundreds of megabytes in size!

Sending the email

Once the image has been successfully resized, you can send the email using your standard email software. Compose and write the email in the normal way and then drag and drop the image (or images) into the message as an attachment. Or you can click on the add button to browse the computer's hard disk to find the photos you require. Click 'choose' to select the pictures, which then appear in your newly composed email as attachments. Your email can now be sent as usual.

If you use a web-based email client, such as those provided by Yahoo or Gmail, the process is the same. In the case of Gmail, you click the paperclip icon at the foot of the compose window, and then browse to the images you want to attach in the same way as described above.

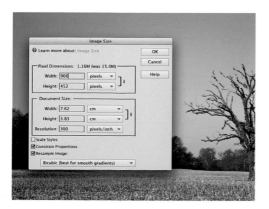

Getting your photos **on-line**

Putting your images on the Internet is an ideal way to showcase your pictures or create a themed website. And it can be much less technical than you might think.

You don't have to let your images languish on your computer's hard disk: you can share them with others via the Internet. It's easy enough to put your images on the web by building your own web gallery (as discussed below), through sites such as Flickr and Facebook or by blogging (as discussed later in the chapter).

You won't have to learn any special programming languages. Most image editing software comes with an automated web gallery building function and on-line photo sharing sites take you through the process step by step.

Constructing a web gallery
Building your own web gallery of images allows you to both publish a growing on-line portfolio and use it as a shop window for your work. You may want to shoot

photographs for pleasure, you may want to build a library of work on a specific photo project or for a local club's activities, or you might want to sell your images as art-style prints. Either way, a web gallery can be a great way to publish your work to the world.

The latest version of Elements uses Adobe's Revel image sharing platform, which allows you to create and share what Adobe calls private web albums and all without the need to have a specific website already set up to add them to. This makes it easier to share your images with others and across all your devices such as smartphones or tablets.

Private web album creation
You can use the private web album sharing feature of Photoshop Elements to create and share galleries of images via email or on the internet, as well as sharing images directly

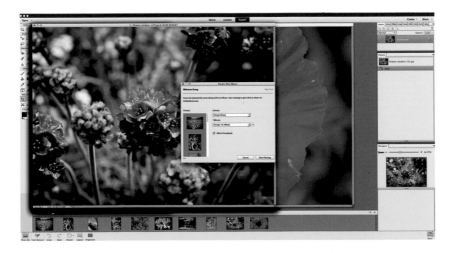

to Flickr, Twitter and Facebook (which we'll expand on overleaf). Follow these steps.

Step 1:

With the images you wish to share open in the Editor, click the **Share** drop-down as shown here and choose the **Private Web Album** option. If you have not shared anything with Revel before, you'll need to authorise Elements to work with it; follow the on-screen instruction to sign in (as shown below left) or create your Revel account, and then you can get posting galleries on-line.

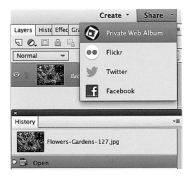

The finished gallery can be viewed in your web browser; click an image or view it in a slide show in the browser. You can download images too, direct from your browser, and view your galleries across all your mobile devices and other computers.

Step 2:

In the private web album dialogue choose your library (it'll make one for you if you've not done so before) and create an album name that you will upload to. If you need to create a new album, click on the plus (+) button next to the album drop-down menu and type a new album name. To remove individual images from the collection being uploaded, click the minus symbol (-) below them in the preview area that appears. If you want to let people download the images from the shared gallery, click the **Allow Downloads** check box. Finally, click **Start Sharing**.

Step 3:

When your selected images have all uploaded, a 'success' box appears with two links: a URL which you can click to view the uploaded photos in your web browser; and an email link. Click this link to start composing a

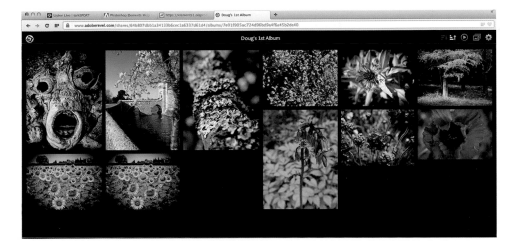

new email containing the URL link to the uploaded album and you can then send your shared image gallery. If the 'Allow Downloads' check box was ticked, as well as browsing, those viewing the gallery will be able to download images directly from the gallery too.

Social media and blogging

There are also other routes to getting images on-line, from dedicated photo-sharing sites such as Flickr – where you can email links of your image albums to your friends, family and other photographers – to popular social networking sites. You simply need an Internet connection.

If you choose to do so, you can share images via Flickr, Twitter or Facebook from your editing software, in this case Elements, by choosing the relevant option from the **Share** drop-down menu. Instead of sharing via the Revel system, you'll be asked to log into or 'authorise' the sharing service you have chosen, and the images will be published there instead.

Flickr

This popular photography social media website is run by Yahoo. You can upload and share images and videos, creating a 'photostream' of your work. Anyone from around the world visiting Flickr will be able to view your images.

Once you've created an account, Flickr makes it easy for you to upload your chosen photos. It launches a window that allows you to browse your PC to find the pictures you want to share. Flickr accepts a variety of image types (TIFF and PNG, for example) but it's advisable to upload JPEG images. (JPEG images are best for the web as they can be highly compressed yet retain good quality.) You can choose to make your photos 'private' (visible to friends and family only, for example) or 'public' (for all to see).

Once uploaded, you can do many things with your images to enhance your Flickr

Advanced Flickr tips

- *You can send images to Flickr groups you join (or who invite you to join them); these are groups of people who are, for example, taking similar images to you. This all helps increase your photography's exposure to the whole Flickr community or simply to others who you'd like to view your images.*

- *Via the 'print and create' link you can create projects to print as normal prints, or select products to have your images printed on.*

- *Although it's best to edit and enhance your images on your PC, you can also edit images on Flickr using Picnik. Click the 'edit photo' button on the chosen picture, agree to allow Picnik to open inside your Flickr and you're ready to go.*

experience. Clicking on Flickr's 'organize and create' feature allows you to access a new set of tools, via the 'batch organize' window, enabling you to get creative with your images. 'Edit photos', for example, allows you to delete or manipulate images: rotating them, adjusting the name of the photo and adding a description if you wish. If there are people in the picture, you can add their name or email address. Flickr also lets you create 'sets': groups of photos organised by themes of your choice, for example, portraits.

You can also add a 'tag', which is a way to group photos by a keyword so that images of a certain type can be quickly searched for. A simple example would be the tag 'tree', which when searched on Flickr would bring up images of trees from your photostream, from your contacts' streams, or from everyone's, depending on the selection you make for the search. The benefit is that it helps you and other Flickr users to quickly find images of a particular sort.

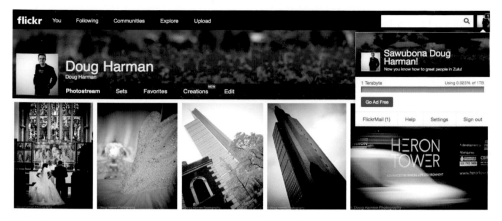

Flickr allows you to upload and share your images with a like-minded photographic community across the globe.

Flickr is often used as a resource by publications looking for good pictures to publish, so good photos, tags, naming and descriptions of your photos might even lead to a picture getting published.

Facebook and Twitter

In case you've missed the social media revolution, Twitter and Facebook are two extremely popular social media tools. Twitter allows you to post images, video and 140-character texts (sometimes called micro-blogging) to friends, family and members of the public that have decided to follow your Twitter updates. Twitter is also good for discovering and 'following' photographers you admire to gather inspiration. Facebook is more of a personal web space tailored to sharing images and content with friends and family who you have allowed to see your page. Facebook allows readers to 'like' what you do too, raising awareness among the people who follow you.

Flickr and Facebook are great for building a network of like-minded photographers, because you can set up your own specific Flickr group or Facebook page on your project or area of photographic interest. Both are good ways to get noticed, build an audience or make contact with other photographers.

Blogging

A blog is a personal web page made by you, formed by placing your own content into a pre-made template, and can be the perfect platform to showcase your work. You can create and write an on-line diary or a gallery of your pictures, since they can easily be uploaded to a blog.

The simplest method is to use a blogging website. There are many available – good examples are Blogger, WordPress, Squarespace or Typepad.

The main differences between using a blogging service such as Blogger, or creating your own WordPress site or blog, is that Blogger tends to be used with simple content that forms a chronological set of articles or images that you 'blog' to the world. WordPress, while essentially a blogging platform, uses an interface that allows you to build an entire website using simple 'widgets' and menus. Its flexibility as a platform (over something more basic such as Blogger) allows you to build and grow either a simple blog or a full-blown website.

With a blogging website you can give your blog a look and feel to match your content by choosing from a number of templates. After you have done the basic set-up, you can customise your pages by giving your blog a headline. You can then begin to post your blogs, either typing text or cutting and pasting text into the blog from another document.

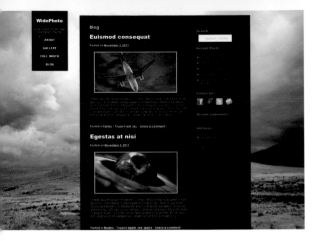

Wordpress offers free photography blog templates such as this, which enable you to view your images at full-screen size (inset).

Uploading images is simple and you can adjust the image size and position on the page too.

You can use your blog to create a photo diary of anything from your favourite holiday photos to a special photo-project you may be doing. Blogging can seem less public than using Facebook or Twitter because it's up to you whether you share it with others, but it fulfils a similar role and effectively gives you your own small website that is unique to you at little or no cost.

Once your blog is up and running, there is more you can do to enhance it, and perhaps even make a little money.

Automatic website software

Once you are an accomplished photographer and would like to develop your professional image, you may want to build your own website. There are various free programs you can download from the Internet that allow you to build simple but professional-looking websites of your images. While such programs are free (you can donate money to the developers if you wish), they contain adverts for the software developer that must always be displayed on any site you make. WebPlus is one (www.freeserifsoftware. com) and another is called SimpleViewer (www.airtightinteractive.com). Both are easy to use and are effective ways of publishing your images on-line.

ⓘ Making the most of your blog

- *You can generate money from your blog by clicking the 'monetize' link on the Blogger settings page. This links to Google's AdSense scheme, whereby ads are placed on your blog that are related to the content (Google checks your blog automatically for content). You can make money when visitors to your blog click on the adverts.*

- *As your blog grows in popularity, people who visit it regularly can, if they so choose, become 'followers', which means they can quickly get updates of your blog via their Google, Twitter, Yahoo or AIM, NetLog and OpenID accounts.*

- *By setting your blog to allow email links, visitors can quickly email your latest blog updates and images to their friends and contacts, which helps get more people to see your images faster and helps the blog grow and the money to flow.*

- *Do update your blog regularly to keep visitors coming back for more. Frequent updates also ensure your blog rises in search listings. All this helps to build popularity and traffic and, of course, money – if that is of particular importance to you.*

Making a **portfolio**

If you're serious about your photography, particularly if you want to sell your images, you'll need to compile a professional portfolio of work.

Creating a portfolio of images is not just a matter of getting all your images together and printing them or putting them on a website. If you intend to make any money, you'll need to cherry-pick the very best of your images and use only those. Being critical is essential as competition is fierce, and unless you focus on your best shots, you're unlikely to succeed. An Internet or on-disc portfolio is a must, but you also need to have a high-quality print portfolio.

Print portfolio
You'll need to get your very best images printed using high-quality photo output and ideally at a large enough size to give the viewer a good impression of what can be achieved with them. Print no smaller than A4 on fade-resistant photo paper and buy a good quality portfolio folder with sleeves to house the prints. Beware: less expensive portfolios often use plastic pages that leak chemicals and can damage your prints over time.

If you have stunning images that you might want to sell or hope to make money from, a portfolio – on-line and print – will be required.

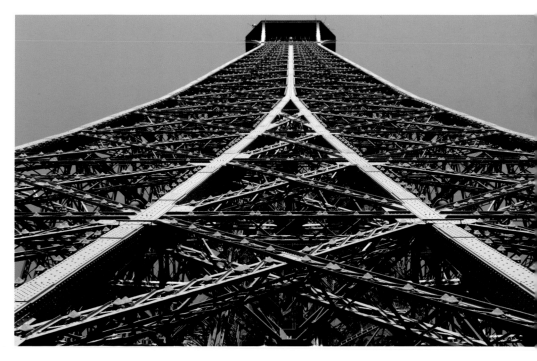

On-line and on-disc portfolios

You'll need to put your portfolio on the Internet (see *Getting your photos on-line*) or on disc (see *Creating slide shows*). Ensure each image is annotated with its technical details, and that the slide show is made at the highest quality possible. Sacrifice the number of images in a show to ensure high quality. It's better to have numerous discs than all the images crammed as low-resolution files onto just one.

Organise all the images by content type: architecture, landscapes, portraits, animals, etc. This makes relevant images easier to find. If you don't have the software to do this, consider getting the portfolio made professionally. Scrimping here could cost you money in the end.

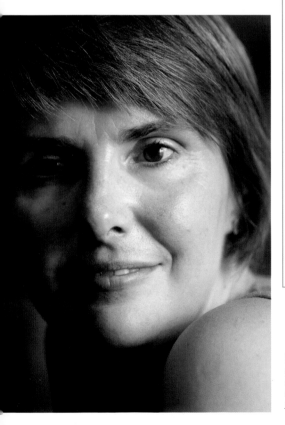

Portraits such as this can be an ideal way to start building a portfolio from your images. Practise on family and friends to help hone your skills and get the perfect photo for the portfolio you're building.

i Including image information

There are key details that should always be associated with your images in any portfolio. Some may seem unnecessary, but all are, in fact, vital. Magazine editors, for instance, are likely to require detailed text information for captions and if it is supplied with the image already it saves them time, making them more likely to use your image over someone else's.

- **Copyright information:** *Include your name and contact details with each image. On prints NEVER write on the back of the print itself. Use special stickers or frame the shots in card borders (from art shops) and include the details on that. Digital images can have the details automatically appended with each image which can then be viewed as the image is displayed.*

- **Image technical data:** *For digital images the shutter speed, focal length, sensitivity setting, image dimensions, file size and lens aperture should all be included. All this information is to be found within the image EXIF data, using your image editing software.*

- **Date and location:** *Include the date the image was made and the location where it was taken or what's in the shot. If you can geotag your image it might be useful.*

Making **money**

Making money from your photography is more achievable than you might think.

Gaining income from your photographs doesn't always mean you'll need professional camera gear and the expense that goes with it. Today, the fastest route to getting your images to market is via the Internet.

But if you want to make money from your photos, family snaps won't be the type of image people want to buy, and you'll need to shoot images that are less personal and more commercial. It's best to have a commercial target market in mind, and then shoot images that are relevant to it.

If, for instance, you want to get your images into magazines, competitions are good ways to start as this helps to discover what's desirable. The classic tropical beach with palm trees you see in holiday brochures would be an ideal example of an ever-popular shot. Landscapes and architecture are always in demand, particularly if you get a novel angle on the subject. Macro-style images of flowers and plants are good too. But what are the routes to making money that you can consider?

Images such as this shot of Egyptian hieroglyphics are classic shots which can be used time and again, from historical publications to holiday brochures.

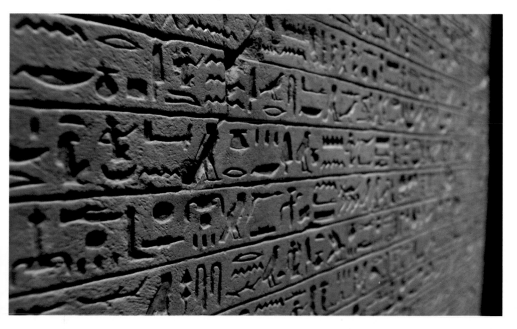

Put your photos on-line

We've already looked at building a website from your images, but if you're going to take this seriously, you'll need to use only the very best of your photos. Eventually you'll need to think about getting a professionally built site, as competition is very stiff. This will cost money but will give you more chance of reaching a wider audience.

Set up an exhibition

An exhibition of your work will raise your profile, but this can be expensive and time-consuming. Look to local businesses such as cafés to see if they would consider hanging framed prints for you with your details on each (there may be a small commission).

Join the professionals

Join your local camera club or a professional photo society. These will offer advice on selling and improving your photography and have connections that will help you get your images out to a wider audience.

Print postcards or calendars

Postcards or calendars of your images are a good way to circulate your photos more widely. However, depending on how many you have printed, the cost can be prohibitive and you'll need to plan in advance who to send them to or where to display them. You could even sell them at local markets.

Join an image library

Image libraries hold photos for many different photographers and act as an agency, selling the use of your images to magazines, for example. You get a fee each time an image is used and the library takes a percentage of that money. Most libraries have websites too. Many image libraries have very specific criteria for the images they want (digital or otherwise and particularly for file size limits), so you'll need to contact them in advance to make sure your images are of the required type and standard.

Timeless images such as this one, shot at the highest possible quality, are best if you want to make money from your photography.

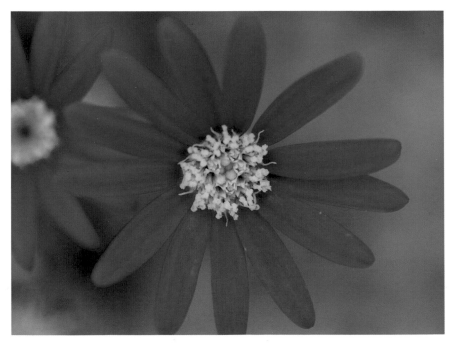

Copyright

You'll need to be aware of copyright issues in our digital age, particularly if you want to sell your photographs.

Copyright is the term describing the law that protects you from the use or abuse of your images by others without your permission. For example, if one of your photos was required for use in a magazine article, the copyright for that image rests with you, the photographer, and the magazine could not use it without a payment to you or your permission to do so.

Anyone who copies or reproduces an image without first paying – or at least getting permission from – the author to do so is said to be breaching the author's copyright. While legal specifics vary from country to country (it's best to check copyright law wherever you sell your work) and can be dependent upon what is negotiated at the time, this is the basic rule of thumb.

This image has the author's name embedded for copyright information, preventing the image being used without payment. This is an ideal tactic for portfolio images off- or on-line. To obtain the image for reproduction, the author must be contacted and the non-marked image then supplied for use.

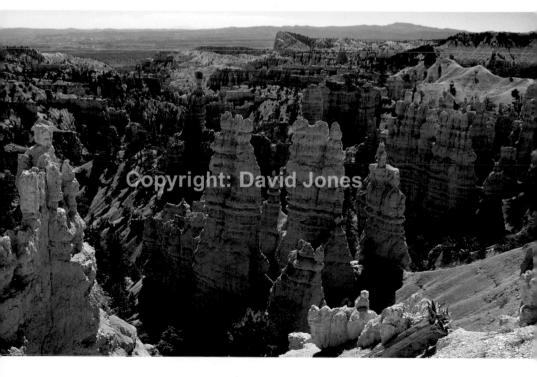

Types of copyright

Some companies might want to buy the entire copyright (called 'all rights') for any image, and this means that from that point on they don't need to pay you again. They have effectively bought the copyright from you and it is theirs to do with as they see fit. Place a higher price on images you sell in this way. Typically, however, most photographers sell 'single-use rights' in their images, which means the photographer retains the copyright and can re-use and re-sell the image repeatedly.

How to get copyrighted

Copyright arises automatically in all works of art, including photography, writing and digital images as they're created. No formal registration is required to receive the basic legal protection this affords in over 140 countries around the world.

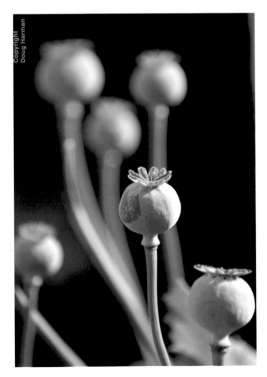

Protecting your images

- While you cannot stop people from downloading your images, you can take precautions to stop them being used elsewhere without payment. Use watermarking technology (it will cost money but embeds a hidden code in the photo which is unique to you and which can be retrieved later using special software) or add your name to the image (as shown below left). This can be done discreetly in a corner of the shot; it's an ideal tactic for portfolios too.

- Ensure any images you put on the Internet are large enough to be viewed at a good size on screen, but small enough in terms of file size to make them useless for printing.

- Watermarking works well on prints too, but you are unable to either reduce the file size or add your name to the print as you can on digital images. You can, however, put a sticker on the reverse of the image with your copyright details. Remember, copying a print (a scan, for example) without payment to you, or your permission, will breach your copyright.

Royalty-free images

These images are photos in which the copyright has been bought outright and which are then assembled, say on a CD, for which there's a charge. These shots can then be used (even commercially in many instances) without incurring another fee to the author for their use. The one-off charge for a royalty-free CD in this example is all that needs to be paid.

If you don't want to 'ruin' an illustrative shot with a big copyright notice, you can also create smaller, less obtrusive text and place it out of the way in a corner of the image as shown here.

Glossary

Aberration Imperfection in an image caused by deficiencies within a lens or optical system.

Ambient Light The natural or available light in a scene.

Aperture The circular opening inside a camera's lens that can change in diameter to control the amount of light reaching the camera's sensor. Apertures are expressed in F-stops; the lower the number, the larger the aperture. For instance, an aperture of F2.8 is larger than one of F8.

App(s) App is short for application and denotes a type of computer program (usually) dedicated to modern tablets and smartphones.

Application A computer program, such as an image editing package or a web browser.

Archival Quality Term used to denote materials having a high degree of permanence. If the longevity of a material (such as printing papers) is said to exceed an acceptable defined time period before starting to degrade, it is said to be of archival quality.

Artefact An unwanted visual aberration within a digital image.

Aspect Ratio The proportions (or ratio) of a picture's width to its height.

Backing-Up Making copies of important computer files in case the originals are damaged and cannot be accessed.

Bit The basic unit of information used in computing. A bit represents a one or a zero, or 'on' or 'off' in a computer.

Blog A blog (a contraction of weB Log) is a type of simple website, usually run and maintained by an individual to post stories, images and commentaries on whatever takes their fancy.

Blu-ray Blu-ray (also known as Blu-ray disc, BD and Blu Ray) is an optical storage disc medium that's set to supersede DVD; its main use is storing high-definition video, video games and other data.

Buffer A memory reservoir built into digital cameras that stores the photos before they are written to the memory card.

Burning (CD/DVD) Creating a copy of your images by electronically saving image files onto an optical disc such as a DVD or CD. (See also Writing)

Burning (image editing)
Selectively darkening part of a photo with an image editing program.

Byte A data 'chunk' made up of eight bits.

Cast The effect of one (unwanted) colour dominating the look of an image. Often caused by exposure errors or incorrect settings of a digital camera's white balance.

CCD Charged coupled device. One of two main types of image sensor (see also CMOS). It is the light-sensitive part of the camera, analogous to the film in older cameras.

CD-R CD-Recordable. A compact disc that holds around 650 to 700MB of digital information. A CD-R disc can only be written once.

CD-ROM Compact disc read-only-memory. A type of CD similar to a normal audio CD but optimised for data storage.

CD-RW CD-Rewritable. Similar to a CD-R, except a CD-RW can be written and erased many times. Suited to back-up tasks, but not long-term storage.

Cloud (Cloud Computing) The Cloud is the generic term for using on-line services and the Internet to store/share data and run Internet-based programs.

CMOS Complementary metal-oxide semiconductor. One of the two main types of image sensors (see CCD above) used in digital cameras.

CMYK Cyan, Magenta, Yellow, Black. The four colours (or ink sets) of many photo-quality printers. Some photo printers use six, seven, eight or more inks to achieve smoother, more photographic prints.

CompactFlash (TYPE I or II)
A common type of digital camera memory card. There are two types of cards, Type I and Type II, varying in thickness. Type I is thinner.

Compression Reducing the file size of digital data files by removing redundant and/or non-critical information within a digital image, helping to maximise storage space.

Contrast The difference between the darkest and lightest areas in a photograph. The greater the difference, the higher the contrast.

Copyright Legal protection against copying and the specific rights allowing copying applying to original works such as photographs. Copyright arises automatically whenever an original work such as a photo is created.

Depth of Field (DOF) The distance between the nearest and farthest points that appear in acceptably sharp focus in a photo. DOF varies with lens aperture, focal length and camera-to-subject distance.

Dodging Selectively lightening part of a photo using image editing software.

Downloading Moving computer data from one location to another. Often used to describe the transfer of data from the Internet or to describe the transfer of photos from a camera to a computer.

dpi Dots per inch. Measurement of the resolution of a digital photo print or digital device such as an inkjet printer. The higher the dpi number, the greater the resolution. (See also ppi)

D-SLR Digital single-lens reflex camera. A lens interchangeable digital camera that allows the scene to be viewed through the lens that will take the photo.

DVD Digital versatile disc. A type of high-capacity optical recording media (similar to CDs) but able to store 4.7 gigabytes of data.

EXIF Exchangeable image file. Image data (such as shutter speed, aperture and ISO) is stored directly in the image file generated by a digital camera. The data can be read by any application that supports JPEG and TIFF file formats, such as web browsers and image editing applications.

Exposure The total amount of light allowed to fall on a digital camera's sensor during the

process of taking a photograph, measured in EV. The higher the EV, the more light there is.

External Flash An accessory flash unit (or flashgun) triggered by the camera or the light from the camera's built-in flash.

Facebook A popular social networking site or on-line community (see also Social Network) allowing individuals or like-minded groups to send messages to other on-line Facebook users sharing images, videos and information.

File A computer document such as an image file.

Fill Flash A flash technique common to most digital cameras used to brighten deep shadow areas, for example, outdoors on sunny days. This mode forces the flash to fire even in bright light.

Filter (photography) A camera accessory made from (usually) optical glass, which is inserted into the optical path to provide a specific effect such as adding an artificial colour.

Filter (software) A software tool that can be used to produce special effects such as sharpening.

Fire Slang term for taking a picture, as in 'fire the shutter'.

FireWire (also known as IEEE 1394) A cabling technology used to transfer data to and from digital devices at high speed as used by many professional digital cameras and memory card readers.

Flickr An image and video hosting website set up with a social network-like structure to create an on-line community of like-minded people and provide image hosting for bloggers. It claims to host over 4 billion images.

Focal Length The distance between the sensor and the optical centre of a lens when that lens is focused on infinity. Focal length is marked in millimetres on the lens (or mount) on those cameras and lenses with adjustable focal lengths.

Formatting The act of writing a file system onto a computer disc or memory card that completely deletes all the previous information and file structure on that disc or card, replacing it with a fresh structure ready for new information. Formatting is the recommended method of clearing a camera's memory card.

F-stop (or F-number) The measure of the size of a camera lens's aperture. The higher the F-stop, the smaller the aperture and vice versa.

Gamut The total range of colours reproduced by a device such as a digital camera.

Geotagging The process of embedding into an image file the GPS coordinates of where the picture was taken. When geotagged images are uploaded to on-line sharing communities such as Flickr, users can search for photos taken in a particular area.

Gif Graphical interchange format file. A bitmap graphical format, ideal for logos, line drawings or images containing solid colours.

Gigabyte (GB) A gigabyte is the amount of memory equal to 1024 megabytes (or 1,073,741,824 bytes) of information.

Greyscale An image made of varying tones of black and white.

HDMI High Definition Multimedia Interface or HDMI is a compact audio and video interface able to transmit raw digital data and is the ideal connection for HDTVs. The latest digital and video cameras capable of shooting HD video have HDMI sockets and can facilitate enhanced features and user controls with compatible equipment.

High Definition High definition (or high-definition video or HDTV [high-definition television]) refers to a video system with a resolution higher than standard definition (which has a 576p resolution), typically with display resolutions of 1280x720 pixels (known as 720p) or 1920x1080 pixels (either 1080i (HD Ready) or 1080p (Full HD)). There are increasing numbers of digital cameras (both compact and D-SLR) able to shoot HD video.

Highlights The brightest parts of a photo.

Histogram A graphic representation of the range of tones from dark to light in a photo. Many digital cameras include a histogram feature facilitating a precise check on the exposure of the photo.

Image Editor A computer program used to alter the appearance of a photo.

Image Resolution The total number of pixels used to make up a digital photo.

Inkjet A type of printer that fires ink droplets onto paper through tiny nozzles.

ISO Sensitivity Digital cameras use the same rating system as was used for film to denote the camera sensor's sensitivity to light. Often a control for adjusting the ISO speed is included; some cameras adjust it automatically depending on the lighting

conditions. The higher the ISO number (100, 200, 400 etc), the more sensitive to light the camera becomes, but as ISO speed climbs, image quality often drops. (See also Noise)

JPEG A standard for compressing image data. A JPEG is not, strictly speaking, a file format; it is a compression method used within a file format (see EXIF). Referred to as a 'lossy' format: some image quality is 'lost' in achieving the JPEG compression.

Kilobyte (KB) A unit of measurement equal to 1000 bytes.

LCD Liquid crystal display. A type of colour screen used on the rear of a digital camera to help with composition and to display the photo once it's taken, and to display setting/control menus.

Megabyte (MB) A measurement of data storage equal to 1024 kilobytes (KB).

Megapixel Equal to one million pixels (or 1MP). The higher the number of megapixels, the higher the resolution of a digital camera is said to be.

Memory Card Generic term for a flash-based storage device for photos and video, such as a CompactFlash card.

Memory Stick A proprietary flash-based storage device developed originally by Sony for digital cameras and other digital devices.

MultiMedia Card A type of flash-based memory card similar to SecureDigital and able to support multiple data types (audio, image or digital movie data, for example).

NiMH Nickel metal-hydride. A type of rechargeable battery, ideal for running digital cameras and flashes.

Noise (in an image) Unwanted random artefacts within an image created by the electronics within a camera and other environmental factors such as heat. Often used together with the term signal-to-noise ratio, which describes the ratio between actual image information (the signal) and the level of background noise.

Off-Site Back-Up An off-site back-up is a back-up performed (usually) over the Internet to remote servers run by a company who supply storage space for your data.

Operating System (OS) The base software needed to manage the hardware and software applications of a computer or other device; examples include Windows and Mac OS.

Panning Photo technique in which the camera follows a moving subject, keeping the subject sharp whilst blurring the background, giving a sense of motion to the photo.

PDF Portable document format. A document file that can be looked at anywhere if you have Adobe Acrobat Reader software.

PICT A file format used primarily for on-screen images.

Pixel A picture element. Digital photographs are composed of millions of them; they are the building blocks of a digital photo and consist of a small light-sensitive photo site, a micro lens and the necessary wiring.

Pixellated Referring to images of poor quality in which the balance between image resolution and output is not correct when printing. For example, if a low-resolution image (say 72dpi) is enlarged by 200% and printed, the pixels become visible – hence pixellated – giving a jagged effect to the printed image.

Plug-In Software program that enhances other computer programs and applications. There are plug-ins for Internet browsers, graphics programs and image editing applications.

ppi Pixels per inch. Measurement of the resolution of a digital image (or of a scan made by a scanner) is made in ppi. The higher the ppi number, the greater the resolution. (See also dpi)

Podcast A downloadable Internet broadcast, be it text, audio or video, for your iPod or other MP3 or music player, which allows you to experience such content on the move.

RAM Random access memory. The type of computer storage whose contents can be accessed in any order, used by your applications for processing and temporary storage. (See also ROM)

RAW Image format in which the data is unprocessed (by the camera) as it comes directly off the CCD. Mostly used by professional photographers (as a digital 'negative') who want to get specific effects from their images. Often provides superior quality (in an image editor) to a camera's internal image processing.

Redeye The reflected red glow from a subject's eyes when light from a flash is coloured by the blood vessels in the retina. Most common when light levels are low indoors, with babies or outdoors at night.

Resolution (of a lens, or resolving power) The ability of a lens or optical system to show fine detail. The higher the resolving power of a lens, the more detail can be captured.

RGB Red, green and blue. The three primary colours into which digital cameras split/convert an image.

ROM Read-only memory. Computer memory whose contents can be accessed and read but cannot be changed. (See also RAM)

Router A device that connects your PC to the Internet (via a phone line) and other PCs either wirelessly or using Ethernet cables plugged into it.

Saturation Measure of how richly colours are rendered in a photo.

SecureDigital A type of flash-memory storage card with built-in copyright security facilities.

Sensitivity see ISO

Sensor see CCD; CMOS

Sharpness The perceived clarity of detail within a photo. Can usually be adjusted in the camera or later using an image editing package.

Shutter Speed Measure of how long the shutter stays open as the photo is taken. The slower the shutter speed, the longer the exposure is said to be. For example, a shutter speed set to 1/250 means the shutter will be open for exactly 1/250th of one second. Shutter speed and aperture together control the amount of light reaching the sensor.

Signal-to-Noise Ratio see Noise

Social Network(ing) A social network – or social networking – is a term used to describe many websites which have vast numbers of individual users – or members, or groups of users – all with similar interests or with the desire to 'meet' and interact on-line using email and instant messaging. These include sites such as Facebook, MySpace and Flickr. They're often termed 'on-line communities'.

Tablet (Tablet PC) A tablet is the name given to the new generation of lightweight, ultra-portable computers that use a large screen as the main interface.

Terabyte (TB) A terabyte is the amount of memory equal to 1000 gigabytes.

Thumbnail A small version of a photo. Image browsers commonly display many thumbnails at a time.

Thunderbolt A new type of super fast PC connection, via a special cable and port. The fastest type of computer connection available at the time of writing.

TIFF Tagged image file format. A widely used file format for images.

USB Universal serial bus. A protocol for transferring data to and from digital devices. Many digital cameras and memory card readers connect to the USB port on a computer.

White Balance A function on the camera that allows compensation for the different colours of light being emitted by different light sources. (See also Cast)

WiFi Wireless Fidelity. A method of wirelessly connecting cameras, printers and PCs.

Writing (a file) The process of outputting a data file to a CD, DVD or Blu-ray disc using a device that 'burns' to the disc.

Index

Photography credits

The publishers are grateful to the following for permission to use their photographs:

All photographs Doug Harman's except:

David Jones pages 2, 15, 20, 21, 27, 50–51, 53, 54–55, 56, 57, 58, 59, 61, 62, 69, 70, 73 (top left), 75, 78, 79, 82, 83, 84, 85, 86, 87, 90, 91, 92, 93, 94, 95, 96, 97, 98, 99, 100, 101, 107, 108, 109, 111, 113, 114, 115, 116, 117, 118–119, 127, 128, 129, 130, 131, 132, 133, 136, 137, 138, 142, 143, 146, 147, 150, 151, 152, 153, 154, 155, 156, 157, 158, 159, 160, 161, 162, 163, 164, 165, 168–169, 190–191, 207, 208, 209, 211.

Special thanks to all the manufacturers who granted permission to use their product shots:

Adobe, Apple, Arcsoft, Aviary, Big Lens, Canon, Camera+, Corel, Devolo, Epson, Fujifilm, Instagram, Iomega, Kodak, Lexar, LG, Maxtor, Microsoft, Nikon, Nik Software, Olympus, Panasonic, Pentax, Philips, Photo Effects Studio, Photosynth, Pixlr, Repix, Roxio, Samsung, Sandisk, Sekonic, Slik, Slow Shutter Cam, Snapspeed, Sony, Transcend, Wacom, Western Digital.

The publishers would like to extend particular thanks to Adobe for permission to use all Adobe Photoshop Elements and Lightroom screen shots.

Special thanks to Samsung for permission to use the Samsung NX2000 image on the front cover; front cover balloon image: © Angi English/FlickR.

The **photographer**

David Jones is a professional photographer with an extensive commercial portfolio, particularly in the fashion and advertising industries. He has also been widely exhibited and contributed photographs to many magazines and books, including *Brunel*, *How to Keep Dinosaurs* and *MasterChef*.

The **author**

Doug Harman has over 23 years' experience as a journalist, author, photographer, and digital camera and technology tester. He has written extensively for a multitude of publications digital photography magazines and web sites, including *The Times Online*, *Amateur Photographer*, *What Digital Camera*, *Total Digital Photography*, *Digital Photographer*, Pocket-Lint.com and fourthirds-user.com, *Professional Photographer*, *Photography Monthly* and *Digital Camera Buyer*.

He's also the author of a pocket guide to better cameraphone photography called *Snap It* (Quercus), first published in January 2006, and the technical advisor to John Freeman on the *Digital SLR Handbook* (Collins).

Doug has his own web site at www.dougharmanphotography.com, he has also written and presented a digital photography DVD show, *Doug Harman's Guide to Digital Photography*, and teaches clients how to get more from their digital cameras and improve their photography.

Doug has built his own fully equipped professional photographic studio. In addition, he is one of the founding directors of media and marketing company US3 Media Ltd (www.us3m.com), and one of the founding editors of the technology, news, reviews and buyer's guide web site www.Best4Reviews.com.

Text by Doug Harman

ISBN 978-1-4351-5687-6

Manufactured in China

2 4 6 8 10 9 7 5 3 1